COLLECTED WRITINGS OF W. D. GANN

VOLUME 2

NUMBER 3 MASTER FORECASTING METHOD

THE MASTER TIME FACTOR

& RAREST STOCK MARKET

FORECASTING COURSES

BY

WILLIAM D. GANN

COSMOLOGICAL ECONOMICS

WWW.COSMOECONOMICS.COM

This Series is Published by the:
Institute of Cosmological Economics

Cosmological Economics
is an imprint of:
Sacred Science Institute
www.SacredScience.com
institute@sacredscience.com
US: 800-756-6141 ϴ Intl: 951-659-8181

Cosmological Economics

The Masters Of Technical Analysis Series

The Masters of Technical Analysis Series brings together a collection of the most important classical and modern works on technical analysis and financial market forecasting. These classic works from the Golden Age of Technical Analysis were carefully selected by the late Dr. Jerome Baumring of the Investment Centre Bookstore in the 1980's, as representing the most valuable and important works in technical analysis ever written. They were included as the foundational source texts for his program in advanced financial market analysis and forecasting, and serve as the ideal foundation for any analyst seeking a thorough education in market theory and technical trading.

The Golden Age of technical analysis was a period from the early 1900's through the 1960's where the foundational theories of modern financial analysis were initially developed. The ideas and technologies developed during this fruitful period have formed the basis for most modern technical market theory, which is considered to be mostly a repetition or reworking of these past ideas and techniques developed by the Old Masters of the Golden Age. In these historical works can be found the timeless trading wisdom which has laid the foundation for all modern investment theory and literature. These techniques are as useful in today's markets as they were in the past, providing rare and valuable insights, tools and strategies that give the modern trader an edge over traders and investors that are unaware of these time honored tools.

Each quality reprint of these classical texts has been reproduced as an exact facsimile of the original text, maintaining the original layout, typeset, charts, and style of the author and time period, helping to preserve and communicate a sense of the feeling of the original work that a reproduction in modern format does not capture. Many of these rare works and courses were originally printed in only very small private editions or as correspondence courses, so that the originals were easily lost or destroyed over time. Our reproductions of these important source works have been printed on acid free paper and bound in a quality hardcover format that will compliment any trading library and help to preserve this important resource for generations to come.

The series is also currently being digitized and archived for permanent digital preservation by the Institute of Cosmological Economics, creating a searchable reference library of market wisdom accessible globally and available in new digital formats to keep the knowledge fresh and accessible through new devices and technology as we advance further into the information revolution. To see our full catalog of hardcover reprints, new publications, and digital editions please visit our website at www.CosmoEconomics.com.

Master No. 3 Forecasting Method
Unpublished Stock Market Forecasting Courses

W. D. Gann

Section I: The Original No. 3 Master Forecasting Method

Section II: Unpublished Stock Market Forecasting Courses

Chapter 1

Learn Before You Lose

Or

Why You Lose Money On Stocks

And

How To Make Profits

LEARN BEFORE YOU LOSE

OR

WHY YOU LOSE MONEY ON STOCKS

AND

HOW TO MAKE PROFITS

LEARN BEFORE YOU LOSE

OR

WHY YOU HAVE LOST MONEY IN STOCKS

AND HOW TO MAKE IT BACK

Why do the great majority of people who buy and sell stocks lose?

There are three main reasons:

1. They over-trade or buy and sell too much for their capital.

2. They do not place stop loss orders or limit their losses.

3. Lack of Knowledge. This is the most important reason of all.

Most people buy a stock because they hope it will go up and they will make profits. They buy on tips, or what someone else thinks, without any concrete knowledge of their own that the stock will advance. Thus they entered the market wrong and did not recognize this mistake or attempt to correct it until too late. Finally they sell because they fear the stock will go lower and often they sell out near low levels, getting out at the wrong time, making two mistakes, getting in the market at the wrong time and getting out at the wrong time. One mistake could have been prevented, they could have gotten out right after getting in wrong. They do not realize that operating in Stocks and Commodities is a business or a profession, the same as engineering or the medical profession.

Why You Should Learn to Determine the Trend of the Market

You may have tried to follow market letters and like many others either lost money or failed to make profits, because the market letters gave a list of too many stocks to buy or sell and you picked the wrong one and lost. A smart man cannot follow another man blindly even though the other man is right, because you cannot have confidence and act on advice when you do not know what it is based on. You will be able to act with confidence and make profits when you can SEE and KNOW for YOURSELF why STOCKS should go UP or DOWN. That is why you should take a Course of Instructions and prepare yourself to act independent of the advice of others.

Why I Teach My Methods

Long years in practical market trading and experience in teaching others has taught me what others need for success in speculation. They must learn a rule and how to apply it before they take up the second lesson or set of Rules. When you first went to school you had to learn your A, B, Cs before you could read and when you started to study arithmetic you had to learn the four fundamental rules, addition, multiplication, division and subtraction.

Then you were prepared to take up higher mathematics, algebra and geometry.

My Course or Lessons starts you in the same way, leading you step by step and adding more rules when you are ready and can understand them.

I have made a success in Wall Street and have all the income that I need, this fact can be proven by the records. I find real pleasure in helping others who are trying to help themselves. Money it not everything in life, when I teach a young man or woman how to protect and preserve their capital I am giving them valuable knowledge that they cannot lose, and no one can steal it or take it from them.

You should never buy a method from a man who has not made money with it.

W. D. GANN

THIRTY-ONE YEARS IN WALL STREET

The Founder and president of W. D. Gann & Son, Inc. has devoted 35 years exclusively to the study of stock and commodity markets and has spent over $300,000.00 developing a worthwhile, practical method of Stock Forecasting.

During the past 31 years W. D. Gann has been in business for himself and under his own name in New York City. He is a member of the Commodity Exchange, Inc. of New York, New Orleans Cotton Exchange and is a Christian and a member of the Masonic fraternity.

The Record of Forecasts—
Highlights through the years

1909—W. D. Gann's record as a forecaster dates back 30 years. We reprint part of an article written by the late Richard D. Wyckoff and published in the Ticker Magazine. This article is dated December 1909 and attests to Mr. Gann's remarkable ability as a forecaster over 30 years ago.

WILLIAM D. GANN

**An Operator Whose Science and Ability Place Him in the Front Rank—
His Remarkable Predictions and Trading Record.**

Sometime ago the attention of this magazine was attracted by certain long pull stock market predictions which were being made by William D. Gann. In a large number of cases Mr. Gann gave us in advance the exact points at which certain stocks and commodities would sell, together with prices close to the then prevailing figures which would not be touched.

For instance, when New York Central was 131 he predicted that it would sell at 145 before 129.

So repeatedly did his figures prove to be accurate, and so different did his work appear from that of any expert whose methods we had examined, that we set about to investigate Mr. Gann and his way of figuring out these predictions, as well as the particular use which he was making of them in the market.

The results of this investigation are remarkable in many ways.

It appears to be a fact that Mr. Gann

has developed an entirely new idea as to the principles governing stock market movements. He bases his operations upon certain natural laws, which, though existing since the world began, have only in recent years been subjected to the will of man, and added to the list of so-called modern discoveries.

We have asked Mr. Gann for an outline of his work and have secured some remarkable evidence as to the results obtained therefrom. We submit this in full recognition of the fact that in Wall Street a man with a new idea—an idea which violates the traditions and encourages a scientific view of the proposition—is not usually welcomed by the majority, for the reason that he stimulates thought and research. These activities said majority abhors.

Mr Gann's description of his experience and methods is given herewith. It should be read with a recognition of the established fact that Mr. Gann's predictions have proved correct in a large majority of instances.

"After years of patient study I have proven to my entire satisfaction as well as demonstrated to others that vibration explains every possible phase and condition of the market."

In order to substantiate Mr. Gann's claims as to what he has been able to do under this method, we called upon Mr. William E. Gilley, an Inspector of Imports, 16 Beaver Street, New York. Mr. Gilley is well-known in the down-town district. He himself has studied stock market movements for twenty-five years, during which time he has examined every piece of market literature that has been issued and procurable in Wall Street. It was he who encouraged Mr. Gann to study out the scientific and mathematical possibilities of the subject. When asked what had been the most impressive of Mr. Gann's work and predictions, he replied as follows:

"It is very difficult for me to remember all the predictions and operations of Mr. Gann which may be classed as phenomonal, but the following are a few: In 1908 when Union Pacific was 168⅛ he told me that it would not touch 169 before it had a good break. We sold it short all the way down to 152⅝, covering on the weak spots and putting it out again on the rallies, securing twenty-three points profit out of an eighteen-point move.

"He came to me when United States Steel was selling around 50 and said 'This Steel will run up to 58 but it will not sell at 59. From there it should break 16¾ points. We sold it short around 58⅜ with a stop at 59. The highest it went was 58¾. From there it declined to 41¼—17½ points.

"At another time wheat was selling at about 89c. He predicted that the May option would sell at $1.35. We bought it and made large profits on the way up. It actually touched $1.35½.

"When Union Pacific was 172, he said it would go to 184⅞ but not an eighth higher until it had had a good break. It went to 184⅞ and came back from there eight or nine times. We sold it short repeatedly with a stop at 185 and were never caught. It eventually came back to 172½.

"Mr. Gann's calculations are based on natural law. I have followed his work closely for years. I know that he has a firm grasp of the basic principles which govern stock market movements, and I do not believe any other man on earth can duplicate the idea or his method at the present time.

"Early this year he figured that the top of the advance would fall on a certain day in August and calculated the prices at which the Dow-Jones averages would then stand. The market culminated on the exact day and within four-tenths of one per cent. of the figures predicted."

"You and Mr. Gann must have cleaned up considerable money on all these operations," was suggested.

"Yes, we have made a great deal of money. He has taken half a million dollars out of the market in the past few years. I once saw him take $130, and in less than one month run it up to cover $12,000. He can compound money faster than any man I ever met."

"One of the most astonishing calculations made by Mr. Gann was during last summer (1909) when he predicted that September wheat would sell at $1.20. This meant that it must touch that figure before the end of the month of September. At twelve o'clock, Chicago time, on September 30th (the last day) the option was selling below $1.08, and it looked as though his prediction would not be fulfilled. Mr. Gann said 'If it does not touch $1.20 by the close of the market it will prove that there is something wrong with my whole method of calculation. I do not care what the price is now, it must go there.' It is common history that September wheat surprised the whole country by selling at $1.20 and no higher in the very last hour of the trading, closing at that figure,

So much for what Mr. Gann has said and done as evidenced by himself and others. Now as to what demonstrations have taken place before our representative:

Durinn the month of October, 1909, in twenty-five market days, Mr. Gann made, in the presence of our representative, two hundred and eighty-six transactions in various stocks, on both the long and short side of the market. Two hundred and sixty-four of these transactions resulted in profits; twenty-two in losses.

The capital with which he operated was doubled ten times, so that at the end of the month he had one thousand per cent. of his original margin.

In our presence Mr. Gann sold Steel common short at 94⅞, saying that it would not go to 95. It did not.

On a drive which occurred during the week ending October 29th, Mr. Gann bought Steel common at 86¼, saying that it would not go to 86. The lowest it sold was 86⅛.

We have seen him give in one day sixteen successive orders in the same stock, eight of which turned out to be either the top or the bottom eighth of that particular swing. The above we can positively verify.

Such performances as these, coupled with the foregoing, are probably unparalleled in the history of the Street.

James R. Keene has said, "The man who is right six times out of ten will make his fortune." Here is a trader, who, without any attempt to make a showing (for he did not know the results were to be published), establishes a record of over ninety-two per cent profitable trades.

Mr. Gann has refused to disclose his method at any price, but to those scientifically inclined he has unquestionably added to the stock of Wall Street knowledge and pointed out infinite possibilities.

We have requested Mr. Gann to figure out for the readers of The Ticker a few of the most striking indications which appear in his calculations. In presenting these we wish it understood that no man, in or out of Wall Street, is infallible.

Mr. Gann's figures at present indicate that the trend of the stock market should, barring the usual rallies, be toward lower prices until March or April, 1910.

He calculates that May wheat, which is now selling at $1.02, should not sell below 99c. and should sell at $1.45 next spring.

On cotton, which is now at about the 15c. level, he estimates that, after a good reaction from these prices, the commodity should reach 18c. in the spring of 1910. He looks for a corner in the March or May option.

Whether these figures prove correct or not, will in no sense detract from the record which Mr. Gann has already established.

Mr. Gann was born in Lufkin, Texas, and is thirty-one years of age. He is a gifted mathematician, has an extraordinary memory for figures, and is an expert Tape Reader. Take away his science and he would beat the market on his intuitive tape reading alone.

Endowed as he is with such qualities, we have no hesitation in predicting that within a comparatively few years Wm. D. Gann will receive full recognition as one of Wall Street's leading operators.

R. D. W.

Note—Since. the above forecast was made, Cotton has suffered the expected decline, the extreme break having been 120 points. The lowest on May wheat thus far has been $1.01⅝. It is now selling at 1.06¼.

In 1912 Mr. Gann forecast the election of Woodrow Wilson and has been correct in forecasting the election of every President since that time. Many of these forecasts have been published in newspapers throughout the country.

In the spring of 1918 Mr. Gann forecast the end of the World War. This forecast was sent out to newspapers throughout the country, and in January, 1919, the New York Herald and other papers gave Mr. Gann credit for forecasting the end of the war and the Kaiser's abdication.

In his 1919 Annual Stock Forecast, issued late in 1918, he forecast a big bull market for 1919 and especially referred to a boom in oil stocks.

His Stock Forecasts for 1920 and 1921 indicated a bear market with sharp declines. The 1921 Forecast called the exact date for bottom on stocks in August, 1921.

In 1923 Mr. Gann wrote "Truth of the Stock Tape" and forecast a big advance in chemical and airplane stocks, which followed during the Coolidge bull campaign. This book has been reviewed by newspapers and magazines throughout the country and favorably commented on by college professors, business men, investors and traders, all of whom agree that it is the best book ever written on the subject.

His Stock Forecasts for 1924 and 1925 outlined the bull market which followed.

In the spring of 1927, Mr. Gann wrote "The Tunnel Thru the Air, or Looking back From 1940," which contained many remarkable forecasts in regard to stocks and commodities and world events which have been fulfilled. In this book Mr. Gann said that from 1929 to 1932 there would be the worst panic in the world's history. Writing under date of "October 3, 1931" on page 323, he said, "The New York Stock Exchange closed to prevent complete panic because the people were panic-stricken and selling stocks regardless of price." It is a matter of history that the New York Stock Exchange did consider closing on October 3 to 5, but decided to stop short selling. The low of that panicky decline was reached on October 5 and a rally of 33 points in industrial stock averages followed to November 9, 1931.

His 1929 Stock Forecast, issued on November 23, 1928, and based on his Master Time Factor, indicated the end of the full market in August and early September, 1929. He stated in no uncertain terms that the panic would start in September, 1929, and that it would be a great deluge with a Black Friday. We quote from the Forecast:

"AUGUST—A few of the late movers will advance this month and reach final high. * * * Unfavorable news will develop which will start declines and the long bull campaign will come to a sudden end. Money rates will be high and final top will be reached for a big bear campaign. Stand from under! Don't get caught in the great deluge! Remember it is too late to sell when everyone is trying to sell. * * *

"SEPTEMBER—One of the sharpest declines of the year is indicated. There will be loss of confidence by investors, and the public will try to get out after it is too late. Storms will damage crops and the general business outlook will become cloudy. War news will upset the market and unfavorable developments in foreign countries. A 'Black Friday' is indicated and a panicky decline in stocks with only small rallies. The short side will prove the most profitable. You should sell short and pyramid on the way down."

In the spring of 1930, Mr. Gann wrote "Wall Street Stock Selector," which was published in June, 1930. In this book he had a chapter headed, "Investors' Panic," which described conditions just as they occurred during 1931, 1932 and 1933. We quote from the book, pages 203-04:

"The coming investors' panic will be the greatest in history, because there are at least 15 to 25 million investors in the United States who hold stocks in the leading corporations, and when once they get scared, which they will after years of decline, then the selling will be so terriffic that no buying power can withstand it. Stocks are so well distributed in the hands of the public that since the 1929 panic many people think that the market is panic-proof, but this seeming strength is really the weakest feature of the market. * * *

"Love of money has been the cause of all financial troubles and depressions in the past, and the coming panic will be the greatest the world has ever known, because there is more money in the United States than ever before, therefore more to fight for."

Thousands of people have bought this book and profited by reading and studying it. The book has been favorably commented on by such papers as The Financial Times of London, England, Wall Street Journal, New York Daily Investment News, Coast Investor, and many other newspapers and magazines throughout the world.

On February 10, 1932, Mr. Gann said that stocks were bottom for a big rally. His 1932 Stock Forecast, issued October 21, 1931, called March 8 for last top for another big decline. During the latter part of June, 1932, and early July he strongly advised buying stocks, stating that final bottom had been reached, as shown by his market letter issued July 8, the day that most stocks reached final bottom. We quote from page 6 of the 1932 Forecast:

"The latter part of June, July, August and September are the most active and bullish months of the year, when sharp advances will be recorded. First extreme high is indicated around September 20 to 21, when stocks should make extreme high for the year. Then follows a decline, reaching bottom around October 4 to 5."

Between July 8 and September 8 many stocks advanced 20 to 60 points. The market reached high of a secondary rally on September 23, from which a big decline followed, making low in the latter part of November and early December, as indicated in the Forecast.

On March 1, 1933, by the use of his Master Time Factor Mr. Gann forecast bottom for stocks and commodities and advised buying for a big advance, as shown by the market letters issued March 1 and 3 given below. This is another proof of the great value of Mr. Gann's discovery of a Master Time Factor.

KEEPING UP TO DATE

Mr. Gann has always been progressive and believes in keeping up to date. In April, 1933, he bought a specially equipped airplane for making crop surveys. Many of the newspapers throughout the country commented on this progressive step. The following article appeared in the New York Daily Investment News, May 26, 1933:

NEW YORK DAILY INVESTMENT NEWS

GANN TO TOUR COUNTRY BY PLANE FOR BROAD BUSINESS SURVEY

Wayne, Mich., May 25.—W. D. Gann, stock market analyst, of 99 Wall St., today left here for New York with the first 1933 model Stinson Reliant plane, piloted by Elinor Smith, woman aviator.

Mr. Gann will use the plane for an extensive tour of the country during which he will study cotton, wheat and tobacco crop and business conditions. He will leave on this tour early in June.

The forecaster expects to make speed in the gathering of first hand information on business conditions by use of the airplane.

The plane is equipped with blind-flying apparatus, extra-large fuel tanks to afford a flying range of 750 miles and with radio receiving equipment. The plane is powered with a Lycoming engine and is capable of 135 miles per hour.

By receiving radio advices on market conditions, Mr. Gann calculates that he will be able at all times to gauge his operations in the markets and send up-to-the-minute advise to his clients, even though he is many miles away from his Wall Street office.

As far as is known, Mr. Gann will be the first Wall Street adviser to use a plane as part of his equipment in studying market conditions.

The recent burst of activity in the markets, following the closing of the banks and leading stock and commodity exchanges, prompted the analyst to buy the plane.

He decided that rapid-changing conditions made it necessary for him to gather his data on crops and business at first hand.

Mr. Gann is a member of the Commodity Exchange, Inc., and also of the New Orleans Cotton Exchange. During his tour of the country he will visit the cotton belt in the south and southwest, the tobacco fields in the south, and the wheat stand in the middle west.

At all times during the trip he will communicate regularly with his office by wire and by radio. He expects to make talks in various cities to Kiwanis and Rotary Clubs, chambers of commerce and other business organizations.

His itinerary will include the following cities:

Washington, D. C.; Richmond, Va; Raleigh, N. C.; Atlanta, Ga; Birmingham, Ala; Memphis, Tenn.; New Orleans, La.; Little Rock, Ark.; Houston and Dallas, Texas; St. Louis, Detroit and Chicago.

1933 STOCK FORECAST:

Mr. Gann's 1933 Stock Forecast called for top July 17 and a sharp decline to July 21. Stocks reached high on July 17 and a wide-open break followed, with the average down 25 points in 4 days.

1934 STOCK FORECAST:

His 1934 Forecast indicated top for February 13th and the high was reached on averages February 5th and 15th. The next low was indicated for May 11th to 12th, and the market made low on May 14th. The next top was indicated for June 22nd; stocks reached high on June 19th. The last low for 1934 was forecast for July 21st to 23rd and the extreme low of the year was reached on July 26th. The Forecast called for the last top for September 8th to 10th, and stocks reached top of the rally on September 6th. A reaction followed to September 17th, the exact date indicated in the Forecast for low. The next top was forecast for October 5th and 6th and the industrial averages reached top October 11th. The next bottom was called for October 23rd to 24th and the lows were reached October 26th. The next top was indicated, accordinq to the Forecast, for December 4th to 5th. The averages reached top on December 6th and a reaction followed. The Forecast indicated high for the end of December and the averages reached high for the month on December 31st.

•

A CROP SURVEY IN SOUTH AMERICA

In the early part of March, 1935, Mr. Gann made a trip to South America to study crop conditions and get first hand information on the increase in production of cotton in Peru, Chile, Argentine, and Brazil. On this trip he covered about 18,000 miles by airplane and more than 1,000 miles by automobile, driving into the country to see the conditions of soil and the possibilities for increased production of Wheat, Corn and Cotton, which will influence prices in the United States market by underselling, due to lower cost of labor in Argentine and Brazil. While in South America, Mr. Gann was interviewed by many newspapers.

We reproduce part of an article which appeared in the Beunos Aires Herald, March 21, 1935.

BEUNOS AIRES HERALD

Thursday, March 21, 1935

SCIENCE AND STOCK

An Astonishing Claims

Records of 1,000 Years

The man who guesses and gambles on hope is sure to lose while the man who follows science makes profits. There is cause and effect for everything and by time element and the cycle theory everything can be mathematically determined.

Mr. W. D. Gann, member of the New Orleans Cotton Exchange and the Rubber Exchange of New York, who stated that he has devoted over 30 years to study of time cycles and spent $300,000 (U.S.) to develop a dependable method based on mathematical science that will determine the trend of stocks and commodities. The success attending his methods he asserts, are borne out by his own good fortune on the American markets, and his accuracy in forecasting the futures markets for the past twenty years has been very widely commented upon in the Press in all parts of the United States.

Mr. Gann told a HERALD reporter yesterday that he has carried his records of grain back over 1,000 years and cotton records nearly 400 years. The former he was able to gather the most accurate information about from old British records, while in his search for cotton cycles he visited Egypt and India. More recently he has used his own aeroplane extensively in America for getting round the country quickly to make forecasts on the cotton crops.

•

1935 Stock Forecast:

His 1935 Forecast indicated first top for January 9th to 10th and the high was reached on January 7th. The next top was forecast for February 13th. The actual highs were reached February 18th, from which a sharp decline followed, making low for the year on March 18th. The Forecast called for the last low on March 28th, and the averages made a second low on March 25th. From the low in March, the Forecast indicated a big advance of at least 32 points in the Dow-Jones Industrial averages.

August 28th and 29th indicated top for a reaction. The averages reached top on August 27th and then reacted. The Forecast called for the next top September 12th to 15th. High on the averages was reached September 11th. The Forecast indicated the next bottom for September 24th to 25th; the last low was made September 20th and 26th.

The Forecast called for top October 26th to 28th, and the averages reached high on October 28th, which was the high of the year up to that time. The Forecast indicated November 15th to 16th as the last high of the year. The actual high of the Dow-Jones 30 Industrial averages was reached on November 20th, from which a reaction of 10 points on averages followed. The Forecast called for low December 9-10th and 23rd. The low of the reaction was made on December 16th and 19th. The Forecast called for a rally to December 31st, and this rally took place.

Mr. Gann has also been issuing Annual Forecast on Cotton, Wheat and other commodities for many years. These Forecasts have shown the same percentage of accuracy that the Stock Forecasts have.

These Annual, Forecasts on Stocks, Cotton, and Grain are issued in October and November each year for the following year.

NEW STOCK TREND DETECTOR

In December 1935, Mr. Gann wrote a new book, NEW STOCK TREND DETECTOR, bringing "Wall Street Stock Selector" up-to-date, with new rules never before published and a method of trading that formerly sold for $1000.00. This book covers changed conditions caused by the new Securities Exchange laws. It gives an example of trading in Chrysler Motors from 1925 to the end of 1935 and new rules on Volume of Sales. This book with the two former books will give you a valuable stock market education.

W. D. GANN MAKES PROFITS TRADING ACCORDING TO HIS OWN METHODS

Many ask the question, "If Mr. Gann can forecast the market accurately, why does he sell service or write market letters?" He has answered that question before, that he finds pleasure in giving his knowledge to help others who need help; money is not everything in life.

Below we publish a record taken from brokers' statements, showing the trades made by Mr. Gann for 3 years. This is proof that he can and does make money by following his own rules and methods. Before you buy a course of instructions, get the record of actual trading by the man who is behind it, if he has not made money following his own advice, why should you pay money for it and follow it and risk your money?

W. D. GANN'S TRADING RECORD FOR 1933

From August 1 to December 31:

Total number of trades—135—of which 112 showed profits and 23 losses.

Percentage of accuracy on the total number of trades........ 83%

Percentage of profits to losses........ 89.9%

Total number of trades for the entire year of 1933: 479 trades, of which 422 were profits and 57 showed losses.

Percentage of accuracy 88.1%

Percentage of profits on capital used........ 4000% or 40 for 1

TRADING RECORD FOR 1934

From January 1 to December 31: Total number of trades—362.

Cotton	—	147	trades,	of	which	135	showed	profits	and	12	losses
Grain	—	170	"	"	"	161	"	"	"	9	"
Rubber	—	23	"	"	"	21	"	"	"	2	"
Silver	—	7	"	"	"	7	"	"	"	0	"
Silk	—	4	"	"	"	3	"	"	"	1	"
Stocks	—	11	"	"	"	10	"	"	"	1	"

Total for yr. 362 trades, of which 337 showed profits and 25 losses.

Percentage of accuracy on the total number of trades........ 93.09%

Percentage of profits to losses........ 93.10%

Percentage of profits on capital used........ 800% or 8 for 1

TRADING RECORD FOR 1935

Commodities:

Total trades in Cotton, Grain and Rubber—98—of which 83 showed profits and 15 showed losses.

Percentage of accuracy on total number of trades........ 85%

Percentage of profits to losses........ 82%

Percentage of profits on capital used........ 336%

Stocks:

Total number of trades—34—of which 29 showed profits and 5 losses.

Percentage of accuracy on total number of trades	85.5%
Percentage of profits to losses	83%
Percentage of profits on capital used	100%

Such a record of accuracy proves that W. D. Gann has discovered a Master Time Factor and Cycle Theory that works and can be depended upon in future.

1936—"New Stock Trend Detector" was written by W. D. Gann. This book was a further advance over "Truth of the Stock Tape" and "Wall Street Stock Selector" and contained an actual trading record for 10 years in Chrysler Motors according to the rules set down in these books.
Bought Special built all-metal Airplane, "The Silver Star" for making crop surveys.

1937—Wrote and published a book, "How to Make Profits Trading in Puts and Calls" Scientific Stock Forecasting again proved equal to the test of predicting a bear year, sharp declines coming in March and September. A maximum decline of 80 points was called for and the actual decline from the March high to the November low was 82 and a fraction points. We reprint an article from the Milwaukee Journal giving further details.

PREDICTED STOCK MARKET CRASHES OF 1929, 1937

Gann Says There'll Be Another Decline in November and an Upturn in December of This Year

NEW YORK, N. Y.—W. D. Gann, who forecast the 1929 stock market crash one year in advance and predicted the exact date, September 3, 1929, when the panic would start, has made another hit.

His 1937 Stock Forecast, issued November 18, 1936, is just as accurate. On page 2 he said—General Outlook for 1937":

This year comes under a time cycle which definitely indicates a bear year in most stocks and a panicky decline in the first half of the year and another panicky decline in the last half of the year. Fluctuations will be wide. Sudden, unexpected events of an unfavorable nature will occur from time to time which will upset the market and rallies will fail to hold. Action by the government and laws changed or passed by congress will have a great influence on business conditions and stock prices.

* * *

"Many people are still buying stocks or holding stocks and hoping for the day when inflation will come and they will be able to sell at high prices. Inflation has been going on ever since 1933 and one of these days people will wake up and find that deflation has set in and then they will realize that inflation had already existed.

* * *

The securities and exchange commission is getting more drastic in its regulations of operations on the exchange and there is likely to be more legislation in 1937. This will cause less support to the market in the future because there will be less buying by floor traders and specialists, and probably less short selling, therefore less support from short sellers when a panic takes place. The final result of all this regulation is likely to do more harm than good as far as the public is concerned."

A Matter of Record

It is a matter of record that the Dow-Jones 30 industrial stock averages reached extreme high on March 8, 1937, and Mr. Gann's forecast called March 6-8 as last high of the year. The decline lasted until June 18, when the Dow-Jones averages were down 32 points. His forecast called for a decline of 32 points and indicated June 23-25 as last low before a rally into August. The forecast said last high would be reached August 25-27 before a panicky decline would start. The Dow-Jones averages reached high August 14, up 27 points from June lows, and on August 25 the market had the last rally and the decline started.

Long Bear Wave

In his forecast for August on page 15 he said: "This should be one of the active months for the stock market. Sudden, unexpected events of an unfavorable nature will cause some sharp breaks and, in fact, this is the month when the market should start on its long bear wave again. The newspapers will try to make it appear that business is improving but it will be far from good. There will be disturbing conditions at Washington and some trouble over crop control or shortage of crops due to government action. Stocks will rally from time to time but the short side is where the big money will be made."

The bear market started in August as predicted. Mr. Gann's forecast called for low October 14-15 and the extreme lows were reached on October 19, just four days later, when there was a panicky decline, culminating in one of the worst declines in the history of the stock exchange, with the Dow-Jones averages down 79.65 points. The most uncanny prediction by Mr. Gann was that the averages could decline a maximum of 80 points.

In his 1937 forecast, page 7, he said: "The range in these industrial averages during 1937 is not likely to be less than 50 to 60 points and may reach a maximum of 80 points."

His forecast called for a sharp advance from October 15 to 30 and the Dow-Jones averages advanced 25 points from October 19 to 30.

Advance in December

Mr. Gann was asked how it was possible to make such an accurate forecast one year in advance. He stated that it was his own discovery of a mathematical master time factor and cycle theory which enables him to tell when certain cycles recur and great panics and booms take place. He said that the extent of an advance was determined by a theory based on the law of averages and that under certain circumstances stocks decline or advance about the same number of points.

* * *

"What about the near future of the stock market?" Gann replied: "My forecast indicates that stocks will back and fill until around November 15, when congress meets. Then they will have another decline and reach low of the reaction about November 26-27, followed by an advance in December."

1938—Predicted bull market to start in the spring or early summer, and called for low of the year for the early part of April. Actual low occurred on March 31st. This Forecast strongly advised buying airplane stocks and said they would lead the market upward. It is now market history that the airplane stocks as a group were the strongest on the New York Stock Exchange, and many of these stocks doubled and tripled in value during 1938.

Again We Repeat:

"Prove all things and hold fast to that which is good."

1939—The Stock Forecast called for high January 3rd, the Dow-Jones Industrial Averages made high January 4th and started to decline.

The Forecast indicated low for January 21st to 23rd, the averages reached low January 26th.

February 4th to 6th indicated high, averages made high February 6th.

February 21st to 23rd indicated low, averages made low February 21st.

March 4th to 6th indicated high, averages made high March 10th.

March 8th to 9th and 24th to 25th indicated low, averages made low March 22nd and 28th.

April 19th to 20th called for last low, averages made low April 11th.

May 16th - 17th indicated high, averages made high May 10th to 15th.

June 7th to 9th indicated high, averages made high June 9th, and a sharp decline followed.

June 23rd to 24th indicated low, averages made low June 29th to 30th.

July 28th to 29th indicated high, averages made high July 25th to 28th.

August 4th to 5th indicated low, averages made low August 5th and 7th.

The 1939 Forecast was issued and mailed to subscribers on November 14th, 1938.

We are sure that anyone will agree that such accurate, long-range forecasting cannot be done by guess-work. You can learn to make forecasts one year or more in advance when you learn how to apply the rules taught with the Master Forecasting Method.

What Others Say of W. D. Gann's Methods:

Below we print copies of letters received from two prominent business men, many other letters on file in our office from people who have used Mr. Gann's Courses of Instruction and followed his advice.

New York, N. Y.
March 16, 1933.

My Dear Mr. Gann:

I am very glad to write you a letter stating my personal observation of the application of your system to trading in Cotton.

On November 30, 1923, starting with a capital of $973.00 you showed a clear profit of over $30,000. at the close of business on January 28, 1924. This profit was made through the purchase and sale of contracts for the delivery and sale of cotton on the New York Cotton Exchange through one of the leading New York brokerage offices. I personally know of all the trades made in this commodity for the account, having received advices of your operations, from the broker on the day following the day each trade was made.

On January 29, 1924, a check for $24,764.04 was drawn against the account and delivered to a person with whom I am personally acquainted.

C. M.

New Bern, N. C.
August 23rd, 1937

I have known Mr. W. D. Gann for many years. I have been in his office on Wall Street, have seen him trade with his method and take the money out of the market. With it he has made a fortune in speculation. And he does not need the money he gets for his method or market service any more than Mr. Ford does for sale of cars.

His method has been used by me since 1927, successfully. In my opinion, it is the only one with which one can make money in the market and keep it. If you will follow his method and the rules he lays down, you will also make a success and I can assure you without it you will make a failure.

This statement is made after having read every book I could find on the subject, including the lives of all the big operators of the past and subscribed to every financial paper published and most of the market services.

C. K.

Results of Trading According To Rules

One of the rules is for trading in fast moves after the market gives a definite signal for a big move up or down. This rule gets you in the market when activity starts and keeps you in until the move has run its course, enabling you to make large profits in a comparatively short period of time.

Trading in the Dow-Jones 30 Industrial Averages beginning June 5th, 1897 to July 25th, 1939 you would have been in the market 1283 weeks or 24⅓ years out of a total of 42 years.

Total number of points profit would have been	2,367.
Average points profit per month	1.84
Profits on 100 shares of stock would have been (without pyramiding or ever trading in more than 100 sh.)	$236,700.00
Figures do not allow for errors in judgment, commission or interest, making a liberal deduction of 25% to cover same	59,175.00
Net profit on 100 shares, or a capital of $3,000	$177,525.00

You could have started trading in 1897 in 100 shares on a capital of $1,000.00 but according to the methods and rules you should have started with a capital of $3,000.00 for trading in 100 shares.

Should you have traded in the active leading stocks at all times, instead of the averages, the profits would have been much greater because the active leaders moved from one to three times as many points as the average.

Dow Jones 20 Railroad Averages May 1897 to March 1914 and Dow Jones 30 Industrial Averages February 1913 to June 1939, trading according to the rules during the above periods, show possible points:

Advances	2,085.52
Possible decline	2,012.42
Total points	4,097.94
Points made on Advance	1,336.78
Points made on Decline	1,236.13
Total	2,572.91

Percentage of total points made to possible points	63%
Percentage of all points made on the up-side or Bull Market	64%
Percentage of points made on the down-side or Bear Market	61.4%

Total number of trades made	177
Total number of years	42
Average number of trades per year (Slightly above 4 per year)	4.2
Net profit per year on 100 shares	$6,125.74
Net profit on 100 shares from 1897 to 1939	$257,291.00
Figuring an original investment of	$5,000.00
Equity as of June 30th, 1939 would be	$262,291.00
Value of $100. invested in 1897 as of June 1939	$5,145.82

COMPARISON OF DOW THEORY AND W. D. GANN'S METHOD

BASED ON DOW JONES 30 INDUSTRIAL AVERAGES

1897 to September 1937

	Dow's Theory:	Mr. Gann's Method:	Advantage of Mr. Gann's Method:
Total points made	718.54	2,118.03	1,399.49
Points made long side	416.37	1,127.40	711.03
Points made short side	302.17	990.63	688.46
Average number of points per year	17.5	51.66	34.16
Total profit made on 100 shares	$71,854.00	$211,803.00	$139,949.00
Profit per year on 100 shares	1,752.54	5,165.92	3,413.38
$100. invested in 1897 equals	3,602.88	5,177.37	1,574.49
Trades per year average	½ trade of 1 every 2 yrs.	3.4	

The Dow Theory as well as Mr. Gann's Method are subject to the human element and errors in determining when the combination occurs naturally will arise. No deduction from the above figures is made for errors or for commission and expenses. The computation and the results of the Dow Theory is based upon what we believe to be the best opinion. Mr. Gann's Method is based upon his own interpretation of his rules.

How You Can Make Profits

You can become a successful trader or investor if you acquire knowledge and learn the mathematical rules which determine the trend of Stocks and Commodity market movements.

The Bible says "Ye shall know the truth and the truth shall make you free". When you have learned the truth about stocks you will no longer buy on hope or sell on fear, you will face facts and be free to act on judgment based on rules that you know always have worked and always will.

Why I Can Teach You To Succeed

I have paid the price in time and money to discover, test and prove, rules that are, practical and get results. You will agree that 36 years experience is valuable in any line of business and that after I have spent that much time in study and research I can teach you the rules that will take the gamble out of Stock Market trading and make it a safe and profitable business. The man who devotes all the time to any business will learn more about it than the man who only studies it a short time.

If the average man or woman would only spend the first few hundred dollars they lose in the market in acquiring knowledge and learning the rules for buying and selling at the right time, they would then make profits—not losses.

Your Son's or Daughter's Future

A man can leave his son or daughter a million dollars or more and they can lose it quickly if they have not learned the rules how to invest it safely. My Course of Instructions will teach any one how to preserve his capital and make profits. They must be willing to study and work hard.

Forecasting Business
Good Positions For Students

Changed conditions due to Government interference, regulations and changes in Europe, make it necessary for every business man to forecast his own business in order to meet competition. It makes no difference whether a manufacturer of raw material or a seller of the finished product, he must be able to forecast future business conditions and guage future demand as closely as possible in order to make a profit in business. This creates a good position for a man who can accurately forecast business conditions and changes. The young man who prepares himself and becomes an expert in forecasting business, Commodities, Stocks and Bonds, will find a demand for his services. Estates must have an expert to handle their investments and once a man has proven his ability to increase the profits of a large estate he will find he can name his own terms as to salary. Money must have brains and experts to increase its earning power. Large estates can and will pay a man who can keep capital intact and prevent losses. The Investment Counsellor will find the future holds a bright outlook for him if he knows his business and has fully prepared himself.

What the Course Consists of

The Complete Course is in Four Lessons:

LESSON I. Form Reading or Picture Method. A great improvement on the Dow Theory. Formations or how to forecast the trend by certain formations by fixed rules which help to make your judgment accurate. Examples are given to prove the rules. With this lesson you learn from the picture or formation and after experience your eyes will recognize a formation and know what it means.

LESSON II. Resistance Levels. Where stocks meet buying or selling and make bottom and top. Definite mathematical rules, practical and proven that make profits. They are easy to learn and apply. All buying and selling points marked plainly on the charts and rules given why to buy or sell at certain points. Anyone should be able to learn this lesson in three days' time and make substantial profits with this Lesson alone. This method keeps you with the trend and enables you to buy near low levels and sell near top.

LESSON III. Time Elements and Time Rules. There is a definite relation between price and time. When time is up stocks make top and start down. When time is up and the time cycle runs out stocks make bottom and start up. It makes no difference how high stocks are selling, they can go higher until time runs out and no matter how low they are they can go lower until time is up.

Time is the most important factor in determining and forecasting market movements. Very few people understand the time element and its value. With this lesson you learn when the right time comes to buy and you know according to time three important buying points:

1. When near extreme low levels. With limited risk.

2. A safer buying point at a certain time period.

3. The safest buying point after the market gives the third time signal.

These rules give the three selling levels according to time. With this method you will be able to make up a forecast one year or more in advance on the average or individual stock.

LESSON IV. Volume of Sales. New, up-to-date, since the Security Exchange regulation and higher margin requirements have changed volume of sales. The Volume of Sales is the driving power that moves the market but time determines when volume will change at top or bottom. The volume rules are proven by charts, rules and forms on volume never published or used by anyone else.

Results from the Methods

1896 to 1939—43 years with Dow Jones Averages.

No. 1 Course of Instructions

CONSISTING OF TWO LESSONS:

1. Form Reading or picture method. Some Time Rules and Formations. B. W. points.

2. Resistance levels make it easier to operate with first lesson. Gives more mathematical confirmations of why to buy and sell at certain points.

In order to help those who are worthy and trying to help themselves, I am making a very reasonable price on these courses so that young students and people of small means can get started on their Investment Education. At a small cost and with a small capital students may start trading after they have gained knowledge and make profits.

The price is $500.00; payable $300.00 cash in advance. Easy terms on the balance, or can be paid after you make profits.

No. 2 Complete Course of Instructions

CONSISTING OF FOUR LESSONS:

This is a more complete course than I have sold for $5,000.00 in former years and it is worth $5,000.00 or more to anyone who will study it and use it. To help others who need help and are trying to make a success, I am making a low price of $1,000.00 for the Complete Course which includes a Weekly High and Low Chart on Dow-Jones 20 Railroad Averages 1896 to 1914, a Weekly High and Low Chart on Dow-Jones 30 Industrial Averages 1914 to date. A swing Chart on 30 Industrials 1896 to date. Weekly High and Low Charts on five active stocks that you select or we select, these Charts will be for two or three years back, according to the stock and market positions at the time.

Terms arranged if you are not in position to pay all cash in advance.

No. 3 Master Forecasting Method

This Method contains all of the Form Rules, Resistance Level and Volume of Sales and my secret discovery of the Master Time Factor and a new way of Forecasting by Mathematical Rules that are simple and practical.

MATHEMATICAL RULES OR REASONS: It is possible to get as many as nine confirmations or reasons why a stock should be bottom or top at a certain time and the greater number of confirmations the surer the chances of making profits. That is why each of my Lessons and Courses teach you more rules to confirm what you learned in the first Course or previous Lessons.

Master Charts that save time and work go with this Course, Master High and Low Charts ten to forty-five years back. This Course gives mathematical proof of how I forecast the 1929 Bull Market and the Panic which followed to 1932.

Price of complete Master Forecasting Course $2500.00 cash in advance. Terms can be arranged with part cash and balance on monthly payments.

Correspondence Course

Anyone can learn a Course by correspondence because everything is made plain. The buying and selling points are marked on the Charts and Rules why we buy or sell at a certain point. However, you can make greater progress if you can arrange for a few days personal instruction.

WHY YOU CAN MAKE MORE PROFITS TRADING IN COMMODITIES THAN STOCKS

In trading according to my Mechanical Method & Trend Indicator or according to my 1936 New Master Forecasting Methods on Cotton, Grain, Rubber and other commodities, there are many advantages over trading in stocks:

1. Commodities follow a seasonal trend and are much easier to forecast. They move with supply and demand.
2. It requires much less work to keep up charts and calculations on Commodities. There are 1200 stocks listed on the New York Stock Exchange and you must keep a separate chart on as many of them as you wish to forecast the trend of. With Cotton, you need one to three charts, and the same with Grain.
3. When you have a forecast made up for Cotton or Grain, if you are right, you are sure to make money because all options follow the same trend. There are no cross-currents as in stocks, with some stocks declining to new low levels and other making new highs.
4. In dealing in Futures, there are no heavy interest charges as there are when long of stocks and no dividends to pay as when short of stocks.
5. Dividends can be suddenly passed or declared which will affect stock prices. This cannot happen to commodities.
6. Pools cannot manipulate a commodity as they can a stock.
7. Facts about commodities are general known while many stocks are mystery stocks all the time and some stocks are subject to false rumors.
8. The stages of the business cycle tell more about the prices of commodities than they do about stocks.
9. Commodities are governed only by demand and supply. This is not always true of stocks.
10. Speculation in commodities is more legitimate than speculation in stocks because you are dealing in a necessity.
11. Commodities are consumed. Stocks are not. This has a bearing upon the ease in forecasting commodity prices.

13. Stock prices tend to move by groups of stocks, while commodities move independently.

14. Notable speculators, like Livermore and Dr. E. H. Crawford, have discovered after long experience that they make money with greater certainty in commodities.

15. Stocks go into receivers' hands and go out of business. Commodities go on forever. Crops are planted and harvested each year.

16. There is always a demand by consumers for commodities, which is not the case with stocks.

17. Since the Securities Exchange Law was passed, marginal requirements are much higher on stocks than on Commodities. Therefore, you can make more money on the same capital trading in Cotton, Wheat, Corn, Rubber or other markets.

18. When you learn the rules for forecasting and trading in Commodities, they never change because we will always have wheat, corn, and cotton crops every year and these crops will be consumed, while stocks change and you have to study new stocks to keep up with changed conditions.

COMMODITY METHODS

The prices of my Commodity Methods are less than Stock Methods because it requires less time to teach them and a small number of charts are needed:

MECHANICAL METHOD AND TREND INDICATION COVERING COTTON OR GRAIN

Price $600.00 Terms: $300.00 cash in advance; balance in monthly payments. Any man can learn this Method easily thru correspondence in a few days. With this Method we furnish weekly charts running back 2 to 3 years, daily charts and a trend chart; instructions how to work the Method; rules for telling where to buy and sell, where to place stop loss orders and when to pyramid. Cotton and Grain Methods combined, price $1,200.00 Terms: $500.00 cash in advance, balance in monthly payments.

FORECASTING METHOD ON COTTON OR GRAIN

Contains Master Time Factor:

Price $1,500.00 Terms: $750.00 cash; balance in monthly payments. With this Method you get charts on cotton back to 1869 (monthly) and with the Grain Method chart running back to 1842 (monthly), also weekly and daily charts, Master tables, Resistance Levels and Resistance Cards. You are taught the Master Time Factor and how to make up a forecast one or more years in advance.

Cotton and Grain Methods combined, price $2,500.00 Terms: $1,500.00 cash in advance, balance in monthly payments.

KNOWLEDGE IS POWER

Webster said: "The man who can teach me something is the man I want to know." You may think my prices are high, but stop to consider that you have the use of these Methods during your entire lifetime and that the knowledge I teach will be worth the money for one week's trading at critical times. You can easily lose in the market the price you would pay for my Course and the market leaves you with no valuable knowledge after your losses. Learn to see and know for yourself what Commodities will do; then you will make a success.

Special Rates in Classes For College Students

I will make a special rate to students where classes of five or more take the course at the same time.

Time Required to Learn the Course

Time required depends on the student. His education, experience and practical knowledge of stocks and commodities. If you have read my books or kept up charts you will learn in a much shorter time than one who has had no experience or special training. However, anyone who can add, subtract, multiply and divide can learn how to apply my rules. School teachers learn easy. The amount of time you put in studying each day or week will determine how soon you can learn the rules and start trading.

Some learn in one week, some in three weeks and others in three months, but one thing is sure, the longer you study the more you learn. Each year you will know more and practice will make you perfect.

Trade on Paper

I recommend that all students start trading on paper until they are sure how to apply the rules. You learn by doing and mistakes made on paper will prevent actual losses later. Never be in a hurry. Be sure you are right, then act and success is sure.

Health Is Wealth

Good health is essential for success in any business and for active trading in Stocks and Commodities. Keeping your health perfect is just as important as protecting your capital.

Why I Live in Miami

I have learned the value of good health and that is why I have a winter home in Miami, Florida. I give personal instruction to individuals or classes in Miami from October 1st to May 1st every year.

W. D. GANN
820 S.W. 26 Road
Miami, Florida

W. D. GANN

P. O. BOX 223
WALL STREET STATION
NEW YORK 5, N. Y.

New York, N. Y.

Chapter 2

Form Reading And Rules For Determining Trends Of Stocks

AUTHOR:
"Truth of the Stock Tape"
"Wall Street Stock Selector"
"New Stock Trend Detector"

W. D. GANN
Statistician and Economist
82 WALL STREET
NEW YORK, N. Y.

2101 N. W. 18th TERRACE
MIAMI. FLA.

MEMBER
New Orleans Cotton Exchange
Commodity Exchange, Inc. N.Y.
American Economic Ass'n
Royal Economy Society

FORM READING

and

RULES FOR DETERMINING TREND OF STOCKS

REQUIREMENTS FOR SUCCESS IN SPECULATION OR INVESTMENT

KNOWLEDGE

One of the vital and most important factors for making a success in speculation or anything else is KNOWLEDGE. The well-posted man or the man who knows his business is the man who succeeds. Therefore, put it down as a rule that hard work in acquiring knowledge will surely bring success in speculation or business.

PATIENCE

After you have acquired knowledge you will need to learn PATIENCE, if you have not already learned the value of patience. You must learn to wait for a definite indication of a change in trend before buying or selling. You must not guess or gamble on hope or fear. You must have ability to act and to act quickly at the right time, acting after you have acquired knowledge and know it is the time to act.

COURAGE

You must have the COURAGE to act. Courage and boldness will come after you have acquired knowledge because you will have confidence in proven rules and confidence in your ability. Therefore, the acquiring of knowledge will give you the courage for action at the time when the real opportunity comes.

STUDY

A man who will not work hard and STUDY and pay in advance for success will never get it. If you will put in the time, study, and go over the records of the Dow-Jones Industrial averages from 1892 to date, you will be convinced that the rules work and that you can make money by following the main trend of the market.

FORM READING

Eighty-five per cent of what any of us learn is from what we see. It has been well said, "One picture is worth a thousand words." That is why FORM READING or the reading of various formations at different periods of time is so valuable. The future is but a repetition of the past. The same formation at tops or bottoms or intermediate points at different times indicates the trend of the market. Therefore, when you see the same picture or formation in the market the second and third time, you know what it means and can determine the trend.

You do not have to accept my word that the rules I give you will work in the future as they have in the past but you owe it to yourself to prove by past records that these rules work; then you will have the faith to follow them and make money.

CAPITAL REQUIRED

The first point to consider in operating any method on the stock market is the amount of capital required, with which you can trade and never lose your capital and over a period of 5, 10 or 15 years be able to make profits, because a method that will make profits and never lose your capital is the kind of a method that every man should follow to make a success.

As a general rule, I have always considered it advisable to use at least $3,000 capital for every 100 shares of stock traded in and to limit stop loss orders to not more than 3 points on every 100 shares. In this way you will be able to make 10 trades on your capital and the market would have to beat you 10 consecutive times to wipe out your capital, which it will not do. Whatever amount of capital you use to trade with, follow this rule: Divide your capital into 10 equal parts and never risk more than 10% of your capital on any one trade. Should you lose for 3 consecutive times, then reduce your trading unit and only risk 10% of your remaining capital. If you follow this rule, your success is sure.

On stocks selling around $15 to $30 per share, you can start with a capital of $1,500. The first trade should be made at a time when you can place a stop loss order not more than 2 points away and you should try to start when your risk will only be 1 point. In other words, with a capital of $1,500 you must figure that you would be able to make at least 7 to 10 trades and the market would have to beat you 7 to 10 consecutive times to wipe out your trading capital. With this Method it is impossible for that to happen, provided you follow the rules and trade on definite indications.

This Method will make the most money trading in high-priced stocks, and for trading in stocks selling above $100 per share, you should use a capital of $4,000 and adhere strictly to all the rules.

If you want to start trading in small units of stock, use a capital of $300 for each 10 shares and never risk more than 3 points on the initial trade. Try to make the first trade, if possible, where your stop loss order will not be more than 1 or 2 points. Never risk more than one-tenth of your capital on any one trade.

KIND OF CHARTS TO USE

A busy man or specialist should keep a weekly high and low chart on the Dow-Jones 30 Industrial averages and the 15 Public Utility averages and should keep weekly high and low charts on 5 to 10 of the leading active stocks in the different groups. He could also keep up monthly high and low charts on a few stocks selling below 20 or below 10 and watch these different low-priced stocks when they indicate a change in trend. By crossing old tops and showing activity, it would indicate a good time to buy them.

MAJOR AND MINOR TRENDS

You will always make the most money by following the main trend of the market, altho to say that you must never trade against the trend means that you will miss a lot of intermediate moves which will make big profits, but your rule must be: When you are trading against the trend, wait until one of your rules gives you a definite indication of a buying or selling point at bottom or top, where you can place close stop loss orders.

There are always two trends--a major trend and a minor trend. The minor trend is a reversal of the main trend, which lasts for a short period of time. When the main trend is down, it is much safer to sell stocks short on rallies at a point where the rules indicate that they are top than it is to buy on a reaction. In a Bull Campaign or advancing market, it is much safer to wait for minor reactions and buy when the rules indicate that it is time to buy than it is to sell short on rallies. You will always make the most money by waiting for a definite indication of the trend before buying and selling.

TREND LINE INDICATIONS

GREEN TREND LINE

This Green Trend Line indicates uptrend, either the minor or the main trend.

We use the GREEN TREND LINE for an advancing market or when a stock, or the averages are making higher tops and higher bottoms each week. The first week that a higher bottom and a higher top is made than a previous week, the Green Trend Line is moved up to the top of that week. Then, as long as the stock or the averages make higher bottoms and higher tops, the Green Trend Line continues to be moved up to the high point of each week.

RED TREND LINE

The first week that a stock or the averages make a lower bottom than the previous week, the Trend Line changes to red and is moved down to the low of that week and continues to be moved down as long as the stock or the averages make lower bottoms. This Red Trend Line means that the minor or the main trend has turned down and that you should follow the RED TREND LINE until it reverses. The first week a higher bottom and a higher top are made, the Trend Line changes again to green.

BUY WHEN THE RED TREND LINE CHANGES TO GREEN

SELL WHEN THE GREEN TREND LINE CHANGES TO RED

For study purposes we have used the Dow-Jones 20 Railroad Stock averages ... weekly high and low ... from 1896 to July, 1914, because the rails were leaders during that period and moved faster, making a wider range, than the Industrial Stocks, therefore, were better trend indicators and more profitable to trade in.

You should follow the Trend Lines and apply the rules given here for buying points:

THREE BUYING POINTS

1 - BUY AT OLD BOTTOMS OR OLD TOPS

When a stock declines to an old bottom or to an old top, it is always a buying point with a stop loss order. In fact, you should never buy unless you can figure where to place a stop loss order 1 to 3 points away and in high-priced stocks never more than 5 points away.

Remember, it is safe to buy when a stock reacts to old tops the first, second or third time, but when it declines to the same level the fourth time, it is dangerous to buy as it nearly always goes lower.

Buy when a stock declines 1 to 3 points under old tops or old bottoms. However, a stock is always strongest if it holds just around the old tops or old bottoms and does not break 1 to 3 points under. Holding slightly higher than these old levels is a still stronger indication.

Stocks selling above $100 a share-- After they cross old tops they can react 5 points under the old tops but not more, and if the market is really strong, they should not go as much as 5 points under, except in very rare cases when the market is in a wide trading range and very active.

2 - SAFER BUYING POINT

Buy when a stock crosses former tops or crosses a series of tops of previous weeks, showing that the minor or the main trend has turned up as indicated by the Green Trend Line.

3 - SAFEST BUYING POINT

Buy on a secondary reaction after a stock has crossed previous weekly tops and the advance exceeds the greatest rally on the way down from the top.

Buy when the first rally from the extreme bottom exceeds in time the greatest rally in the preceding Bear Campaign.

Buy when the period of time exceeds the last rally before extreme lows were reached. If the last rally was 3 or 4 weeks, when the advance from the bottom is more than 3 or 4 weeks, consider the trend has turned up and stocks are a safer buy on a secondary reaction. Examples later will prove this rule.

THREE SELLING POINTS

When we refer to selling points we mean to either sell out long stocks or sell short.

1 - SELL AT OLD TOPS OR OLD BOTTOMS

An important point to sell out longs and go short is at old tops or when a stock rallies to old bottoms the first, second or third time. As a rule, it

is risky to sell the fourth time that a stock advances to the same level because it nearly always goes higher. When you sell short, place stop loss orders 1, 2, or 3 points above old tops or old bottoms.
When prices are at high levels above $100, the averages can go 5 points above old tops or 5 points above old bottoms without changing the main trend. But this seldom happens, as a study of previous tops and bottoms will prove. As a rule, when the market is weak and the main trend down, the rally stops right under old bottoms and should not go more than 2 points above them. If it goes 3 points above, it is an indication that the market is strong and likely to go higher. If it declines under these old levels, this indicates that the market is very weak.

2 - SAFER SELLING POINT

Sell when a stock breaks the low of a previous week or a series of bottoms of previous weeks as indicated by the Trend Line.

3 - SAFEST SELLING POINT

Sell on a secondary rally after the stock has broken the previous bottoms of several weeks or has broken the bottom of the last reaction, turning trend down. This secondary rally nearly always comes after the first sharp decline in the first section of a Bear Campaign.

Sell after the first decline exceeds the greatest reaction in the preceding Bull Campaign or the last reaction before final top.

Sell when the period of time of the first decline exceeds the last reaction before final top of the Bull Campaign. Example: If a stock has advanced for several months or for one year or more and the greatest reaction has been four weeks.... which is an average reaction in a Bull Market ... then after top is reached and the first decline runs more than 4 weeks, it is an indication of a change in the minor trend or the main trend. The stock will be a safer short sale on any rally because you will be trading with the trend after it has been definitely defined.

FORMATIONS AT BOTTOMS AND TOPS

By studying stock formations of the past you will be able to determine what is going to happen when similar formations occur in the future, just as you know that there is going to be a rainstorm when you see a heavy dark cloud form.

After accumulation or distribution at bottom or top has been completed, there is a BREAKAWAY POINT. When you buy or sell stocks at this point, you make money very quickly.

Study the volume of sales, the space and price movements and the last and most important time period. Similar action of the market occurs around the same month years apart. When we come to the Lesson on "Volume" it will give you more rules and information.

Study the different types of bottom formations-- Sharp, double, triple, flat and ascending bottoms.

SINGLE "V" OR SHARP BOTTOM

This formation can be a sharp, fast decline followed by a fast advance, or even a slow decline followed by a quick rally from the bottom with no secondary reactions until it advances to higher levels.

Example: July 26, 1910, the Dow-Jones 20 Railroad averages had a sharp decline to 105¾; then rallied sharply to 114¾ ... a 9-point advance with no reactions ... and did not later go back to make a double bottom.

"U" BOTTOM OR FLAT BOTTOM

This "U" bottom is a formation where a stock remains for 3 to 10 weeks or more in a narrow trading range, making about the same top and bottom levels several times; then when it crosses the intermediate tops, it has formed a "U" or flat bottom and is at the breakaway point ... a safe place to buy.

Example: March 12 to April 30, 1898 ... The 20 Railroad averages held between 56 and 60, hitting the bottom level 4 times. This was a flat bottom and when they crossed 60, the averages indicated higher prices.

"W" BOTTOM OR DOUBLE BOTTOM

When a stock declines and makes bottom; then rallies for 2 to 3 weeks or more; declines and makes a bottom around the same level the second time; then advances and crosses the previous top, it has formed a "W" or double bottom. It is safe to buy when it crosses the top or middle of the "W" ... which is the BREAKAWAY POINT.

Example: December 23, 1899, low 72½. June 23, 1900, low 73.

"W V" BOTTOM OR TRIPLE BOTTOM

This is a third higher bottom after a double bottom or three bottoms near the same level. It is safe to buy when a stock has formed a "W" and a "V" on the side and crosses the second top of the "W".

Example: Dec. 23, 1899 - 1st bottom at 72½
Jun. 23, 1900 - 2nd bottom at 73
Sep. 29, 1900 - 3rd bottom at 73¾
This formed a "W V" bottom and after the averages advanced above 78.. the BREAKAWAY POINT ... a runaway advance followed, the market advancing 44 points in 28 weeks.

"W W" BOTTOM OR 4-BOTTOM FORMATION

This formation shows first, second, third and fourth bottoms. The safest point to buy is at the BREAKAWAY POINT or when a stock crosses the middle point of the second "W".

Example: Aug. 8, 1903, low 90¾ .... rallied to 98¾ on Aug. 22, 1903
Oct. 17, 1903, low 89-3/8 .... rallied to 99-5/8 on Jan. 23, 1904
Mch. 19, 1904, low 91¼ .... rallied to 97¾ on Apr. 16, 1904
May 21, 1904, low 93½

When the averages crossed $97\frac{3}{4}$, the middle of the second "W" they went on thru the top of 99-5/8, top of the first "W". This was the BREAK-AWAY POINT and the market advanced 27 points without reacting to 99 again.

TOP FORMATIONS

You should study the various types of tops-- Sharp, flat, double, triple, and descending tops.

SINGLE "A" OR SHARP TOP

After a prolonged advance or at the end of a Bull Campaign, the averages or individual stocks often make a single sharp top ... advancing 17 to 26 weeks or more with only small reactions lasting sometimes 10 days to two weeks ... then follows a sharp, quick decline. It is safe to sell on a subsequent or secondary rally and safer to sell when it breaks the last leg of the "A" or when it breaks the bottom of the first sharp decline.

Example: The 20 Railroad averages advanced from $117\frac{1}{2}$ to $129\frac{1}{4}$ in 16 weeks from May 24 to September 13, 1902; then had a sharp decline to October 18, and only rallied to $123\frac{1}{4}$. When they broke $118\frac{3}{4}$, it was an indication of weakness and the Bear Market continued.

"⊓" TOP OR FLAT TOP

When the market makes several tops near the same level and the bottoms on reactions are near the same level ... holding in a narrow trading range ... it forms a "⊓" top or flat top. It is safe to sell short when it breaks under the series of weekly bottoms.

Example: May 13 to July 29, 1911, the Railroad averages held in a range of $2\frac{1}{2}$ points for 8 weeks, forming a flat top, and the market was a safe short sale when the averages broke 121, under the low point of this narrow range.

"M" TOP OR DOUBLE TOP

When a stock or the averages reach top after a substantial advance; then react 3 to 7 weeks or more and rally again to around the same top, an "M" or double top is formed. Then, when it declines and breaks under the low of the last reaction or under the middle of the "M", it is safe to sell short.

Example: 1906, September 15 high $137\frac{3}{4}$; November 17 low $131\frac{1}{2}$; December 15 high $137\frac{1}{2}$; then followed a quick decline, breaking the low of $131\frac{1}{2}$, and a Bear Market followed.

"M A" TOP OR TRIPLE TOP

This formation occurs when a stock or the averages make 3 tops near the same level or the 2nd and 3rd tops are slightly lower. When these formations are made at tops after a long advance, they are signals for a major decline. The more time between tops, the stronger the indications for a big decline. It is safe to sell when a stock breaks the last bottom or breaks the end of the "M" and safer when it breaks the bottom of the "A" ... which is the BREAKAWAY POINT.

Example: 1st top - Jan. 19, 1906, high 138-3/8 ... end of Bull Market;
May 5, 1906, sharp decline to 120¼;
2nd top - Sep. 22, 1906, high 137¾, slightly lower than Jan. 1906 top
Nov. 17, 1906, low of 6-point reaction;
3rd top - Dec. 15, 1906, high 137½, near same level ... a signal for a big decline. Panic followed in 1907 and the averages declined 57 points in 11 months.

"M M" OR 4-TOP FORMATION

This formation occurs when a stock or the averages make 4 tops at the same level or slightly lower. It is safest to sell short when a stock breaks the second point of the second "M" or the low of the last reaction.

Example: 1st top - July 22, 1911, high 124;
2nd top - Aug. 17, 1912, high 124;
Sep. 14, 1912, reacted to 120½;
3rd top - Oct. 5, 1912, high 124-3/8;
Nov. 2, 1912, reacted to 119-5/8;
4th top - Nov. 9, 1912, last rally to 122¾;
When the averages broke under 119-5/8, low of the last reaction, this was the BREAKAWAY POINT and a big decline followed.

SECTIONS OF MARKET CAMPAIGNS

A Bull or Bear Campaign in stocks or the averages runs out in 3 to 4 sections--

BULL MARKET

1st Section - Advance after final bottom; then a secondary reaction

2nd Section - Advance to higher levels, above the highs of previous weeks and of the first advance; then a reaction.

3rd Section - Advance to new high for the move. In many cases this means the end of the campaign, but you must watch for a definite indication before deciding that the 3rd run up means a change in the main trend.

4th Section - Often four sections are run out and this 4th move or run-up is the most important to watch for the end of a Bull Campaign and a change in trend.

Minor Bull Campaigns of short duration, running one year or less, often run out in two sections, especially if the first section is from a sharp bottom. Therefore, always watch the action of the market after the second advance to see if it is forming a top and gives indications of a change in trend.

BEAR MARKET

A Bear Campaign runs opposite to a Bull Campaign--

1st Section - There is a sharp, severe decline which changes the main trend; then a secondary rally on which stocks are safer short sales. That marks the end of the 1st Section.

2nd Section - Then there is a second decline to lower prices, followed by a moderate rally.

3rd Section - A third decline or move to still lower prices, which may be the end of the campaign.

4th Section - There is often a 4th move, when you must watch closely for bottom. In determining whether it is final bottom, you use all of the other rules ... watching old tops and old bottoms for definite indication that the main trend is ready to change.

Minor Bear Campaigns of short duration, running one year or less, often run out in two sections, especially if the 1st Section is from a sharp top. Therefore, always watch the action of the market after the 2nd decline to see if it is forming a bottom and gives indication of a change in trend.

In extreme cases, like 1929 and the Bear Campaign which followed from 1929 to 1932, there are as many as 7 sections up or down, but this is abnormal and unusual and only occurs many years apart.

Go back over all of the campaigns we have worked out and you will see how these sections or moves run out.

HOW TO DETERMINE CHANGE IN THE MAIN TREND

SPACE MOVEMENT

RULE FOR DETERMINING CHANGE IN TREND ACCORDING TO SPACE MOVEMENTS--

When a decline in points exceeds the greatest decline of a previous reaction by one or more points, it is an indication of a change in trend.

When the market has run out 3 or more sections in a Bull Campaign, go back over the record and find out what the greatest reaction has been in any section, whether 10, 15, 20, 30 points or more. Suppose the averages have been advancing for a long time and the greatest reaction in the Bull Market has been 10 points and the market has reached the 3rd or 4th Section of the campaign. Then the first time the averages or the price of a stock breaks back more than 10 points, or more than the greatest reaction, it is an indication that the main trend has changed or will change soon. This does not mean that a rally cannot take place after this definite signal of reversal has been given, as usually after the first signal of a change in trend is given, there is a secondary rally in a Bull Market and time has to be allowed at top for distribution to take place. Therefore, just because you get a definite indication that the main trend has changed, do not jump to the conclusion that you can sell short right at that time and that there will be no rally. Always sell on rallies, if possible, altho there are times that you can sell at new low levels or when bottoms are broken. Judge this by applying all of your rules.

TIME PERIOD -- Another way to tell when the main trend is changing.

RULE-- When a campaign has only 3 or 4 sections and the TIME period on a reaction exceeds the greatest time of a previous reaction, consider that the main trend has changed.

Go back over the record and find the greatest time period from any minor top or the duration of a reaction in previous sections of the Bull Market. If you find that the greatest reaction has been about 4 weeks, then the first time the market declines consecutively for 5 weeks or more, it is an indication that the main trend has changed and that stocks will be short sales on a secondary rally.

Apply the same rules in a Bear Market. When the SPACE movement or number of points that a stock or the averages have rallied during a Bear Campaign is exceeded, the trend is changing. When the TIME period of the greatest reverse movement is exceeded, then the main trend is changing and a Bull Campaign is starting.

A reversal in SPACE movement after the second run or 2nd Section in a Bull or a Bear Market, would not mean as important a change in trend as if it came after the 3rd or 4th Section had run out, either up or down.

Examples of all these rules will be referred to in the working out of each Bull and Bear Campaign from 1892 to 1939 so that you will know just how to apply the rules in future market movements.

MANY WEEKS IN NARROW RANGE

When a stock or the averages hold for 2 to 6 weeks or 10 to 13 weeks in a narrow range, then cross tops or break bottoms of previous weeks, the trend has changed and you should go with it. The longer the period of time in a narrow range, the greater the advance or the decline when they break out of the range, either up or down.

Example: 1897, January 16 to March 20, the Railroad averages held in 2-point range; then broke the low of 52 and went lower. 1897, April 10 to May 22, held in a 2-point range for 6 weeks; then crossed the top at 51 and the Bull Market started.

ACCUMULATION OR DISTRIBUTION ON SIDE

After a market has advanced to the 3rd or 4th Section, then has a sharp decline and rallies, it will often remain for a long period of time in a range while DISTRIBUTION is taking place ON THE SIDE. The top of the range may be several points below the extreme high. In FORM READING it is very important to note the range from high to low in this zone of distribution. The stock is a short sale at the top of this range of distribution on the side and a safer sale when it breaks the low point of this range ... which is the BREAKAWAY POINT.

At the end of a Bear Campaign, after the first sharp advance there is a secondary reaction; then a long period of ACCUMULATION ON THE SIDE, with several moves up to the top of the range and back to the bottom of the range of accumulation. The market is a buy at the bottom of this range and a safer buy when the tops of this range are crossed as that is the BREAKAWAY POINT and a signal for a fast advance.

Examples of these sideways accumulation and sideways distribution will be shown in the different campaigns worked out.

LAST STAGE OF BULL OR BEAR MARKET

In fast, advancing markets in the last stage of the campaign reactions get smaller as stocks work to higher levels, until the final section or run has ended. Then comes a sharp, quick reaction and a reversal in trend.

In the last stage of a Bear Market, after all old bottoms and resistance levels have been broken, rallies get less or smaller as prices work lower. Therefore, people who buy have no chance to sell on rallies until the final bottom has been reached and the first rally takes place.

This is why it never pays to buck the trend in the last stage of a Bull Market or the last stage of a Bear Market.

RANGE OF BOTTOMS

Never consider that a major or a minor trend has reversed or changed until the bottoms of previous weeks have been broken or the tops of previous weeks have been crossed. The number of points that a stock or the averages should decline below a bottom to indicate a change in trend to lower levels, varies according to the price at which the averages or the stock is selling. We consider a range within 1 to 3 points a double or triple bottom or a double or triple top. In a strong market a stock will break only 1 point under a bottom and then rally and, in extreme cases, not more than 2 points. As a rule when bottoms are broken by 3 full points it is an indication for lower prices before any rally of importance.

RANGE OF TOPS

The same at the top. The range for double tops is about 3 points. These tops can be in a range of 1 to 3 points and still be considered double and triple tops. Advancing 1 to 2 points above an old top does not always indicate that the main trend has changed and that stocks are going up immediately but advancing 3 points above old tops is nearly always a definite indication that higher prices will follow before much reaction. At the end of Bull or Bear Markets some false moves are often made and quick reversals follow.

HOW FAR SHOULD STOCKS DECLINE BELOW OLD TOPS AFTER THEY ADVANCE ABOVE THEM?

In order to still show uptrend, after a stock or the averages have advanced above old tops, then reacted, when in strong position they will stop right around the old tops or sometimes go 1 to 2 points below the old tops but seldom more than 3. Regardless of how high a stock is selling, a decline of more than 5 points below the old top would indicate that the trend had reversed and at that immediate time the stock would not go higher but would go lower for awhile. It can decline 5 points under old tops and still be in a Bull Market, all depending on what section the market is in. A signal in the last section is most important.

HOW FAR STOCKS CAN GO ABOVE OLD BOTTOMS IN BEAR MARKETS

Reverse this rule in a Bear Market. When stocks advance to old bottoms, they are short sales because bottoms become tops and tops become bottoms. They should not go more than 1 to 2 points above the old bottoms and on an average should not go more than 3 points. Therefore, even when stocks are at high levels if they advance more than 5 points above an old bottom, it is an indication that they are going higher and are not going to work lower immediately with the main trend.

SEVERAL FAST MOVES UP OR DOWN OVER A RANGE OF 5 TO 7 OR 10 TO 12 POINTS

Whether the market is very active or in a slow trading range, all indications are more accurate and more valuable when the market is quite active.

After a stock or the averages have been advancing for some time and have run out 3 or 4 section, if there are several moves of 10 to 12 points up or down in a range, making several bottoms and several tops in this range, it indicates either accumulation or distribution. When the bottoms in a range of this kind are broken it is an indication of lower prices and when the tops in a range of this kind are crossed, it is an indication of higher prices. Note the range on sideways accumulation and the range on sideways distribution.

An advancing market may have several reactions of 10 to 12 points; then have a reaction of 20 to 24 points;then after an advance if it declines from any top more than 20 points, it will usually run 30 to 40 points. Go over the stocks or averages when they have been selling at very high levels and prove to yourself the value of this rule.

WHEN THE MARKET IS IN STRONGEST POSITION OR IN WEAKEST POSITION

A stock or the averages are in the strongest position after there has been a prolonged decline and the market starts making higher bottoms, especially after a sharp, fast decline, when rallies have been small. After the 2nd or 3rd higher bottom has been made and then the top of a previous rally has been crossed, the stock is in the strongest position. Rising bottoms always indicate strength and an advance usually starts from the 3rd or 4th higher bottom, that is, the big advance which runs for a long time with only small reactions. You make money quickest when you get in on a move of this kind.

Reverse this rule in a Bear Market. A market is weakest when it is making lower tops. The 3rd or 4th lower top is the safest place to sell. After the 3rd or 4th lower top, when it breaks the last low or previous bottom, it is in the weakest position and indicates that the main trend is down and declines will be faster.

HOW TO DETERMINE CHANGE IN MINOR TREND

MINOR ADVANCE

When a market is advancing and makes a top around the same level for 2 or more weeks, especially when the range is very narrow near top levels, then prices break under the bottom of 2 weeks or more, the minor trend has turned down and you would follow it until there is another definite indication of a change in trend.

MINOR REACTION

After the averages or a stock has been declining for several weeks or several months and prices make bottom 2 weeks or more around the same level and hold in a narrow trading range for 2 weeks or more and then cross the tops of 2 or 3 weeks on the upside, the minor trend has changed, at least temporarily, and you should go with it.

DULL MARKET

A dull market, in a narrow trading range at any point, indicates that it is getting ready for some kind of a change and you should follow it whichever way it breaks out, up or down, after these narrow, dull periods.

DURATION OF MINOR MOVES

RULE FOR TIME OF MINOR REACTION IN BULL MARKETS--

In an advancing market or Bull Campaign when indications are given for a minor reaction, prices will react 3 to 4 weeks but as a rule in the 4th week they will rally and close higher. In some cases there will only be a sharp, quick reaction of 2 weeks and then the main trend will be resumed, but after a decline of 3 to 4 weeks should the market have a minor rally; then break back under the bottom of the 3rd or 4th week, it will be an indication of a greater change in the trend and probably a change in the main trend.

In extreme cases, after a secondary rally in a Bull Market, prices will decline as much as 6 to 7 weeks, seldom more, before the main trend is resumed.

RULE FOR TIME OF MINOR RALLIES IN BEAR MARKETS--

These rules are reversed in a Bear Market. Rallies in a Bear Market last 2 to 4 weeks. Should a rally hold into the 5th week, it is likely to run into the 6th or 7th week; then you can watch for an important change in trend.

After a rally of 3 to 4 weeks and a secondary reaction in a Bear Market, should the market advance and cross the level made at the end of the 3 or 4 weeks' rally, then the trend is changing, at least temporarily, and higher prices .. even in a Bear Market ... are indicated.

HOW TO DETERMINE FIRST CHANGE IN TREND BY OPENING AND CLOSING PRICES

The Weekly high and low Chart with the opening and closing prices on it is one of the best charts to use for determining trend of stocks or the averages. That is why we have used the Weekly Chart on the Dow-Jones 30 Industrial averages and given all the indications according to it.

The closing price at the end of the week or at the end of any day is most important because regardless of how high or how low stocks have been during the week or during the day, the closing price shows exactly what they have lost or gained at the end of the period.

After a stock or the averages have been advancing for a considerable period of time and have reached an old top or a section of the campaign which indicates that a change in trend could take place, it is very important in very active markets to watch the opening price on Monday morning. Should the averages or a stock not sell more than one point above the opening price on Monday morning and then decline and close at or near the low levels of the week on Saturday, it is the first indication of a change in trend on the Weekly Chart. But don't fail to use your other rules and wait for the proper declines in TIME or SPACE or until previous weekly bottoms have been broken before deciding that there is a definite change in trend.

Reverse this rule at the bottom of a decline or after there has been a sharp, fast decline in a very active market. Watch the opening price on Monday morning. Should a stock decline rapidly to around the middle or latter part of the week, then after making bottom, reverse and rally quickly and on Saturday close at or near the opening on Monday morning or above this opening, it is an especially strong indication that the trend is reversing and that prices are going higher temporarily. But use all of your other rules ... the crossing of previous weekly tops ... the reversal of the SPACE movement in points ... also reversal in TIME .. before deciding that a definite change in trend is indicated.

It is also very important at the end of the week if prices close under old bottoms or under bottoms of previous weeks or close above old tops or above tops of previous weeks as it is an indication of weakness or strength.

WHEN STOCKS ADVANCE INTO NEW HIGH GROUND OR DECLINE INTO NEW LOW GROUND

When stocks advance to higher levels than they have been before in their previous history or decline to lower levels than they have ever sold before in their history, they are in new high or new low ground and you must have a rule to follow when stocks reach new high or new low record prices.

First, apply all of your other rules and do not buy or sell until there is a definite indication of a change in the main trend.

When a stock or the averages advance to a new high level that they have never sold at before in their history, it is an indication of an advance of 7, 10, 15, 20 to 24 points or more, especially if it is in the 1st or 2nd Section of the Bull Campaign. Should new highs be made in the 3rd or 4th Section, then the advance into new high ground may not be very many points before final high is reached and the trend changes.

You should watch the action of the market when it has advanced 7 points into new high territory, 10 points, again around 15 points, and on an extreme advance watch around 20 to 24 points, where there is likely to be resistance and top made. These are average moves and it depends upon the activity and the price of a stock whether it will stop on any of these points. By following the trend indications and rules you will be able to determine when the first move into new high territory has run out and the trend has changed.

Reverse the above rules in a Bear Campaign.

When the averages or stocks selling between 50 and 125 advance into new high ground, these average movements of 7, 10, 15, 20 and 24 points, work out quite accurately. After stocks advance above 125, they move faster and go higher than they do below 125. Above 200, the movement increases and the range is much wider. The same when stocks or the averages get above 300 ... they have a still greater range and faster moves, all of which depends upon how long the campaign has been running and how many moves or sections the campaign has run out and how high the stocks are from the last bottom or how far down from the last top.

WHEN TO USE DAILY HIGH AND LOW CHART

When markets are very active and fluctuating over a wide range, especially in the last stages of a Bull Market or the last fast decline in a Bear Market, you should keep up a Daily high and low Chart on the averages or individual stocks and put on the Trend Lines, applying the same rules as used for the Weekly Chart, because the Daily Chart will give you the first change in the minor trend, which may later be confirmed by the Weekly Chart into a change of the main trend. Full instructions will follow under "Resistance Levels."

Again I remind you ... Don't try to get ahead of the market. Don't guess if it is making a change in trend and be wrong. Wait until it shows a definite change in trend. You will be right when you form your judgment after definite indication is given according these rules.

July 6, 1939

DOW-JONES 20 RAILROAD AVERAGES

BOTTOM AND TOP FORMATIONS

1896 - 1914

1896	Aug. 8	Sharp bottom or single "V" - Low 42.
1897	Jan. 16	to 23 and March 20 - Flat double top "M".
	Apr.	Sharp bottom and 4 weeks narrow on side in 1-point range.
	Sep.	Sharp or "A" top at 1/2 point from 42 to 92.
	Nov.	Sharp or "V" bottom.
1898	Feb.	Flat top ... 2 weeks in 1-point range.
	Mch. 5	to April 23 - Flat bottom ... triple bottom near same level.
	Aug.	Sharp top.
	Oct. 1	to Nov. 5 - Flat bottom ... 6 weeks in 1-point range.
1899	Apr. 1	to 29 - Flat top ... 5 weeks in 2-point range.
	Jun. 3	Sharp bottom.
	Jul. 29	to Sep. 9 - Flat top ... 7 weeks in 2-point range; 1st lower top after April.
	Nov.	Sharp top ... 4 weeks on side in 2-point range ... 2nd lower top.
	Dec. 23	Sharp bottom.
1900	Apr. 7	Sharp top ... 4th lower top.
	Jun. 23	Sharp bottom ... 1st higher bottom and double bottom against Dec. 1899 low.
	Aug. 18	Flat intermediate or middle top.
	Sep. 29	Sharp bottom ... a triple bottom and 3rd higher bottom ... strong and good buying point.
1901	May 4	Sharp top.
	May 9	Sharp bottom ... panic.
	Jun. 15	Sharp top ... 2 narrow eeks on side ... a double top.
	Aug. 10	Sep. 14 and Oct. 12 - Sharp bottoms ... triple bottoms with 2nd and 3rd bottoms higher than the 1st ... strong.
1902	Sep. 13	A sharp top and sharp decline followed.
	Nov. 15	and Dec. 13 - Two sharp bottoms ... double bottoms.
1903	Jan. 10	Sharp top with 5 weeks on side in 2-point range.
	Jul. 11	Sharp top ... 2 weeks rally followed.
	Aug. 22	Sharp top ... 3 weeks on side in 2-point range.
	Sep. 19	to Nov. 14 - Triple bottoms ... 3rd bottom higher.
1904	Jan. 23	Sharp or "A" top.
	Feb. 27	to Mch. 19 - Flat bottom ... 3 weeks in 2-point range.
	Dec. 3	Sharp top ... 3 weeks' reaction.
1905	Mch. 18	and Apr. 15 - A double flat top.
	May 27	Sharp bottom.
	Sep.	to Nov. - Flat top but only declined 4 points.
1906	Jan. 19	Final sharp top ... sharp decline followed.
	May 5	Sharp bottom ... sharp rally followed.
	Jun. 16	Sharp top ... sharp decline followed.
	Jul. 7	Sharp bottom ... sharp rally followed.
	Sep. 18	to Oct. 13 - Flat top ... 7 weeks in 2-point range, just under January top.
	Nov. 17	to Dec. 22 - Flat top ... 4 weeks in 3-point range. A panicky decline followed this 3rd lower top.

BOTTOM AND TOP FORMATIONS 1896 - 1914 (Continued)

1907	Mch. 14	to 25 - A sharp bottom.
	Apr. 6	to May 11 - Sharp double tops.
	Jun. 8	Flat bottom ... 4 weeks in 2-point range.
	Jul. 6	to 27 - Flat top ... 4 weeks in 3-point range.
	Nov. 23	Sharp bottom and sharp rally followed.
1908	Jan. 18	Sharp bottom and sharp decline followed.
	Feb. 15	to Mch. 7 - Flat narrow bottom ... 3 weeks in 1½-point range.
	May 23	Sharp top.
	Jun. 27	Sharp bottom.
	Sep. 12	Sharp top.
	Sep. 22	Sharp bottom ... quick, sharp rally followed.
1909	Jan. 2	Sharp top.
	Feb. 27	Sharp bottom.
	Aug. 14	Sharp top followed by sharp reaction.
	Sep. 11	Sharp bottom.
	Sep. 18	to Oct. 9 - Flat top ... 4 weeks in 2-point range ... 1st lower top.
1910	Jul. 26	Sharp bottom ... end of Bear Market ... quick rally followed.
	Oct. 22	Sharp top.
	Dec. 10	Sharp bottom.
1911	Feb. 4	to 18 - Flat top ... 3 weeks in 2-point range.
	Mch. 11	and Apr. 22 - Double bottoms.
	Jun. 10	to Jul. 29 - Flat narrow top ... 7 weeks in 2-point range.
	Sep. 30	Flat bottom ... 4 weeks in 2-point range.
1912	Aug. 17	to Oct. 3 - Double tops ... narrow range ... 3rd top from July 22, 1911. A prolonged decline followed.
1913	Jun. 14	Sharp bottom.
	Nov. 15	to Dec. 20 - Flat double bottoms.
	Sep. 13	to 27 and
1914	Jan. 24	to Feb. 7 - Double flat tops ... narrow range.
	Apr. 25	A sharp bottom ... slow rally followed.
	May 23	to July 11 - Flat top ... 9 weeks in 2-point range ... a panicky decline followed.

BREAKAWAY POINTS IN BULL & BEAR MARKETS
DOW-JONES 30 INDUSTRIAL AVERAGES
STUDY THESE POINTS ON THE CHART

YEAR					WEEKS	POINTS
1897	June	5	to	Sept. 4	12	16
1897	Oct.	2		Mch. 26, 1898	10	14
1898	May	7		Aug. 28	12	15
1898	Dec.	3		Apr. 29, 1899	9	20
1899	Dec.	9		Dec. 23	3	15
1900	Oct.	20		Apr. 20, 1901	10	18
1901	July	13		Oct. 14	15	14
1903	Mch.	28		Oct. 17	29	25
1904	July	9		Apr. 15, 1905	40	33
1905	June	24		Jan. 19, 1906	30	28
1906	Feb.	17		May 5	8	14
1906	July	28		Oct. 13	11	8
1907	Feb.	9		Mch. 25	7	16
1907	July	6		Nov. 15	19	25
1908	Feb.	29		Aug. 14	23	25
1909	Apr.	3		Oct. 2	25	16
1910	Jan.	3		Feb. 12	6	13
1910	Apr.	30		July 26	13	16
1910	Oct.	1		Oct. 29	4	6
1911	Aug.	5		Sept. 30	8	12
1911	Nov.	11		Sept. 7, 1912	46	15
1912	Dec.	7		Mch. 22, 1913	15	12
1913	Apr.	26		June 14	7	9
1913	July	19		Sept. 13	8	8
1913	Oct.	4		Dec. 20	11	6
1913	Dec.	27		Mch. 24, 1914	12	5
1914	July	25		Dec. 24	21	27
1915	Mch	20		May 1	6	13
1915	July	24		Dec. 30	32	28
1916	Jan.	22		Apr. 29	14	10
1916	Aug.	12		Nov. 14	14	13
1916	Dec.	9		Feb. 3, 1917	8	12
1917	June	16		Dec. 22	26	30
1918	Jan.	5		Oct. 19	41	14
1919	Feb.	22		July 19	21	30
1919	Aug.	2		Aug. 23	3	10
1919	Aug.	30		Nov. 8	10	18
1919	Nov.	15		Feb. 28, 1920	17	23
1920	Mch.	6		Apr. 10	5	10
1920	Apr.	24		May 29	5	14
1920	July	24		Dec. 25	23	23
1921	May	21		Aug. 24	15	13
1921	Sept.	10		Oct. 28, 1922	59	13
1923	Mch.	24		Aug. 4	19	16
1923	Nov.	10		Feb. 9, 1924	13	10
1924	Mch.	23		May 24	10	9
1924	June	14		Aug. 23	18	14
1924	Nov.	8		Mch. 14, 1925	18	16

BREAKAWAY POINTS IN BULL & BEAR MARKETS
DOW-JONES 30 INDUSTRIAL AVERAGES (Cont.)
STUDY THESE POINTS ON THE CHART

YEAR				WEEKS	POINTS
1925	May 9		Feb. 27, 1926	41	36
1926	Mch. 1		Apr. 17	9	19
1926	June 5		Aug. 21	11	18
1926	Sept. 12		Oct. 16	5	12
1927	Apr. 16		Sept. 24	22	31
1927	Sept. 30		Oct. 15	2	14
1928	Mch. 17		May 12	8	14
1928	Aug. 18		Oct. 8	15	68
1928	Oct. 8	to	Oct. 22	2	24
1928	Oct. 22		Feb. 9, 1929	16	40
1929	Mch. 22		Mch. 30	1	4
1929	Apr. 30		May 11	2	8
1929	May 18		June 8	3	9
1929	July 6		Sept. 3	8	38
1929	Sept. 7		Nov. 13	9	160
1929	Nov. 16		Dec. 14	4	46
1930	Jan. 25		Apr. 17	13	38
1930	Apr. 19		July 5	11	64
1930	Sept. 20		Nov. 15	8	62
1930	Nov. 29		Dec. 20	3	27
1931	Feb. 7		Feb. 24	3	20
1931	Mch. 7		Jun. 2	12	64
1931	Jun. 9		Jul. 27	2	27
1931	Jul. 2		Aug. 8	5	20
1931	Aug. 31		Oct. 3	5	45
1931	Oct. 10		Nov. 9	4	24
1931	Nov. 16		Jan. 9, 1932	8	42
1932	Mch. 19		July 8	17	38
1932	July 16		Sept. 8	8	31
1932	Sept. 7		Oct. 30	7	16
1933	Feb. 4		Feb. 27	3	8
1933	Apr. 8		Jul. 17	17	44
1933	July 18		Jul. 21	1	18
1933	Sept. 23		Oct. 21	4	15
1933	Nov. 18		Feb. 5, 1934	12	15
1934	May 5		Jul. 26	12	17
1934	Nov. 24		Feb. 23, 1935	14	8
1935	Apr. 13		Apr. 6, 1936	52	54
1936	Apr. 10		Apr. 30	4	15
1936	May 30		Nov. 21	25	32
1936	Nov. 28		Dec. 26	4	4
1937	Jan. 16		Mch. 8	8	8
1937	Mch. 27		Jun. 17	14	22
1937	Jul. 3		Aug. 14	6	20
1937	Aug. 21		Oct. 19	9	65
1937	Oct. 19		Oct. 29	1	18
1937	Nov. 23		Jan. 15, 1938	7	15

BREAKAWAY POINTS IN BULL & BEAR MARKETS
DOW-JONES 30 INDUSTRIAL AVERAGES (Cont.)
STUDY THESE POINTS ON THE CHART

YEAR					WEEKS	POINTS
1938	Mch.	10	Mch.	31	3	28
1938	Jun.	25	Jul.	25	4	24
1938	Sept.	17	Sept.	26	1	10
1938	Sept.	28	Nov.	10	7	25
1939	Jan.	14	Jan.	28	2	14
1939	Mch.	18	Apr.	11	3	25
1939	Apr.	12	Jun.	9	8	15
1939	Jun.	10	Jun.	30	3	7
1939	Jun.	30	Jul.	25	3	12

TIME PERIODS FOR DIFFERENT FORMATIONS

DOW JONES 20 RAILROAD AVERAGES

The RUN OR ADVANCES

AFTER BREAKAWAY

IN A BULL MARKET

EXAMPLES:

Nov. 1898 to April 1899, in 21 weeks advanced 38 points after the breakaway.
Mar. 1902 to Sept. 1902, in 21 weeks advanced 15 points.
July 9, 1904 to Mar. 1905, in 36 weeks advanced 29 points.
June 24, 1905 to Jan. 19, 1906, in 27 weeks advanced 19 points.
Mar. 7, 1908 to Sept. 12, 1908, in 26 weeks advanced 20 points.
Mar. 20, 1909 to Aug. 14, 1909, in 21 weeks advanced 16½ points

BREAKAWAY POINTS

IN A BEAR MARKET

EXAMPLES:

Feb. 21, 1903 to Oct. 13, 1903, in 33 weeks declined 30 points.
Dec. 22, 1906 to Mar. 25, 1907, in 15 weeks declined 36 points.
Aug. 10, 1907 to Nov. 21, 1907, in 15 weeks declined 24 points.
Jan. 15, 1910 to July 26, 1910, in 27 weeks declined 22 points.
Aug. 5, 1911 to Sept. 30, 1911, in 8 weeks declined 12 points.
?Dec. 7, 1912 to June 14, 1913, in 27 weeks declined 17 points.
July 18, 1914 to Dec. 23, 1914, in 22 weeks declined 11 points.

CHAPTER 3

RESISTANCE LEVELS

AUTHOR:
"Truth of the Stock Tape"
"Wall Street Stock Selector"
"New Stock Trend Detector"

W. D. GANN
Statistician and Economist
82 WALL STREET
NEW YORK, N. Y.

2101 N. W. 18th TERRACE
MIAMI. FLA.

MEMBER
New Orleans Cotton Exchange
Commodity Exchange, Inc. N.Y.
American Economic Ass'n
Royal Economy Society

RESISTANCE LEVELS

If we wish to avert failure in speculation we must deal with causes. Everything in existence is based on exact proportion and perfect relation. There is no chance in nature, because mathematical principles of the highest order lie at the foundation of all things. Faraday said: "There is nothing in the Universe but mathematical points of force."

Every stock makes a top or bottom on some exact mathematical point in proportion to some previous high or low level.

The movement of a stock between extreme high and extreme low, either in a major or a minor move, is very important and by a proper division of this range of fluctuation, we determine the points where resistance or support will be met on a reverse move, either up or down. By carefully watching these Resistance Levels in connection with your Trend Lines, you can make a greater success and trade with closer stop loss orders. You can tell by the Resistance Points why the averages or a stock should receive support or meet selling at old tops or bottoms.

RANGE OF FLUCTUATIONS

1/8 POINTS

Take the extreme low and extreme high of any important move; subtract the low from the high to get the range; then divide the range of fluctuation by 8 to get the 1/8 points, which are Resistance Levels or buying and selling points. When a stock stops around these levels and makes bottom or top on or near them and shows a turn on the Trend Line, this is the place to buy or sell. Sometimes the averages or a stock will hold for 3 to 7 days, making bottom or top around these important Resistance Levels, and at other times may hold for several weeks around them.

1/3 and 2/3 POINTS

After dividing a stock by 8 to get the the 1/8 points, the next important thing to do is to divide the range of fluctuation by 3 to get the 1/3 and 2/3 points. These 1/3 and 2/3 points are very strong, especially if they fall near other Resistance Points of previous moves or when they are divisions of a very wide move.

HIGHEST SELLING PRICE

Next in importance is the division of the highest price at which a stock has ever sold and each lower top.

Divide the highest selling price by 8 to get the 1/8 points and also divide by 3 to get the 1/3 and 2/3 points.

This is very important as a stock, after breaking the half-way point of the fluctuating range, will often decline to the half-way point of the highest selling price, and will also work on the other Resistance Points in the same way.

When a stock is advancing, it will often cross the half-way point of the highest selling point and then advance to the half-way point of the fluctuation and meet resistance.

MOST IMPORTANT STOCK MOVEMENTS TO CONSIDER

The first and most important point: Consider the Resistance Levels between the extreme high and extreme low of the life of a stock.

Next important point to consider: Resistance Points or divisions of the highest price at which the stock has ever sold.

Then consider the fluctuation of each campaign which runs one year or more. Take the range between extreme high and extreme low and divide into 8 equal parts to get the Resistance Points.

Then take a third or fourth lower top and divide it by 8 to get the Resistance Points.

SECONDARY BOTTOMS AND TOPS

After the market has made final top in a Bear Campaign and the first rally takes place, then follows a secondary reaction, making a higher bottom, the half-way point between the high of the first rally and the low on secondary decline is very important to figure Resistance Levels from. The half-way point between the top of the first rally and the bottom of the secondary reaction is a strong support point.

Example: Dow-Jones Industrial averages - 1932 Bear Market
Jul. 8, 1932 final low 40-1/2;
Sep. 8, 1932 high of first rally 81-1/2;
Feb. 27, 1933 bottom of secondary reaction 49-1/2;
half-way point 61.

After final top in a Bull Campaign has been reached and the first sharp decline takes place and a secondary rally follows, making a lower top, this lower top is an important point to figure Resistance Levels from. The half-way point between the bottom of the first reaction and the secondary top is a strong Resistance Level.

Example: 1937, Mch. 8 high 195-1/2;
Jun. 17 low of first decline 163;
Aug. 14 high of secondary rally 190-1/2;
half-way point 179-1/4.

Also figure the half-way point between the secondary bottom of 49-1/2 made on February 27, 1933 and the secondary top of 190-1/2 reached on August 14, 1937.

This was 120, a very important Resistance Level. The low of April 11, 1939 was 120, where the trend turned up again. There were many other bottoms and tops formed around this level in the past.

ORDER OF RESISTANCE LEVELS

When a stock is advancing and crosses the 1/4 point, the next most important point to watch is the half-way point (1/2 point) or gravity center, or the average of the move or fluctuation.

Then the next point above the half-way point is the 5/8 point.

The next and strongest point after the half-way point is crossed is the 3/4 point.

Then, if the range is very wide, it is important to watch the 7/8 point of the move. This will often mark the top of an advance.

But in watching these Resistance Points, always watch your Trend Lines on the Weekly Chart and follow rules given on Formations. If the stock starts making tops or bottoms around these Resistance Points, it is safe to sell or buy.

THE AVERAGE OR HALF-WAY POINT

Always remember that the 50% reaction or half-way point of the range of fluctuation or of the extreme highest point of a stock or any particular move is the most important point for support on the down side or for meeting selling and resistance on the way up. This is the balancing point because it divides the range of fluctuation into two equal parts.

To get this point, add the extreme low of any move to the extreme high of that move and divide by 2.

When a stock advances or declines to this half-way point, you should sell or buy with a stop loss order 1, 2, or 3 points according to whether the stock is selling at very high or very low levels.

The wider the range and the longer the time period, the more important is this half-way point when it is reached.

You can make a fortune by following this one rule alone. A careful study and review of past movements in any stock or the averages will prove to you beyond doubt that this rule works and that you can make profits following it.

Buy or sell at the most important half-way point of the major move and place stop loss orders 1 to 3 points under the half-way point or 1 to 3 points above the half-way point. By major moves we mean the half-way point between the extreme low and extreme high when the range runs 25 to 100 points or more. A minor half-way point would be the 1/2 point between a minor top and a minor bottom. Reactions usually run back half of the last move or to the half-way point.

When the range between the 1/2 point and the 5/8 point is 5 to 10 points or more and the stock crosses the half-way point, it will go to the 5/8 point and meet resistance and then react or decline. The 5/8 point is a very important point to watch for top or reaction. A stock will often react from the 5/8 point back to the half-way point and be a buy again.

The same rule applies when a stock is declining. If the range is 5 to 10 points or more between the 1/2 point and the 3/8 point, then the stock breaks the half-way point, it will decline to the 3/8 point and make bottom and rally to the 1/2 point or higher.

When a stock is in a narrow trading range, it will often fluctuate between the 5/8 point on the upside and the 3/8 point below the half-way point, making bottoms and tops around the half-way point and at the 5/8 and 3/8 points, moving in 1/4 of the full range of fluctuation. See examples of 1/2, 3/8, 5/8 points on the Dow-Jones 20 Railroad averages 1896 to 1914 and the 30 Industrial averages 1903 to 1939.

When a stock advances to a half-way point and reacts several points from this level, then finally goes thru it, you can expect it to make the next resistance point indicated on your Resistance Level Card or the next old top.

The same applies when a stock declines and receives support several times on a half-way point, then breaks thru it. It will then indicate the next resistance point on your Resistance Level Card or the next important bottom.

The greatest indication of strength is when a stock holds one or more points above the half-way point, which shows that buying or support orders were placed above this important Resistance Level.

A sign of weakness is when a stock advances and fails to reach the half-way point by one or more points; then declines and breaks the Trend Line or other Resistance Points.

NEXT RESISTANCE LEVELS AFTER THE MAIN HALF-WAY POINT HAS BEEN BROKEN

The next Resistance Level to watch after the main half-way point has been broken is the next half-way point of some previous move. By main half-way point I mean, the half-way point of the extreme fluctuating range of the life of a stock.

Another very important Resistance Level after the main half-way point is crossed is the half-way point or 1/2 of the highest selling price. This is a stronger support level than the half-way point of minor fluctuating moves because it cuts the highest selling price in half, and is a strong buying or selling point until it is crossed by 1, 2, or 3 points, according to the price of a stock, whether it is very high-priced, medium or low-priced.

RESISTANCE POINTS NEAR SAME LEVELS

When two half-way points or any other two Resistance Points, either in the range of fluctuation or the division of the highest selling price, occur near the same level, you should add these two points together and divide by 2, as the half-way point between these two points will often be a support point on a decline or a selling point on a rally.

HOW TO LOOK UP RESISTANCE LEVELS

When you find an important Resistance Level or the strongest one - the half-way point - at a certain level, look to see if any other Resistance Level, whether it be 1/8, 1/4, 3/8, 5/8 or 2/3 point, falls around this same price. You may find 3 or 4 Resistance Levels around the same price. The more you find, the stronger resistance the stock will meet when it reaches this level. Then take the highest Resistance Level around this same price and the lowest, and add them together to get the average point of resistance.

Watch the activity of the stock when it reaches these Resistance Levels. If it is advancing very fast or declining very fast on large volume, do not consider that it is going to stop around these Resistance Levels unless it stops or holds one or two days around these levels; then sell or buy with stop loss orders. Also consider whether the market is in 3rd or 4th section from bottom or in 3rd or 4th section from top down.

AVERAGE AND EXTREME FLUCTUATIONS

In normal markets the rallies and reactions on the Dow-Jones 30 Industrial averages run 10 to 12 points and when they exceed this number of points they run 20 to 24 points and then 30 to 40 points. When there are great extremes between main tops and main bottoms, like August 8, 1896, low 28-1/2 to September 3, 1929, high 386, and from 386 high to a low of 40-1/2on July 8, 1932, you can divide by 16 and 32 to get closer mathematical points instead of dividing by 8 to get the 1/8 points. These points will correspond to minor tops and bottoms of other movements.

Use all the rules and figure that the important tops and bottoms will come out on the strongest points, like the 1/3, 2/3, 1/4, 3/8, 1/2, 5/8 and 3/4 points.

Do not overlook the fact that it requires time for a market to get ready at the bottom before it advances and requires time to distribute at the top. The longer a market has been running, the more time it will require to complete accumulation or distribution.

WHEN STOCKS DECLINE UNDER OLD TOPS

When stocks drop back under old tops of previous campigns, the Resistance Levels between old bottoms and these old tops will be important points for support and resistance.

Example: After the 1929 high the averages dropped back below 119-5/8, the top of 1919, and declined to 85-1/2 in October, 1931, which was also the low of October 27, 1923. On November 9, 1931, they rallied to 119-5/8, the old top of 1919. After that, as long as the averages stayed below 120, you would watch the old Resistance Levels from 28-1/2 low, 38-1/2 low, 42 low, 52 low to 119-5/8 high. Then, when the averages advanced above 120, you would watch Resistance Levels to higher tops. The important ones were at 195-1/2 to 197.

SMALL GAINS IN LAST STAGE OF BULL OR BEAR MARKET

When a bull or advancing market is nearing the end of a campaign, the gains or runs will often get smaller, which is a sign that the averages or stocks are meeting with greater selling pressure.

Example: Suppose a stock is moving up and crosses a previous top and advances 20 points, then reacts 10 points; then crosses the last top and advances 15 points and reacts 5 to 7-1/2 points; again advances above the last top but only goes 10 points above it and reacts 5 points or more, this would be a sign of weakness or that the top was near because each move was making a smaller gain. In very active fast markets, when volumes of sales are large, the last run may be a greater number of points. Reverse this rule in a declining market.

If a stock has made several moves down of 10, 15 or 20 points and each one gets shorter or when the stock breaks bottom and the declines get smaller, it is a sign that the selling pressure is decreasing and that a change in trend is near, but in fast panicky markets the last decline may be a large number of points with very small rallies. This is a final wave of liquidation.

In the last stages of Bull or Bear Campaigns use only the half-way point of short or minor moves. It is most important to watch the Resistance Levels of the final move, which may run several weeks or months, particularly the half-way point. When it is exceeded by 3 full points, the trend usually reverses.

LOST MOTION

As there is lost motion in every kind of machinery, so there is lost motion in the stock market due to momentum, which drives a stock slightly above or below a Resistance Level. The average lost motion is 1-7/8 points.

When a stock is very active and advances or declines fast on heavy volume, it will often go from 1-7/8 points above a half-way point or other strong Resistance Level and not go 3 points. The same rule applies on a decline. It will often pass an important Resistance Point by 1-7/8 points but not go 3 full points beyond it.

This is the same rule that applies to a gravity center in anything. If we could bore a hole thru the earth and then drop a ball, momentum would carry it beyond the gravity center, but when it slowed down, it would finally settle on the exact center. This is the way stocks act around these important centers.

A study of the Resistance Levels between bottoms and tops of individual stocks or the averages will prove how accurate the market works out to these important points.

July 6, 1939

RESISTANCE LEVELS

DOW JONES 30 INDUSTRIAL AVERAGES

COMPARATIVE BOTTOMS AND TOPS

Resistance points are figured to show you why bottoms and tops were made around these levels. You can use your resistance cards and levels in the same way to determine future bottoms and tops.

1896 Aug. 8	Low 28½	was 3/8 of 78 3/4	the Last High	
1896 Nov. 12	High 45	was 1/2 of 78 3/4	to 28½	
1898 Mar. 19	Low 42	was 1/4 of 94½	to 28½	
1898 Aug. 7	High 61	was 1/2 of 94½	to 28½	
1898 Oct. 22	Low 51 5/8	was 1/2 of 78 3/4	to 28½	
1900 Sept. 29	Low 53	was 1/2 of 77 5/8	to 28½	

From 42 Low to 78 5/8 the 1/2 point was 60 1/4
From 53 Low to 78 1/4 the 1/2 point was 65 6/8
From 53 Low to 78 1/4 the 5/8 point was 68 3/8

1902 Apr. & Sept.)
1904 Feb.) Tops 68 1/2 to 67 3/4 was 5/8 of 53 to 78 1/4

1904 Broke 65 6/8 was 1/2 of 53 to 78 1/4
1903 Nov. 9 Low 42 1/8 an old bottom of March 1898 and was 1/4 of 28½ to 78 3/4
Later crossed 53 5/8 was 1/2 of 28½ to 78 3/4 and a big Bull Market followed.

1906 Jan. 19 High 103 A sharp decline followed.
1906 May 5 Low 86½ was 3/4 of 38½ to 103
1906 July 14 Low 85½ was 3/4 of 28½ to 103
1906 Aug. 13 High 96
1907 Jan. 12 High 96 3/4 was 7/8 of 53 to 103
and 3/4 of 76½ to 103
Later broke 85
declined to 78 was 1/2 of 53 to 103
A Bear Market followed.

1907 Nov. 23 Low 53 (same as 1900) was 1/3 of 28½ to 103
and 1/4 of 38½ to 103
(Note: 1/2 of 103 is 51½. Holding above this 1/2 point was a strong support and buying point at 53, the old bottom.)

1908 Jan. 18 High 86 3/4 was 5/8 of 103 to 53
1908 Sept. 22 Low 77 1/4 was 1/2 of 103 to 53
1909 Oct. 2 High 100½ was
(Note: 3 bottom at 96 was 7/8 of 53 to 103
and 94½ was 7/8 of 53 to 100½
Then broke 96 and 96½ and declined fast.)

RESISTANCE LEVELS, Cont'd

DOW JONES 30 INDUSTRIAL AVERAGES

COMPARATIVE BOTTOMS AND TOPS

1910 July 26	Low	73 5/8	was 1/2 of	42	to 103
1911 June 24	High	87	was 1/2 of	73 5/8	to 100½
1911 Sept. 25	Low	73	was 1/2 of	42	to 103
	and same low as July 26, 1910.				
	A double bottom and place to buy.				
1912 Oct. 10	High	94	was 3/4 of	73 5/8	to 100½
Made several bottoms around		88	was 3/4 of	53	to 100½
Later Broke		87	was 1/2 of	73 5/8	to 100½
1913 June 14	Low	72 1/8	was 3/8 of	53	to 103
			and 1/2 of	42	to 103
	A third time at this level - a buying point.				
1913 Sept. &) 1914 March)	High	83 3/8	was 1/2 of	72 1/8	to 94 1/8
			and 3/8 of	73	to 100½
1914 July declined to		71 1/4	under three old bottoms		
	and under		1/2 of	42	to 103
	and		3/8 of	53	to 103
	A sure sign of lower prices.				
1914 Dec. 24	Low	53 1/8	This was third time at this level.		
	1900-- Low 53				
	1907-- Low 53				
	1914-- Low 53 1/8				
	Holding above	51½	the 1/2 of	103	
			and 1/3 of	28½	to 103
			and 1/4 of	38½	to 103
	Made this a good support and buying point in a panic.				
	The War Bull Market Followed.				
1915 May	High	71 3/4	just under the 3/8 of	53	to 103
	and under three old bottoms.				
1915 June	Low	60½	a secondary reaction		
		60½	was 1/3 of	38½	to 103
	and	62 3/8	was 1/2 of	53 1/8	to 71 3/4
1919 Jan.	High	99			
1916 Apr.	Low	85	was 5/8 of	53	to 103
1916 Nov. 21	High	110 1/8	a sharp reaction followed.		
1917 Feb. 2	Low	87	was 5/8 of	53 1/8	to 110 1/8
1917 June 9	High	99	was 7/8 of	28½	to 110 1/8
			and 1/2 of	85	to 110
	Later broke all important 1/2 points				
	including	81½	was 1/2 of	53	to 110 1/8

RESISTANCE LEVELS, Cont'd

DOW JONES 30 INDUSTRIAL AVERAGES

COMPARATIVE BOTTOMS AND TOPS

1917	Dec. 19		Low 66	was 1/3 of 42	to 110 1/8
				and 3/8 of 38½	to 110 1/8
1918	Oct. 19		High 89	was 3/4 of 28½	to 110 1/8
				and 5/8 of 53	to 110 1/8
1919	Feb. 8		Low 79 1/8	was 1/2 of 53	to 110 1/8
				and 5/8 of 28½	to 110 1/8
			A Big Bull Market followed.		
1919	Nov. 3	A New High	119 5/8	A sharp decline followed.	
1920	Feb. 25		Low 90	was 3/4 of 28½	to 110 1/8
				and 5/8 of 42	to 119 5/8
				and 2/3 of 28½	to 119 5/8
1920	Apr. 8		High 105	was 5/8 of 79 1/8	to 119 5/8
				and 3/4 of 66	to 119 5/8
				and 1/2 of 90	to 119 5/8
			Later declined, to 99	was 1/2 of 79 1/8	to 119 5/8
1921	Aug. 24		Low 64 Just 2 points under 1917 Lows.		
			" 64	was 1/3 of 38½	to 119 5/8
			62 5/8	was 3/8 of 28½	to 119 5/8
			This was a final low and the greatest Bull Market in history followed.		
			(Note: When averages crossed 80 they were above	1/2 of 42	to 119 5/8
			and	1/2 of 38½	to 119 5/8

Note: 91 7/8 was 1/2 of 119 5/8 to 64 and after averages crossed 92 did not reach 91 before they advanced to 105 5/8

1923	Mar. 20	High 105 5/8	was 3/4 of 64	to 119 5/8
1923	Oct. 27	Low 85 3/4	was 3/8 of 64	to 119 5/8
			5/8 of 28½	to 119 5/8
			1/2 of 53	to 119 5/8
		A Strong Support Point.		
1924	May 20	Last Low 88 3/8	was 2/3 of 28½	to 119 5/8
1924	Dec.	Crossed old top of 1919 at 119 5/8		
		A Big Bull Market followed.		

In view of the fact that the averages made - High 103 in 1906 and in 1916 made a new High of 110 1/8 and in 1919 another record High 119 5/8 and in 1921 decline to 64, holding more than 4 points above 1/2 of 119 5/8, was a strong indication of much higher prices because of such a long period of time between these top levels. From January 1906 to December 1924, when averages went above 119 5/8, was nearly 19 years. You could figure they would first double the highest selling price or made 240. After that figure was crossed, you figure three times 119 5/8 of about 360.

RESISTANCE LEVELS, Cont'd

DOW JONES 30 INDUSTRIAL AVERAGES

COMPARATIVE BOTTOMS AND TOPS

1929 Sept. 3 — High 386
If you take the range from extreme Low 28½ to 119 5/8 the range was 91 1/8. Multiply this range by 4 and we get 364½ as a probable top. The proper procedure after the averages were in new high, was to follow the trend and use all rules until there was a change in the main trend.

1926 July — High 162½
1926 Apr. — Low 135 1/8 was just under 1/2 of 115 to 162½
150 5/8 was 1/2 of 162½ to 135 1/8
When the averages crossed this level the second time they went right up to new highs.

1927 Oct. — High 199 7/8
1927 Oct. — Low 179 was 1/2 of 165 3/4 the last low to 199 7/8
189 3/8 was 1/2 of 119 7/8 to 179
When crossed this level never sold below 190½ again.

1928 Dec. — High 299
1928 Dec. 12 — Low 254½ was near 250 the 1/2 of 200 7/8 to 299
Holding above the 1/2 of last move indicated higher.

1929 Jan. — High 324½
1928 Mar. 30 — Low 281½
279 was 1/2 of 234 to 374½ the last low, and holding above 1/2 point was strong.

1929 May — High 331 Last reaction before top
End of " — Low 290 3/4 of 281½ to 331 was 287½
holding above this indicated support.
Then when crossed — 306 the 1/2 of 281½ to 331
and crossed — 310½ the 1/2 of 331 to 290
indicated higher.
1929 Sept. 3 — High 386 Final Top.

After the trend turned down, we calculated the Resistance Points from bottoms from 1896 to date, to get points to watch on the way down. The first 1/2 point of the last move from 281½ to 386, making 333 3/4, - this was broken on the first decline to 321, which was 1/2 of 255 to 386.

1929 Oct. Last Rally — 358 the 1/2 of 386 to 321 was 253½, did not go 5 points above it -- then broke wide open.
1929 Oct. 29 — Low 213 was 1/2 of 38½ to 386
1929 Oct. 31 — High 273½ was 2/3 of 42 to 386
and 2/3 of 53 to 386
and just under 2/3 of 64 to 386

RESISTANCE LEVELS, Cont'd

DOW JONES 30 INDUSTRIAL AVERAGES

COMPARATIVE BOTTOMS AND TOPS

1929 Nov. 13 — Low 195½
This was a very important panic bottom and there was a strong mathematical point which indicated they should stop around this level.
When 225 was 1/2 of 64 to 386 was broken
219½ was 1/2 of 53 to 386
214 was 1/2 of 42 to 386
207½ was 1/2 of 28½ to 386

The extreme high according to our rules is the next important point, or 1/2 of 386 the highest selling point - which is 193 - and the averages held 2½ points above this strong point, indicating bottoms for a big rally.

1930 Apr. 17 — High 296 3/8 was 3/4 of 28½ to 386
and just 5 points above
291 the 1/2 of 386 to 195 3/8
when the averages dropped back under 290
they never rallied to 291 again
245 3/4 was 1/2 of 195 3/8 to 296 3/8, they never broke this 1/2 point, never sold at 250 again.

1930 June to Aug. Bottoms at — 208 to 214 which was 1/2 of 28½ to 386
and 42 to 386

1930 Sept. 10 — Last High 247 was 1/2 of 195 3/8 to 296 3/8
Then followed a big decline breaking all main 1/2 points and when the average broke 193 the 1/2 of 386 in Oct. 1930 they never sold above 198½ again.

1930 Dec. 17 — Low 155½ was 1/3 of 38½ to 386
1/3 of 42 to 386

1931 Jan. — High 175½ was 3/8 of 53 to 386
1/3 of 64 to 386

1931 Jan. 24 — Low 160 was 1/4 of 85 3/4 to 386
165½ was 1/2 of 155½ to 175½
When it crossed this level it never sold at 163 until it made next Top.

1931 Feb. 24 — High 197½ was just above
193 the 1/2 of 386 and under low of Nov. 1929 and last Top of Nov. 1930 - making this a safe point to Sell Short.

The next important point to watch... 176 7/8 was 1/2 of 155½ to 197½

1931 Mar. 14 — Low 175 3/4 was 1/2 of 155½ to 197½

1931 Mar. 20 — High 189 was 5/8 of 297
1/3 of 85 3/4 to 386
3/8 of 64 to 386

Latter part of Mar. broke 176 the 1/2 of 155½ to 197½
and a panic decline followed.
Later broke 161 which was 1/4 of 85 3/4 to 386
Then broke Low 155½ and declined fast.

RESISTANCE LEVELS, Cont'd

DOW JONES 30 INDUSTRIAL AVERAGES

COMPARATIVE BOTTOMS AND TOPS

Year	Month	Day		Price		To
1931	June	2	Low	120	was 1/4 of 85 3/4	to 386
					and 3/4 of 157½	
			and back to 1919 Top. A strong support for a rally.			
1931	June	27	High	157½	was 1/3 of 42	to 386
			and just under		1/2 of 197½	to 120
			and at Lows of Dec. 1930 made this a Sure Selling Level.			
1931	Oct.	5	Low	85½	Same Low as Oct. 27, 1923	
				85	was 1/8 of 386	to 42
1931	Nov.	9	High	119 5/8	was under 1/2 of 157½	to 85½
					and 1/4 of 28½	to 386
					and 1/8 of 85 3/4	to 386
			A sharp decline followed.			
1932	Jan.	7	Low	70	was 1/8 of 28½	to 386
1932	Mar.	8	High	89½	was 3/8 of 119 5/8	to 70
				79 3/4	was 1/2 of 70	to 89½
			When it broke under 79 it declined fast.			
1932	July	8	Low	40½		
			Final Low - End of Great Bear Market		Down to Lows of 1898.	
1932	Sept.	8	High	81½	was 1/2 of 119 5/8	to 40½
					under 3/8 of 386	to 40½
					1/3 of 157½	to 40½
				61	was 1/2 of 40½	to 81½
1933	Feb.	27	Low	49½	was 3/4 of 40½	to 81½
1933	Mar.	18	High	64½	was 1/2 of 49½	to 81½
1933	Apr.	1	Last Low 54 3/4 not 3 points under		1/2 of 49½	to 64½
			A rapid advance followed,			
			crossed		1/2 of 49½	to 81½
			and		1/2 of 40½	to 81½
1933	July	17	High	110½	was 3/8 of 296 3/4	
			just under		5/8 of 146½	to 40½

Why did prices of the Dow Jones 30 Industrial Averages make High at 110½ and 111½ in 1933 and 1934?

The highest selling point in 1929 was 386. 1/3 of this is 128 5/8. 1/4 of 386 is 96½. The half-way point between 1/3 and 1/4 points is 112½. This is one of the reasons that so many tops were made around this level for such a long period of time before they were crossed.

RESISTANCE LEVELS, Cont'd

DOW JONES 30 INDUSTRIAL AVERAGES

COMPARATIVE BOTTOMS AND TOPS

Why 82½ Low, October, 1933?

In September 1932, the old Top 81. From the low of 49½ to 111½, the half-way point is 80½. From the breakaway point 55½ to 111½ the half-way point is 83½. The fact that the averages held above the extreme half-way point was a sign of strength and good support. From 111½ to 82½, the half-way point was 97.

In March, 1935, the averages started up from 95½, not 3 points under this half-way point and on March 31, 1939, the averages declined to 97½ which was also the half-way point of the highest selling point 195½ in 1937.

Year	Month	Day	
1933	Oct.	21	Low 82½ was above 1/2 of 49½ to 110½ and 1/8 of 386 to 40½ and 1/2 of 54 3/4 to 110½ Holding above these important 1/2 points, indicated strong support.
1934	Feb.	5	High 111½ Low 82½ to 111½ made 97 the 1/2 point.
1934	Mar.	31	Low 97 rallied to 107
1934	July	26	Low 84½ was 3/8 of 157½ to 40½ From 111½ To 84½ the 1/2 point was 98
1935	Feb.	18	High 108½
1935	Mar.	18	Low 95½ just under 1/2 of 87½ to 111½ and 1/2 of 195½ and 1/4 of 386 From 108 To 95½ the 1/2 was 101 3/4 Crossed this minor 1/2 point and crossed Old Tops 110½ to 111½ and Big Bull Market followed.
1936	Apr.	6	High 163½ was 3/8 of 28½ to 386 was 3/8 of 386 to 49½
1936	Apr.	30	Low 141½ was 7/8 of 40½ to 157½ Just 3 points under 1/2 of 176½ to 163½
1937	Mar.	10	High 195½ Same as Low Nov. 13, 1929 and Last High Oct. 1930. Just under High of Feb. 1931. This was not 3 points above 193, the 1/2 of 386 and a sure place to go Short.
1937	June	17	Low 163 was 3/8 of 28½ to 386 was 1/2 of 141½ to 195½

RESISTANCE LEVELS, Cont'd

DOW JONES 30 INDUSTRIAL AVERAGES

COMPARATIVE BOTTOMS AND TOPS

1937 Aug. 14	High	190½	just 2½ points under 1/2 of 386 and a lower Top- a sign of weakness.		
	The 1/2 point from 163 to 195 was 179¼ and 163 to 190½ was 176 3/4. When these levels were broken a panicky decline followed.				
1929 Oct. 19	Low	115½	was 1/2 of	195½	to 40½
1929 Oct. 29	High	141½	was 2/3 of	195½	to 40½
	and under		3/8 of	386	
1937 Nov. 23	Low	112½	was 3/8 of	196 3/4	
1938 Jan. 15	High	134½	was 3/8 of	40½	to 296 3/4
			and 3/8 of	95½	to 195½
1938 Mar. 31	Low	97½			
Final Bottom of Panic		97½	was 1/2 of	195½	
			and 3/8 of	40½	to 195½
			and 1/3 of	296 3/4	
			and 1/4 of	386	
	This was a safe buying point.				
1938 Apr. 18	High	121½	just above 1/2 of	40½	to 195½
			and 2/3 of	157½	to 140½
			and 5/8 of	195½	
1938 May 27	Low	106½	just above 1/4 of	40½	to 296 3/4
			and 1/8 of	195½	to 97½
		109¼	was 1/2 from	97½	to 121½
	When it crossed 110 showed strong up and advanced fast.				
1938 July 25	High	146¼	was 1/2 of	195½	to 97½
1938 Sept. 26	Low	128	was 1/3 of	386	
			and 1/3 of	195½	to 97½
			and 1/2 of	106½	to 146¼
	A Strong Support Level and Buying Point.				
1938 Nov. 10	High	158 3/4			
	When the averages crossed			146¼	
			1/2 of	97½	to 195½
	indicated the 5/8 point at 158 3/4.				
	158 3/4		was 5/8 of	97½	to 195½
			and 1/3 of	40½	to 386
			and 3/4 of	195½	to 40½
	Making this a sure point to Sell Short.				

DOW JONES 30 INDUSTRIAL AVERAGES

COMPARATIVE BOTTOMS AND TOPS

1939	Nov.	28	Low	145	was 1/2 of 195½	to 97½
					and 3/4 of 195½	
					1/2 of 128	to 158 3/4
					3/8 of 97½	to 158 3/4
					and 5/8 of 40½	to 195½
1939	Mar.	10	High	152½	was 7/8 of 97½	to 158 3/4

Last Low 136 1/8
to 158 3/4 the 1/2 was 148½
and 1/3 of 136 1/8 to 152½
was 144½
When broke this 1/2 point declined fast.

1939	Apr.	11	Low	120	was 3/8 of 97½	to 158 3/4
					and 3/4 of 158 3/4	
			Note	118	was 1/2 of 40½	to 195½

This was the strongest 1/2 point and the averages held 2 points above, also 118½ was
1/4 of 28½ to 386

1939	May	10	High	134 5/8	was 3/8 of 158 3/4	to 120
					also 3/8 of 195½	to 97½
1939	May	17	Low	128 3/8	was 1/2 of 97½	to 158 3/4
1939	June	9	High	140 3/4	was 1/2 of 120	to 158 3/4
1939	June	30	Low	129	was 1/2 of 97½	to 158 3/4
					and 1/3 of 386	

A strong support point and buying level.
The Market rallied and crossed 139 3/8
the 1/2 of 120 to 158 3/4
and on July 25th advanced to 145 3/4 just
under 1/2 of 97½ to 195½
and 2/3 of 120 to 158 3/4

RESISTANCE LEVELS, Cont'd

DOW JONES 20 RAILROAD AVERAGES

Aug. 8, 1896 .... Low 42 WHY?

46 was 1/2 of 92, the last high

49½ was 1/2 of 99, the extreme high

Apr, 1897 Low of reaction 48¼ was 1/2 of 54¼ to 42

Sept. 1897 ....High 67½ was 1/2 of 42 to 92

Nov. 1897 .... Low 57½ was 1/2 of 48¼ to 67¼

Apr. 1898 .... Low 58 3/4 was 1/2 of 42 to 67¼

Aug. 1898 .... High 70¼ was 1/2 of 42 to 99

Oct. 1898 .... Low 65 3/4 was 1/2 of 42 to 92 close

After averages crossed 70¼, the 1/2 of 42 to 99 never sold lower and advanced to 138 3/ Jan. 19, 1906.

Apr. 1899 .... High 87 was 7/8 of 99

and 2/3 of 42 to 99

June 1899 .... Low 77¼ was 1/2 of 66 to 87

Dec. 1899 .... Low 72½

just above 1/2 42 to 99

and 1/2 of 56 to 87

(Note triple bottom near this level)

June .... Low 73

Oct. .... Low 73 3/4

(Note) .... 79 3/4 was 1/2 87 to 72½

and 80½ was 1/2 of 62 to 99 and in

Nov. 1899 the breakaway came when averages crossed 80½ after making triple bottoms above the 1/2 of 42 to 99, - later crossed 99, the old top advancing quickly to 117 3/4 May, 1901 and on Sept. 30, 1902 made high at 129¼.

May 9, 1901 .... Low 103¼ was 1/8 of 42 to 117 3/4

and 1/4 of 56 to 117 3/4

and 1/3 of 72½ to 117 3/4

(Note) .... 106½ was 1/4 of 72½ to 117 3/4

and on secondary reaction after double top, the market made 3 bottoms: 105, 105¼, 106¼, starting up from 106¼ and advancing to new highs.

Sept. 10, 1902 .... High 129¼

Dec. 1902 .... Low 113¼

just above 3/4 of 56 to 129¼

Jan. 1903 .... High 121¼ at 1/2 of 110¼ to 129¼

(Note) 101¼ was 1/2 of 72½ to 129½, broke this level and rallied 2 points above, then broke under and declined further.

Oct. 1903 .... Low 89 3/8 at 1/2 of 48¼ to 129¼

Jan. 1904 .... High 99 3/4 at 1/4 of 129¼ to 89 3/8

and under 1/2 of 72½ to 129¼

Aug. 1904 crossed old top and crossed 1/4 of 129¼ to 89 3/8, then came the breakaway and rapid advance to new highs.

Later crossed 1/2 point 129¼ to 89 3/8

RESISTANCE LEVELS, Cont'd

DOW JONES 20 RAILROAD AVERAGES

Mar.&Apr. 1905 made double tops at 127
July 1905 .... Low 114½ at 3/4 of 89 3/8 to 129¼, later crossed
121 above 1/2 of 114½ to 127 advanced to
138 3/8 Jan.19, 1906.
May 1906 .... Low 120¼ (This was first sharp reaction).
....at 3/4 of 89 3/8 to 129¼
Last Low 114½ .... to 138 3/8, the 1/2
point.............................. 126½ and 1/2 of 138 3/8 to 120¼ was 129.
The first rally was to............ 131
Then secondary reaction........... 121 3/4
Then crossed...................... 129
And advanced to................... 137 3/4, making triple tops.

Showed down when they broke the .... 1/2 of 120¼ to 138 3/8 and was
still weaker when they broke .... 1/2 of 98 3/8 to 138 3/8.

Mar. 14, 1907.............. Low 98 3/8 at 3/8 of 138 3/8 to 72¼
and 1/2 of 56 to 138 3/8
May 1907..............High 110 3/8 at 1/4 of 98 3/8 to 138 3/8
and 2/3 of 56 to 138 3/8

(Note.. 1/2 of 98 3/8 to 110 3/8 was 104.
When they broke this level, they declined to new lows.

Nov. 23, 1907 ....Low 81 3/8 at 3/8 of 48¼ to 138 3/8
Jan. 1908 ....High 95 3/4 at 1/2 of 81 3/8 to 110 3/8, and later
a secondary reaction to....... 86¼
Just under 1/2 of 81 3/8 to 95 3/4. Later
crossed top at................ 95 3/4 and 1/4 of 138 3/8 to 81 3/8.

Sept. 1908 ....High 110¼ at 1/2 of 138 3/8 to 81 3/8
Sept. 22, 1908 reacted to 103 3/8 the 1/2 of 98 to 110 3/8
Jan. 1909 ....High 120 3/4 at 2/3 of 138 3/8 to 81 3/8
Mar. 1909 ....Low 113 3/4 above 1/2 of 103 3/8 to 120 3/4
Aug. 14, 1909 ....High 134¼
(Note)............................ 131 was 1/8 of 138 3/8 to 81 3/8
Last move up 113 3/4 to 134¼
the 1/2 at 124.
When the averages broke this level they never sold above......... 125 3/4
Until declined to 105 5/8
On July 26, 1910. This Low was just under 1/8 of 81 3/8 to 134¼

Oct. 1910 ....High 118 3/8 the 1/2 of 105 5/8 to 118 3/8 was 112
Dec. 1910 ....Low 111½
good support @ 1/2 point
July 1911 ....High 124 at 2/3 of 105 5/8 to 134¼
.... 3/4 of 81 3/8 to 134 3/8 at 121
and... 1/2 of 105 5/8 to 134¼ at 120
When this level was broken, sharp decline followed.

DOW JONES 20 RAILROAD AVERAGES

Sept. 25, 1911 ....Low 109 3/4 at 3/8 of 105 5/8 to 124
(Note)........................ 117 was 1/2 of 124 to 109 3/4.
Averages advanced to.......... 119
Reacted to.................... 115
Then crossed the 1/2 at 117 and went higher.

Oct. 1912............High 124 5/8 at 2/3 of 105 5/8 to 134¼
(Note) .... 117 was 1/2 of 109 3/4 to 124 5/8
When averages broke this level never rallied above.......118
June 1913 ....Low 100½ at 3/8 of 81 3/8 to 134¼
Sept. 1913
and
Jan. 1914 ....High 109¼ at 3/8 of 105 5/8 to 124 5/8
..........................and under .... 1/2 of 124 5/8 to 100½
Later broke under.............. 105 the 1/2 of 100½ to 109¼
and declined with very small rallies.

July 30, 1914 ....Low 89½

(Note) From 1896 ....Low 42
to
Jan. 19, 1906 ....High 138 3/8 the 1/2 was 90 1/8
and on July 30, 1914 the averages closed under the 1/2 point from exteeme low to the extreme high, closing, in a panic under this strongest point indicated lower prices later.

When Exchange opened in December 1914, the 20 RAILROAD AVERAGES declined to 87½.

CHAPTER 4

VOLUME OF SALES

AUTHOR:
"Truth of the Stock Tape"
"Wall Street Stock Selector"
"New Stock Trend Detector"

W. D. GANN
Statistician and Economist
82 WALL STREET
NEW YORK, N. Y.

2101 N. W. 18th TERRACE
MIAMI, FLA.

MEMBER
New Orleans Cotton Exchange
Commodity Exchange, Inc. N.Y.
American Economic Ass'n
Royal Economy Society

VOLUME OF SALES

After considering the three important factors ... FORMATIONS, TIME, and RESISTANCE LEVELS ... the fourth and next very important factor is the VOLUME OF SALES AT TOPS AND BOTTOMS.

The VOLUME OF SALES is the real driving power behind the market and shows whether Supply or Demand is increasing or decreasing. Large buying or selling orders from professional traders, the public or any other source of supply and demand, are bound to be registered on the tape and shown in the volume of sales.

Therefore, a careful study of the VOLUME OF SALES will enable you to determine very closely a change in trend, especially if you apply all of the other rules for judging position according to the Formations, Resistance Levels and Time.

RULES FOR DETERMINING CULMINATIONS BY VOLUME OF SALES

1 - At the end of any prolonged Bull Campaign or rapid advance in an individual stock, there is usually a large increase in the volume of sales, which marks the end of the campaign, at least temporarily. Then, after a sharp decline on heavy volume of sales, when a secondary rally takes place and the volume of sales decreases, it is an indication that the stock has made final top and that the main trend will turn down.

2 - If the stock holds after making a second lower top and gets dull and narrow for some time, working in a sideways movement, and then breaks out on increased volume, it is a sign of a further decline.

3 - After a prolonged decline of several weeks, several months, or several years, at the time a stock is reaching bottom, the volume of trading should decrease and the range in fluctuation should narrow down. This is one of the sure signs that liquidation is running its course and that the stock is getting ready to show a change in trend.

4 - After the first sharp advance (when the trend is changing from a Bear Market to a Bull Market) the stock will have a secondary reaction and make bottom, just the same as it had a secondary rally after the first sharp decline. If the volume of sales decreases on the reaction and then the stock moves up, advancing on heavier volume, it will be an indication of an advance to higher levels.

These rules apply to the general market, that is, to the total sales traded in on the New York Stock Exchange——daily, weekly or monthly——as well as to individual stocks.

SUMMARY: SALES INCREASE NEAR THE TOP AND DECREASE NEAR THE BOTTOM, except in abnormal markets, like October, and November, 1929 when the market was moving down very fast and culminated on large volume of sales, making a sharp bottom, from which a swift rebound followed. As a rule, after the first sharp rally, there is a secondary decline on decreased volume, as described above under Rule 4.

MONTHLY RECORD OF VOLUME OF SALES ON NEW YORK STOCK EXCHANGE 1930 - 1935

To understand the importance of Volume, a study of the total number of shares traded in on the New York Stock Exchange is necessary.

1 9 3 0

JUNE Sales were 80,000,000 shares, with the market moving lower.

JULY & AUGUST On a small rally the total sales were only 80,000,000 shares for two months.

SEPTEMBER The market was slightly higher early in the month; then a decline started, which carried prices to new low levels, sales of 50,000,000 shares being recorded.

OCTOBER The market broke to new low levels. Stocks at this time broke the low levels of November, 1929 and sales increased to 70,000,000 shares.

DECEMBER The Dow-Jones Industrial Averages declined 46 points under the low levels of November, 1929. Total sales this month were 60,000,000 shares.

1 9 3 1

JANUARY A rally started and in January, 1931 the sales were 42,000,000 shares.

FEBRUARY The market made top of the rally on sales of 64,000,000 shares, which showed that the volume of trading was increasing on the rally and that stocks were meeting resistance. Note that this top was just under the low levels of November, 1929, which showed that stocks met selling when they moved up under the old low levels of the panic.

MARCH A decline started in March and the sales were 64,000,000 shares, a heavier volume, with prices moving lower.

APRIL Sales were 54,000,000 shares.

MAY Sales 47,000,000.

JUNE There was a sharp decline on a volume of sales totaling 59,000,000, which carried the Averages down to new low levels, reaching 120, the old top of 1919 and the last low of May, 1925. A quick rally followed to the end of June and early July, the Averages reaching 157½, but failing to cross the high level made in May, 1931.

JULY The sales were smaller, only 33,000,000, and the market narrowed down.

AUGUST The sales were 24,000,000, still a narrow, dull market, not making much progress on the upside.

SEPTEMBER Activity started and sales reached 51,000,000. On this increased volume the Averages declined 45 points during the month of September. This showed great weakness and indicated a further decline.

OCTOBER A sharp decline occurred which carried the Averages down to 85 on sales of 48,000,000 shares.

NOVEMBER A rally followed, culminating on November 9th. The averages reached 119½, back to the old top of 1919, to the last low of 1925, and to the bottom of a previous rally. Failing to penetrate these old bottoms and cross the previous top, the market showed weakness and indicated that the trend was still down. Sales in November were 37,000,000, the volume decreasing on the rally.

DECEMBER The Averages declined to a new low for the move, making 72 on sales of 50,000,000 shares, the largest since September, 1931. This indicated that big liquidation was still going on.

1 9 3 2

JANUARY The Averages reached a low of 70 on sales of 44,000,000 shares for the month.

FEBRUARY Rallied to 89¾ on sales of 31,000,000 shares.

MARCH The Averages made about the same high on sales of 33,000,000 shares. Then the market went dead on the rally, stocks narrowing down.

APRIL The Dow-Jones 30 Industrial Averages broke 70, the low of January; and declined to 55 on sales of 30,000,000 shares.

MAY The Averages broke 53, the old low levels of the panic of 1907 and 1914, which indicated lower prices; then declined to 45 on sales of 23,000,000 shares.

JUNE The range between extreme high and extreme low averaged 10 points and the averages reached a new low on sales of 23,000,000 shares.

JULY On July 8, 1932, the extreme low was reached, with the Averages down to 40½. The volume was very small and the Averages and individual stocks moved in a very narrow trading range, indicating the last stages of a bear market. Late in the month the Averages crossed the high of June, which indicated that the trend was turning up. Sales were 23,000,000 shares. The range was about 13 points on Averages.

At the low in July the Averages were down 345 points from 1929 high. The volume of sales for the three months—May, June and July—aggregated only 69,000,000 shares, the smallest since 1923, in contrast to over 100,000,000 shares per month at the top in September, 1929 and 141,000,000 in the month of October, 1929. This indicated that after such a drastic decline, liquidation had run its course and the trend was changing. The market really had been sold to a standstill. Traders and investors sold out everything because they feared things were going to get worse. It was the same old story: A bull market begins in gloom and ends in glory. All of the indications were plain: The small volume of sales and narrow range of fluctuations indicated that the end had been reached and that a change in trend was certain.

During the latter part of July, 1932, the advance started.

AUGUST There was a sharp rally in August on sales of 83,000,000 shares, more than for the entire three months past. This was on short covering and wise investment buying.

SEPTEMBER Top of the rally was reached on sales of 67,000,000 shares, with the Averages up 40 points from the low of July 8. After this advance to September on a large volume, distribution took place and the trend turned down. (Note that the total volume from July 8 to the top in September was 168 million shares.) The Averages failed to go higher in the third month. At no time from April, 1930 to July, 1932 had the Averages or most of the individual stocks rallied over two months. Therefore, to show a change in trend to a prolonged bull market, they would have to advance three full months or more.

OCTOBER After September stocks worked slowly down on a smaller volume of sales. In October the sales were 29,000,000.

NOVEMBER Sales were 23,000,000.

DECEMBER Sales 23,000,000.

1 9 3 3

JANUARY Sales were 19,000,000 shares.

FEBRUARY The whole country was in a state of panic. Banks were failing right and left. People were panic stricken and selling stocks and bonds regardless of price. There were business failures, and when President Roosevelt was inaugurated on March 1, he immediately acted and closed all the banks in the United States. This marked the end of the secondary decline and started a constructive movement.

The Dow-Jones Industrial Averages declined to 50 in February, which was 9 points higher than the low of July, 1932. Sales were only 19,000,000 shares, the smallest volume of any time in over 10 years and the smallest volume for any month since the top in September, 1929, a sure sign of bottom.

MARCH A rally started on increased sales. The volume was 20,000,000 shares.

APRIL The United States went off the gold standard. This started a rapid advance in stocks and commodities. Sales on the New York Stock Exchange were 53,000,000 shares this month.

MAY The advance continued and the volume of trading reached 104,000,000 shares.

JUNE The volume increased to 125,000,000.

JULY The sales were 120,000,000 sales.

From March low to July high, 1933, the total number of shares traded in on the New York Stock Exchange was 422,000,000 shares and the Averages at the top in July were up 60 points from the low of February, 1933. Very few people keep records and study enough to understand what the enormous volume of 422,000,000 shares meant. This was the greatest volume of sales of any bull campaign in the history of the New York Stock Exchange. It was greater than the last advance in 1929. (From the last low in May, 1929 to September, 1929, the Averages advanced 96 points and the total sales on the New York Stock Exchange were 350,000,000 shares.) It was one of the wildest buying waves in history. Commodities advanced by leaps and bounds. People bought stocks regardless of price. Just think about it: Sales of 350,000,000 in three months—May, June, and July, 1933—equal to the volume from May, 1929 to September, 1929. The signs were plain that volume was telling the story of a wave of inflation. Commodities and stocks had advanced so rapidly and everybody had bought on such thin margin that a wide-open break occurred in four days from July 18th to 21st, carrying the Dow-Jones Averages down 25 points to 85. Cotton and Wheat broke badly at the same time on heavy liquidation. At this time Dr. E. A. Crawford failed. He was involved in commodities, said to be the largest amount carried ever known.

AUGUST & SEPTEMBER After the sharp decline in July, a rally followed in August and September, which carried the Averages to within two points of the July high, making a double top. The volume of sales on this second rally was smaller. In August the sales were 42,000,000 and in September 43,000,000 shares. In these two months the volume was only two-thirds of the total volume for July, 1933.

OCTOBER The Dow-Jones 30 Industrial Averages declined to $82\frac{1}{2}$, the last low before the start of a long advance. Sales decreased to 39,000,000 and the market became very dull and narrow. A slow rally started from the October lows.

NOVEMBER Sales were 33,000,000 shares.

DECEMBER Sales 35,000,000.

1 9 3 4

JANUARY The sales this month were 54,000,000.

FEBRUARY Sales 57,000,000 shares, with the top in February only slightly above the high of January. The Averages failed to get over one point above the high of July, 1933, making a double top. Sales of 111,000,000 shares in two months and the third time at the same level was a signal of top. Individual stocks especially showed plainly by the large volume and the slow progress they were making in February that they were getting ready to start down. The trend turned down in the latter part of February.

MARCH Sales reached 30,000,000 shares.

APRIL There was a slight rally on 29,000,000 shares.

MAY Prices were lower on 25,000,000 sales.

JUNE There was a small rally and the volume decreased to 16,000,000 shares for the month.

JULY On July 26, 1934, stocks made bottom on sales of nearly 3,000,000 shares for the day, with the Dow-Jones Averages down to 85, slightly above the low level of October, 1933.

For the month of July, 1934 total sales were only 21,000,000 shares. Individual stocks moved in a narrow trading range, which showed that bottom was being made and the foundation laid for another bull campaign. The fact that an extreme high was reached in July, 1933 was an indication that you should watch for a change in trend in July, 1934, according to my rules to watch for a change in trend one year, two years, or three years from any important top and bottom.

AUGUST The market rallied 11 points on averages on sales of 16,000,000 shares.

SEPTEMBER The market reacted within one point of the July low. Sales were down to 12,000,000 shares, a sure sign of bottom, being the smallest sales per month in many years.

OCTOBER The market rallied in October on a slightly increased volume of sales, 16,000,000 shares.

NOVEMBER The sales increased to 21,000,000 shares.

DECEMBER Prices were higher on sales of 23,000,000 shares for the month.

1 9 3 5

JANUARY There was increased activity on sales of 19,000,000 shares.

FEBRUARY The market reached the top of the rally. Sales only 14,000,000 shares, which was a sign that there was not enough buying power to carry prices thru.

MARCH There was a big decline, which was the last before the market advanced to new highs. Sales were 16,000,000 shares.

APRIL Increased activity shown and stocks started advancing. Volume of sales was 22,000,000 shares, which showed that a bull market was under way.

MAY The Dow-Jones 30 Industrial Averages crossed the high levels of 1933 and the top of February, 1934, on sales of 30,000,000 shares. Individual stocks showed increased sales and many of them moved up to new high levels.

JUNE The Averages crossed 120, which was above the last high of November 9, 1931, a sure indication of higher prices. The sales for June were 22,000,000 shares.

JULY New highs were reached for individual stocks and the Averages. Sales for the month were 29,000,000 shares.

AUGUST More new highs for individual stocks and new highs for the Industrial

Averages. Sales reached 43,000,000 shares, the highest since January and February, 1934.

SEPTEMBER The advance continued and sales were 35,000,000 shares.

OCTOBER The Dow-Jones 30 Industrial averages advanced to 142. The total sales for the month were 46,000,000 shares. During the week ending October 26, sales on the New York Stock Exchange were 14,000,000 shares, the largest for any week since September, 1934, which was an indication that you should begin to watch for top in stocks that had had big advances.

NOVEMBER During the week ended November 2 the sales were 11,000,000 shares and during the week ended November 9 ... a 5-day week ... the sales were 12,000,000 shares. On November 8 the sales were 3,350,000, the largest for any day since the bottom of July 26, 1934.

JULY, 1934 to NOVEMBER, 1935

The total sales from the low of July 26, 1934 to the high of November 8, 1935 were 383,000,000 shares. The total number of points which the Dow-Jones Industrial averages advanced from July, 1934 to November 8, 1935 was 61 points. Note that the total advance from the low of March, 1933 to the top in July, 1933 was 60 points. Therefore, with the averages in November, 1935 up 61 points, as much as in the 1933 campaign, it was time to watch for at least a temporary change in trend.

Note that the volume of sales during this 15-months campaign from July, 1934 to November, 1935 was about 39,000,000 shares less than the 5 months' campaign from March, 1933 to July, 1933. This shows that since the Securities Administration has been operating, it has reduced trading considerably.

DECEMBER Volume of sales 57,462,000 shares and a 10-point reaction occurred, a normal reaction in a Bull Market.

LARGEST VOLUME OF SALES BEFORE FINAL TOP

By going over the records you will find that the largest volume of sales often comes before final top is reached; that when the actual high is made, the volume of sales is smaller than in previous months, weeks or days. This is due to the fact that the public often loads up heavily, buying all they can carry, when the market gets very active; then as the market nears top, their demand having been supplied, they buy less. Example:

1 9 3 6

JANUARY Sales 67,500,000, the largest since the low was reached in July, 1934.

FEBRUARY Sales 60,884,000.

MARCH Sales 51,000,000.

APRIL High was reached on April 6 for a reaction. A sharp decline followed. Low April 30, with the Dow-Jones 30 Industrial averages down 21 points. Sales for the month, 39,610,000. The volume on this reaction was smaller than for many months past. You will see that the largest volume came in January before the reaction in April, the public having loaded up on the January rise.

1 9 3 7

JANUARY Sales 58,671,000, the largest since January, 1936 ... a signal to watch for a change in trend in the near future.

FEBRUARY Sales 50,248,000.

MARCH Dow-Jones averages reached final high at 195½ on March 8. Sales for the month were 50,346,000 and the averages broke back 15 points before the end of the month. This again proves that the public loaded up on stocks in January, as the volume was less in February and when top was reached in March, the public was unable to buy in large volume.

JULY, 1934 to MARCH, 1937

From July 26, 1934 to October 31, 1936, the total volume was 866,988,000 shares and the market had advanced 94 points on the Dow-Jones averages. This was an average of 88,860 shares per point. From October 31, 1936 to March 8, 1937, when final high was reached, the total volume was 258,392,000 shares and the market had advanced 17 points. This was an average of 151,197 shares per point, showing that the market was meeting with almost twice as many shares per point as it did up to October 31, 1936. This increased volume on a smaller gain was an indication that the market was nearing top. The total sales in the entire Bull Campaign from July 26, 1934 to March 8, 1937 was 1,125,380,000 shares or about one-third of the total shares listed on the New York Stock Exchange.

1 9 3 7

After the high in March, 1937, the volume decreased on the decline.

MAY Sales 18,562,000.

JUNE Sales 16,457,000. Low was reached on June 17 with the averages down 32 points. This decreasing volume indicated that a secondary rally was due.

JULY Sales 20,721,000.

AUGUST High of secondary rally. Dow-Jones averages reached 190½, up 27½ points. Sales 17,212,000. This will prove that on the secondary rally to within 5 points of the old top the volume was not more than one-third the sales at the first top in March, 1937 ... a sure indication of decreasing demand and a signal to sell the market short.

SEPTEMBER Sharp decline followed. Sales 33,854,000 shares, almost double the volume in August.

OCTOBER Panicky decline. Sales 51,250,000.

NOVEMBER Further decline to lower levels, but the volume decreased. Sales, 21,250,000.

1 9 3 8

JANUARY There was a rally to January; then decline was resumed. Sales for the month, 24,151,000. This was light volume on the rally, showing that there was not enough buying to turn the trend up.

FEBRUARY Sales 14,522,000.

MARCH Sales 23,995,000. This was light volume, considering the fact that the averages declined over 25 points. Final low reached March 21.

MARCH 1937 to MARCH, 1938

From March 10, 1937 to March 31, 1938 the averages declined 98 points. The total volume of sales was 346,192,000 or an averages of 35,325 shares per point, showing a much smaller volume on the decline than when the market advanced in the previous Bull Campaign and more proof of the thin markets due to Securities Exchange regulations.

1 9 3 8

APRIL Sales 17,119,000. This was on a 20-point rally in the averages.

MAY Sales 14,000,000, very small volume on a secondary reaction. The market became very dull and narrow at the bottom when the averages declined to around 106½. This was the same kind of a signal on a secondary reaction that the market was making bottom for an advance as the signal which came in August, 1937, on the secondary rally when the market was making top and getting ready for a big decline.

JUNE Sales increased to 24,668,000.

JULY A further great increase to 38,880,000.

AUGUST Sales 20,788,000. The market made top in July and August; then reacted.

SEPTEMBER Sales 23,876,000. Low of reaction. The fact that the volume increased on this reaction in September indicated that there was good buying.

OCTOBER Heavy buying and a great increase in volume this month. Sales were 41,558,000.

NOVEMBER Sales 27,922,000. November 10, final high; Dow-Jones 30 Industrial averages reached 158¾. The market made a very small gain over the high in October, when there was such large volume. During the first 10 days of November the total volume was 11,800,000, indicating that stocks were meeting some heavy selling and that distribution was taking place.

MARCH, 1938 to NOVEMBER, 1938

From March 31 to November 10, 1938 the total advance was 61¼ points. Total volume of sales 192,685,000 or 32,080 shares per point, a little less than the same number of shares per point on the decline during 1937 and early 1938.

DECEMBER Sales 27,492,000, just slightly lower than the sales in November, 1938.

1 9 3 9

JANUARY Sales 25,182,000, just a little more than the total sales in Jan.1938.

FEBRUARY The market narrowed down and the volume was very small, 13,873,000.

MARCH Sales 24,560,000. A sharp decline followed after March 10.

APRIL Sales 20,246,000. April 11, low.

NOVEMBER, 1938 to APRIL, 1939

From November 10, 1938 to April 11, 1939 the Dow-Jones 30 Industrial averages declined 38-5/8 points. Total sales 115,232,000 shares. Average volume per point decline was 30,324 shares, slightly less than on the advance to November 10, 1938, but the advance was a greater number of points.

MAY A rally followed this month but the volume was small. Sales 12,935,000

JUNE Top of rally was reached on June 9 and a decline of 20 points followed, market reaching low June 30. Sales for the month, 11,963,000. This was a secondary reaction on small volume ... an indication to buy stocks.

JULY A rally followed on increased volume. Sales in July, 18,067,000.

APRIL to JULY, 1939

From April 11, 1939 to July 31, 1939 the averages advanced 25¾ points. Total sales were 55,211,000 shares. Average sales per point, 21,234 shares, indicating a thin market, the market being able to advance on a much smaller number of shares than on its decline from November 10, 1938 to April 11, 1939.

If you continue to study the Volume of Sales on the New York Stock Exchange and watch the position of the Dow-Jones Industrial Averages on Formations and at Resistance Levels, you will be able to determine culminations with greater accuracy.

A STUDY OF WEEKLY VOLUME

CHRYSLER MOTORS 1928-35

A study of each individual stock, noting its decrease or increase in Volume and the points at which it narrows down into a slow trading range with small volume and then the other extreme when it advances on large volume and makes a rapid advance, will enable you to determine when tops and bottoms are being made. For example: CHRYSLER MOTORS

1 9 2 8

On January 21, 1928 Chrysler made low at 54½; June 2, high 88½. Then followed a decline to June 23, making low at 63-5/8, down 25 points in three weeks, on a volume of sale of 1,012,000 shares.

Then followed the final grand rush lasting 15 weeks. During this time the stock never broke the low of a previous week at any time from the bottom at 63⅝ to 140½, where it reached high on October 6, up 87 points in 15 weeks, on total sales of 9,741,800 shares. During the last two weeks of this rapid advance the sales were 2,768,000.

The total number of shares of Chrysler listed on the New York Stock Exchange is 4,484,000. Thus, you see that on this last great advance the total capitalization changed hands more than twice, and in the last two weeks more than half of the total outstanding stock was traded in. This large volume indicated that during the second advance the stock was making top. During the week ended October 6, the total sales were 1,741,500. This was the largest volume of sales for one week in the history of Chrysler Motors, nearly half of the total stock outstanding.

The following week the price of the stock was lower. It never rallied again to this top until it declined to 5. If you were making a study of the volume of sales, you would see the handwriting plain on the wall and know that this was a final top, especially after it gave all the other indications of a change in trend to the downside.

1929 TO 1932

After Chrysler reached high in October, 1928 there was a panicky decline to the week of November 16, 1929, when the ending of the first section of the bear market was recorded on Averages. The sales during the period were 22,533,000 shares, or over 5½ times the total stock outstanding.

On the rally from the week of November 16, 1929 to April, 1930, when the stock sold at 43, the total number of sales was 3,916,000 on a rally of 17 points. This volume of sales almost equalled the entire outstanding stock.

From April, 1930 high to the low of 5, which was reached in the week ended June 4, 1932, the total number of sales was 14,814,422.

The grand total of sales from the high at 140½ in the week ended October 6, 1928 to the low of 5 in June, 1932 was 41,263,622 shares. Thus, the capital stock changed hands nearly 10 times in this campaign.

1929 - 1935

COMPARISON: DECLINE FROM 88 TO 5 AND ADVANCE FROM 5 TO 88

It is important to review the total number of shares traded in from the time Chrysler sold at 88 in the week ended May 11, 1929 to the low in the week ended June 4, 1932, when it declined to 5. This review is important because we want to make a comparison with the total sales from the low of 5, reached in the week ended June 4, 1932, to the time when Chrysler sold at 88¾ again in October, 1935.

In the week ended May 11, 1929, Chrysler declined below 88 and then failed to get above this level again until it declined to a low of 5 in June, 1932. The total number of sales was 25,154,622 on this decline.

From the extreme low of 5 in the week ended June 4, 1932 to October, 1935, when the stock advanced to 88¾ again, we find that the total volume of sales was 30,628,200, or 5½ million shares more than the total number of shares traded in on the decline from May, 1929 to June, 1932, covering the same range in price.

We know that under normal conditions the volume is always greater when a stock is advancing than when it is declining, because there are more wash sales, pool operations and manipulation. The fact that Chrysler made this advance on only five million shares more than was required to go down the same number of points showed that the operations of the Securities Exchange Commission had reduced the volume of trading in an advancing market, especially when we consider that from the week ended June 4, 1932 to March, 1933 low there was a period of accumulation, the stock advancing from 5 to 22 and then declining to 7¾ again in March, 1933, on a volume of 5,105,000 shares. Therefore, deducting this from the total sales for the period from June, 1932 to October, 1935, it would bring the volume of trading down to 25 million shares on this advance, or near the same number of shares traded in on the decline of an equal number of points, from 88 to 5.

1 9 3 3 - 1 9 3 5

From the low of 7¾ in the week ended March 4, 1933 to the high at 60⅜ in the week ended February 24, 1934, Chrysler advanced 52⅝ points. Total sales, 15,219,800 shares, over three times the total amount of stock outstanding. Study this first section of the bull campaign and the distribution that took place- then apply the same rules to any other stock in order to determine a change in trend.

RANGE OF DISTRIBUTION: In the week ended January 6, 1934, Chrysler reached a high of 59½; then reacted to 50, and rallied in the week of February 3 to 59⅝; then reached top at 60⅜ in the week ended February 24, 1934. After three weeks it had failed to gain one point over the high in the week of February 3 and the first high of 59½ in January, which showed that there was real distribution taking place and the stock was meeting with heavy selling. The distribution took place between 50 and 60⅜, or in a range of 10⅜ points. In this range of distribution, there was a total number of 2,776,300 shares traded in, or over half of the total shares outstanding, which indicated that after an advance of 52 points, the stock was making top for at least a sharp decline.

SIDEWAYS DISTRIBUTION: It is interesting to study a sideways distribution. After a stock turns the minor trend down; then rallies and cannot reach the old highs again, distribution often takes place on the side, which we call a sideways movement. People buy the stock on the reaction because they think it is cheap and don't know that it is getting ready to turn the main trend down. For example:

From the week ended March 3, 1934 to the week ended April 28, 1934, the price range for Chrysler was 49¼ to 56. Total number of shares traded in 1,225,800. Adding this to the distribution at the top, the total volume was 4,002,100, or practically the entire capital stock traded in in this 10-point range of distribution. After an advance of over 50 points, when the entire capital stock turned over in a range of 10 points, it certainly was a sign of a change in trend.

It is also interesting to consider that after the advance of 52⅝ points in 51 weeks, the stock was nearing the Time period of one year. One of my rules is to always watch for a change in trend at the end of a year.

A decline followed in Chrysler after this sideways distribution.

BEAR CAMPAIGN - FEBRUARY TO AUGUST, 1934: From the high at 60⅜ in the week ended February 24, 1934 to the low at 29¼ in the week ended August 11, 1934, the range was 31⅛ points. The total volume of sales was 3,033,900, nearly three-fourths of the capital stock changing hands on this decline, Compared with the large volume on the advance, this volume on the decline, which was a secondary reaction, showed that the pressure of sales was decreasing and that the stock was reaching bottom, at least for a rally. Study this bottom and the volume of sales per week, Also note that the low of 29¼ was practically one-half of 60⅜, the high point.

BULL CAMPAIGN - AUGUST, 1934 TO NOVEMBER, 1935: From the low of 29¼ in the week ended August 11, 1934 to the high of 42½ reached in February, 1935, the sales were 2,196,500, a smaller volume on the rally. Then the trend turned down again and the stock reached a low of 31 in the week ended March 16, 1935, making a higher bottom than that of August, 1934. The price was down 11½ points from 42½ in three weeks on a small volume of 286,600 shares, which indicated that it was the last decline and that the stock was getting ready to change trend to the upside, especially as it did not go lower in the fourth week of the decline.

LONG UPSWING AFTER SECONDARY BOTTOM: From the low of 31 in the week of March 16, 1935 to the high of October 25, 1935, when the stock sold at 88¾, making a total range of 57¾ points, the number of shares traded in was 5,091,000 shares, about 3/4 million over the total capital stock outstanding. From the low of 29¼ in August, 1934 to the high of 88¾ in October, 1935, the total range was 59½ points and the total sales 7,287,500, the total number of outstanding shares changing hands nearly twice.

The most important last long swing to consider was from the low of 7¾ in March 1933 to 88¾ in October, 1935, an advance of 81 points on total sales of 25,523,200 shares, which showed that the stock traded in equalled nearly six times the amount of stock outstanding.

When the stock was near the low in March, 1935, the sales per week were around 75,000 shares to as low as 46,000 shares per week until April 27, when the volume was 235,000 shares in the week. After that they were running higher right along. Then, beginning the week of August 31, sales were as high as 229,000 shares a week, 233,000, 254,000, 149,000, 223,000, 209,000, 260,000 in the week of October 19, and during the week ended October 26, when Chrysler reached 88¾, the sales were 256,000. Thus, you see how the volume of sales was increasing rapidly when this stock made a sharp advance to 88¾ from the low of the last reaction around 69.

In determining the extreme high and low points, you will find it will help you to study the Volume of Sales on each individual stock, especially the active leaders, and follow the rules.

Regulations against specialists, pool operators, and against member os the New York Stock Exchange trading for their own accounts have cut down the volume of sales probably as much as 50%. When the Government makes business bad in Wall Street, it hurts business throughout the nation.

The day will come when these roforms and regulations will cease because they are doing harm and helping no one. After these restrictions are taken off, then the market will show a larger volume of sales per point and there will be a more normal market.

When once again we have a free market and everybody is permitted to trade who can put up the money, there will be better business and general prosperity. Let us all pray that the day of reform and regulations will soon cease as it is best for all concerned that they should.

August 12, 1939

CHAPTER 5

MASTER TIME FACTOR
AND
FORECASTING BY MATHEMATICAL RULES

W. D. GANN
88 WALL STREET
NEW YORK

SCIENTIFIC ADVICE
AND ANALYTICAL REPORTS
ON STOCKS AND COMMODITIES
AUTHOR OF "TRUTH OF THE STOCK TAPE"
"WALL STREET STOCK SELECTOR"
AND "THE TUNNEL THRU THE AIR"

MEMBER
AMERICAN ECONOMIC ASS'N
ROYAL ECONOMIC SOCIETY
CABLE ADDRESS
"GANWADE NEW YORK"

FORECASTING

Every movement in the market is the result of a natural law and a Cause which exists long before the Effect takes place and can be determined years in advance. The future is but a repetition of the past, as the Bible plainly states:

> "The thing that hath been, it is that which shall be; and that which is done is that which shall be done, and there is no new things under the sun." Eccl. 1: 9.

Everything moves in cycles as a result of the natural law of action and reaction. By a study of the past, I have discovered what cycles repeat in the future.

MAJOR TIME CYCLES

There must always be a major and a minor, a greater and a lesser, a positive and a negative. In order to be accurate in forecasting the future, you must know the major cycles. The most money is made when fast moves and extreme fluctuations occur at the end of major cycles.

I have experimented and compared past markets in order to locate the major and minor cycles and determine what years in the cycles repeat in the future. After years of research and practical tests, I have discovered that the following cycles are the most reliable to use:

GREAT CYCLE - MASTER TIME PERIOD - 60 YEARS:

This is the greatest and most important cycle of all, which repeats every 60 years or at the end of the third 20-year Cycle. You will see the importance of this by referring to the war period from 1861 to 1869 and the panic following 1869; also 60 years later—1921 to 1929—the greatest bull market in history and the greatest panic in history followed. This proves the accuracy and value of this great time period.

50-YEAR CYCLE:

A major cycle occurs every 49 to 50 years. A period of "jubilee" years of extreme high or low prices, lasting from 5 to 7 years, occurs at the end of the 50-year cycle. "7" is a fatal number referred to many times in the Bible. It brings about contraction, depression and panics. Seven times "7" equals 49, which is shown as the fatal evil year, causing extreme fluctuations.

30-YEAR CYCLE:

The 30-year cycle is very important because it is one-half of the 60-year cycle or Great Cycle and contains three 10-year cycles. In making up an annual forecast of a stock, you should always make a comparison with the record 30 years back.

20-YEAR CYCLE:

One of the most important Time Cycles is the 20-year cycle or 240 months. Most stocks and the averages work closer to this cycle than to any other. Refer to analysis of "20-year Forecasting Chart" given later.

15-YEAR CYCLE:

Fifteen years is three-fourths of a 20-year cycle and most important because it is 180 months or one-half of a circle.

10-YEAR CYCLE:

The next important major cycle is the 10-year cycle, which is one-half of the 20-year cycle and one-sixth of the 60-year cycle. It is also very important because it is 120 months or one-third of a circle. Fluctuations of the same nature occur which produce extreme high or low every 10 years. Stocks come out remarkably close on each even 10-year cycle.

7-YEAR CYCLE:

This cycle is 84 months. You should watch 7 years from any important top and bottom. 42 months or one-half of this cycle is very important. You will find many culminations around the 42nd month. 21 months or 1/4 of this cycle is also important. The fact that some stocks make top or bottom 10 to 11 months from the previous top or bottom is due to the fact that this period is 1/8 of the 7-year cycle.

There is an 84-year Cycle, which is 12 times the 7-year Cycle, that is very important to watch. One-half of this cycle is 42 years- 1/4 is 21 years, and 1/8 is $10\frac{1}{2}$ years. This is one of the reasons for the period of nearly 11 years between the bottom of August, 1921 and the bottom of July, 1932. A variation of this kind often occurs at the end of a Great Cycle or 60 years. Bottoms and tops often come out on the angle of 135° or around the 135th month or $11\frac{1}{4}$-year period from any important top or bottom.

5-YEAR CYCLE:

This cycle is very important because it is one-half of the 10-year cycle and 1/4 of the 20-year cycle. The smallest complete cycle or work-out in a market is 5 years.

MINOR CYCLES:

The minor cycles are 3 years and 6 years. The smallest cycle is one year, which often shows a change in the 10th or 11th month.

RULES FOR FUTURE CYCLES

Stocks move in 10-year cycles, which are worked out in 5-year cycles — a 5-year cycle up and a 5-year cycle down. Begin with extreme tops and extreme bottoms to figure all cycles, either major or minor.

Rule 1 - A bull campaign generally runs 5 years — 2 years up, 1 year down, and 2 years up, completing a 5-year cycle. The end of a 5-year campaign comes in the 59th or 60th months. Always watch for the change in the 59th month.

Rule 2 - A bear cycle often runs 5 years down—the first move 2 years down, then 1 year up, and 2 years down, completing the 5-year downswing.

Rule 3 - Bull or bear campaigns seldom run more than 3 to $3\frac{1}{2}$ years up or down without a move of 3 to 6 months or one year in the opposite direction, except at the end of Major Cycles, like 1869 and 1929. Many campaigns culminate in the 23rd month, not running out the full two years. Watch the weekly and monthly charts to determine whether the culmination will occur in the 23rd, 24th, 27th or 30th month of the move, or in extreme campaigns in the 34th to 35th or 41st to 42nd month.

Rule 4 - Adding 10 years to any top, it will give you top of the next 10-year cycle, repeating about the same average fluctuations.

Rule 5 - Adding 10 years to any bottom, it will give you the bottom of the next 10-year cyclo, repeating the same kind of a year and about the same average fluctuations.

Rule 6 - Bear campaigns often run out in 7-year cycles, or 3 years and 4 years from any complete bottom. From any complete bottom of a cycle, first add 3 years to get the next bottom; then add 4 years to that bottom to get bottom of 7-year cycle. For example: 1914 bottom - add 3 years, gives 1917, low of panic; then add 4 years to 1917, gives 1921, low of another depression.

Rule 7 - To any final major or minor top, add 3 years to get the next top; then add 3 years to that top, which will give the third top; add 4 years to the third top to get the final top of a 10-year cycle. Sometimes a change in trend from any top occurs before the end of the regular time period, therefore you should begin to watch the 27th, 34th, and 42nd months for a reversal.

Rule 8 - Adding 5 years to any top, it will give the next bottom of a 5-year cycle. In order to get top of the next 5-year cycle, add 5 years to any bottom. For example: 1917 was bottom of a big bear campaign; add 5 years gives 1922, top of a minor bull campaign. Why do I say, "Top of a minor bull campaign?" Because the major bull campaign was due to end in 1929.

1919 was top; adding 5 years to 1919 gives 1924 as bottom of a 5-year bear cycle. Refer to Rules 1 and 2, which tell you that a bull or bear campaign seldom runs more than 2 to 3 years in the same direction. The bear campaign from 1919 was 2 years down—1920 and 1921; therefore, we only expect one-year rally in 1922; then 2 years down—1923 and 1924, which completes the 5-year bear cycle.

Looking back to 1913 and 1914, you will see that 1923 and 1924 must be bear years to complete the 10-year cycle from the bottoms of 1913-1914

Then, note 1917 bottom of a bear year; adding 7 years gives 1924 also as bottom of a bear cycle. Then, adding 5 years to 1924 gives 1929 top of a cycle.

FORECASTING MONTHLY MOVES

Monthly moves can be determined by the same rules as yearly:

Add three months to an important bottom, then add 4, making 7, to get minor bottoms and reaction points.

In big upswings a reaction will often not last over two months, the third month being up, the same rule as in yearly cycle—2 down and the third up.

In extreme markets, a reaction sometimes only lasts 2 or 3 weeks; then the advance is resumed. In this way a market may continue up for 12 months without breaking a monthly bottom.

In a bull market the minor trend may reverse and run down 3 to 4 months; then turn up and follow the main trend again.

In a bear market, the minor trend may run up 3 to 4 months, then reverse and follow the main trend, altho, as a general rule, stocks never rally more than 2 months in a bear market; then start to break in the 3rd month and follow the main trend down.

FORECASTING WEEKLY MOVES

The weekly movement gives the next important minor change in trend, which may turn out to be a major change in trend.

In a bull market, a stock will often run down 2 to 3 weeks, and possibly 4, then reverse and follow the main trend again. As a rule, the trend will turn up in the middle of the third week and close higher at the end of the third week, the stock only moving 3 weeks against the main trend. In some cases the change in trend will not occur until the fourth week; then the reversal will come and the stock close higher at the end of the fourth week.
Reverse this rule in a bear market.

In rapid markets with big volume, a move will often run 6 to 7 weeks before a minor reversal in trend, and in some cases, like 1929, these fast moves last 13 to 15 weeks or 1/4 of a year. These are culmination moves up or down.

As there are 7 days in a week and seven times seven equals 49 days or 7 weeks, this often marks an important turning point. Therefore you should watch for top or bottom around the 49th to 52nd day, altho at times a change will start on the 42nd to 45th day, because a period of 45 days is 1/8 of a year. Also watch for culminations at the end of 90 to 98 days.

After a market has declined 7 weeks, it may have 2 or 3 short weeks on the side and then turn up, which agrees with the monthly rule for a change in the third month.

Always watch the annual trend of a stock and consider whether it is in a bull or bear year. In a bull year, with the monthly chart showing up, there are many times that a stock will react 2 or 3 weeks, then rest 3 or 4 weeks, and then go into new territory and advance 6 to 7 weeks more.

After a stock makes top and reacts 2 to 3 weeks, it may then have a rally of 2 to 3 weeks without getting above the first top; then hold in a trading range for several weeks without crossing the highest top or breaking the lowest week of that range. In cases of this kind, you can buy near the low point or sell near the high point of that range and protect with a stop loss order 1 to 3 points away. However, a better plan would be to wait until the stock shows a definite trend before buying or selling; then buy the stock when it crosses the highest point or sell when it breaks the lowest point of that trading range.

FORECASTING DAILY MOVES

The daily movement gives the first minor change and conforms to the same rules as the weekly and monthly cycles, altho it is only a minor part of them.

In fast markets there will only be a 2-day move in the opposite direction to the main trend and on the third day the upward or downward course will be resumed in harmony with the main trend.

A daily movement may reverse trend and only run 7 to 10 days; then follow the main trend again.

During a month, natural changes in trend occur around

6th to 7th	14th to 15th	23rd to 24th
9th to 10th	19th to 20th	29th to 31st.

Those minor moves occur in accordance with tops and bottoms of individual stocks.

It is very important to watch for a change in trend 30 days from the last top or bottom. Then watch for changes 60, 90, 120 days from tops or bottoms. 180 days or six months—very important and sometimes marks changes for greater moves. Also around the 270th and 330th day from important tops or bottoms, you should watch for important minor and often major changes.

January 2nd to 7th and 15th to 21st:

Watch these periods each year and note the high and low prices made. Until these high prices are crossed or low prices broken, consider the trend up or down.

Many times when stocks make low in the early part of January, this low will not be broken until the following July or August and sometimes not during the entire year. This same rule applies in bear markets or when the main trend is down. High prices made in the early part of January are often high for the entire year and are not crossed until after July or August. For example:

U. S. Steel on January 2, 1930 made low at 166, which was the half-way point from 1921 to 1929, and again on January 7, 1930 declined to 167¼. When this level was broken, Steel indicated lower prices.

July 3rd to 7th and 20th to 27th:

The month of July, like January, is a month when most dividends are paid and investors usually buy stocks around the early part of the month. Watch these periods in July for tops or bottoms and a change in trend. Go back over the charts and see how many times changes have taken place in July, 180 days from January tops or bottoms. For example:

July 8, 1932 was low; July 17, 1933, high; and July 26, 1934 low of the market.

HOW TO DIVIDE THE YEARLY TIME PERIOD

Divide the year by 2 to get 6 months, the opposition point or 180° angle, which equals 26 weeks.

Divide the year by 4 to get the 3 months' period or 90 days or 90° each, which is 1/4 of a year or 13 weeks.

Divide the year by 3 to get the 4 months' period, the 120° angle, which is 1/3 of a year or 17-1/3 weeks.

Divide the year by 8, which gives $1\frac{1}{2}$ months, 45 days and equals the 45° angle. This is also $6\frac{1}{2}$ weeks, which shows why the 7th week is always so important.

Divide the year by 16, which gives $22\frac{1}{2}$ days or approximately 3 weeks. This accounts for market movements that only run 3 weeks up or down and then reverse. As a general rule, when any stock closes higher the 4th consecutive week, it will go higher. The 5th week is also very important for a change in trend and for fast moves up or down. The 5th is the day, week, month, or year of Ascension and always marks fast moves up or down, according to the major cycle that is running out.

BULL AND BEAR CALENDAR YEARS

By studying the yearly high and low chart and going back over a long period of time, you will see the years in which bull markets culminate and the years in which bear markets begin and end.

Each decade or 10-year cycle, which is 1/10th of 100 years, marks an important campaign. The digits from 1 to 9 are important. All you have to learn is to count the digits on your fingers in order to ascertain what kind of a year the market is in.

No. 1 in a new decade is a year in which a bear market ends and a bull market begins. Look up 1901, 1911, 1921.

No. 2 or the 2nd year, is a year of a minor bull market, or a rally in a bear market will start at some time. See 1902, 1912, 1922, 1932.

No. 3 starts a bear year, but the rally from the 2nd year may run to March or April before culmination, or a decline from the 2nd year may run down and make bottom in February or March, like 1933. Look up 1903, 1913, 1923.

No. 4 or the 4th year, is a bear year, but ends the bear cycle and lays the foundation for a bull market. Compare 1904, 1914.

No. 5 or the 5th year, is the year of Ascension, and a very strong year for a bull market. See 1905, 1915, 1925, 1935.

No. 6 is a bull year, in which a bull campaign which started in the 4th year ends in the Fall of the year and a fast decline starts. See 1896, 1906, 1916, 1926.

No. 7 is a bear number and the 7th year is a bear year, because 84 months or 84½° is 7/8 of 90. See 1897, 1907, 1917, but note 1927 was end of a 60-year cycle, so not much decline.

No. 8 is a bull year. Prices start advancing in the 7th year and reach the 90th month in the 8th year. This is very strong and a big advance usually takes place. Review 1898, 1908, 1918, 1928.

No. 9 the highest digit and the 9th year, is the strongest of all for bull markets. Final bull campaigns culminate in this year after extreme advances and prices start to decline. Bear markets usually start in September to November at the end of the 9th year and a sharp decline takes place. See 1869, 1879, 1889, 1899, 1909, 1919, and 1929—the year of greatest advances, culminating in the fall of the year, followed by a sharp decline.

No. 10 is a bear year. A rally often runs until March and April; then a severe decline runs to November and December, when a new cycle begins and another rally starts. See 1910, 1920, 1930.

In referring to these numbers and years, we mean the calendar years. To understand this, study 1891 to 1900, 1901 to 1910, 1911 to 1920, 1921 to 1930, 1931 to 1939.

The 10-year cycle continues to repeat over and over, but the greatest advances and declines occur at the end of the 20-year and 30-year cycles, and again at the end of the 50-year and 60-year cycles, which are stronger than the others.

IMPORTANT POINTS TO REMEMBER IN FORECASTING

TIME is the most important factor of all and not until sufficient time has expired does any big move, up or down, start. The Time factor will overbalance both Space and Volume. When Time is up, space movement will start and big volume will begin, either up or down. At the end of any big movement—with monthly, weekly or daily—Time must be allowed for accumulation or distribution.

Consider each individual stock and determine its trend from its position according to distance in time from bottom or top. Each stock works out its 1, 2, 3, 5, 7, 10, 15, 20, 30, 50 and 60-year cycles from its own base or bottoms and tops, regardless of the movements of other stocks, even those in the same group. Therefore, judge each stock individually and keep up weekly and monthly charts on them.

Never decide that the main trend has changed one way or the other without consulting the angles from top or bottom and without considering the position of the market and cycle of each individual stock.

Always consider the annual forecast and whether the big time limit has run out or not before judging a reverse move. Do not fail to consider the indications on Time, both from main tops and bottoms, also Volume of Sales and position on Geometrical Angles.

A daily chart gives the first short change, which may run for 7 to 10 days; the Weekly Chart gives the next important change in trend; and the Monthly the strongest. Remember, weekly moves run 3 to 7 weeks, monthly moves 2 to 3 months or more, according to the yearly cycle, before reversing.

Yearly bottoms and tops: It is important to note whether a stock is making higher or lower bottoms each year. For instance, if a stock has made a higher bottom each year for five years, then makes a lower bottom than the previous year, it is a sign of reversal and may mark a long down cycle. The same rule applies when stocks are making lower tops for a number of years in a bear market.

When extreme advances or declines occur, the first time the market reverses over 1/4 to 1/2 of the distance covered in the previous movement, you consider that the trend has changed, at least temporarily.

It is important to watch space movements. When Time is running out one way or the other, space movements will show a reversal by breaking back over 1/4, 1/3 or 1/2 of the distance of the last move from extreme low to extreme high, which indicates that the main trend has changed.

Study all the instructions and rules that I have given you; read them over several times, as each time they will become clearer to you. Study the charts and work out the rules in actual practice as well as on past performance. In this way you will make progress and will realize and appreciate the value of my Method of Forecasting.

HOW TO MAKE UP ANNUAL FORECASTS

I have stated before that the future is but a repetition of the past; therefore, to make up a forecast of the future, you must refer to the previous cycles.

The previous 10-year cycle and 20-year cycle have the most effect in the future, but in completing a forecast, it is best to have 30-years past record to check up, as important changes occur at the end of 30-year cycles. In making up my 1935 Forecast on the general market, I checked the years 1905, 1915, and 1925. For the 1929 Forecast, I compared 1919—10 years back, 1909—20 years back, 1899—30 years back, and 1869—60 years back, the Great Cycle.

You should also watch 5, 7, 15, and 50-year periods to see if the market is repeating one of them closely.

MASTER 20-YEAR FORECASTING CHART

1831 - 1935

In order to make up an annual forecast, you must refer to my Master 20-year Forecasting Chart and see how these cycles have worked out and repeated in the past.

As stated before, the 20-year cycle is the most important cycle for forecasting future market movements. It is one-third of the 60-year cycle and when three 20-year cycles run out, important bull and bear campaigns terminate.

In order for you to see and study how these cycles repeat, I have made up a chart of 20-year cycles, beginning with the year 1831. To show all of the cycles from 1831 to date, we have carried thru on this chart the monthly high and low on railroad and canal stocks from 1831 to 1855. Beginning with 1856 we have used the W. D. Gann Averages on railroad stocks until the beginning of the Dow-Jones Averages in 1896. After that we have used the Dow-Jones Industrial Stock Averages.

After the end of the 20-year cycle in 1860,
the next cycle begins at 1861 and runs to 1880,
the next cycle begins at 1881 and runs to 1900,
the next cycle begins at 1901 and runs to 1920,
the next cycle begins at 1921 and runs to 1940.

By placing the monthly high and low prices for each of these 20-year periods above each other, it is easy to see how the cycles repeat. The year of the cycles are marked from "1" to "20." Study the chart and note what happened in the 8th and 9th year of each cycle—that extreme high prices have always been reached. For example:

1929 FORECAST:

According to my discovery of the 60-year cycle, I had figured that 1929 would repeat like 1869, 1909, and 1919. Looking back 20 years, we find that top was reached in August, 1909, and 60 years before, top was reached in July, 1869. If you will read my Annual Forecast for 1929, you will see that I had figured the top must come not later than the end of August and stated that a "Black Friday" would come in September. Following strictly the 1869 top, the top would have come in July, 1929, and some stocks did make top at that time. Following the 1909 top, we could expect top in August, and the actual high of the averages and many individual stocks was reached on September 3, 1929. Going back to 1919, we find that the Averages made first top in July and a big decline followed, but extreme high was made in the early part of November.

From all of those tops—1869, 1909, and 1919—sharp declines followed in the fall of the year, just as they did in 1929. Therefore you see how easy it was to follow this great advance and determine when it would culminate. There is no other way, outside of using the 20 and 60-year cycle that we could have forecast this great bull campaign and its culmination so closely in 1929.

1869-73 VS. 1929-33:

After the 1869 top, stocks continued to decline and reached low in November, 1873. See how many other bottoms were reached around this time in other cycles. After the big decline from 1929, notice that in October, 1933 the last low was reached on the Dow-Jones Averages; thenfollowed an advance to new high levels, crossing the top of July, 1933.

1935 FORECAST:

Figuring out the Forecast for 1935, we see on this 20-year Chart that we are running against 1855, 1875, 1895, 1915; therefore, we look to see what happened in those years. We find that in 1895 the high was reached in September, in 1915

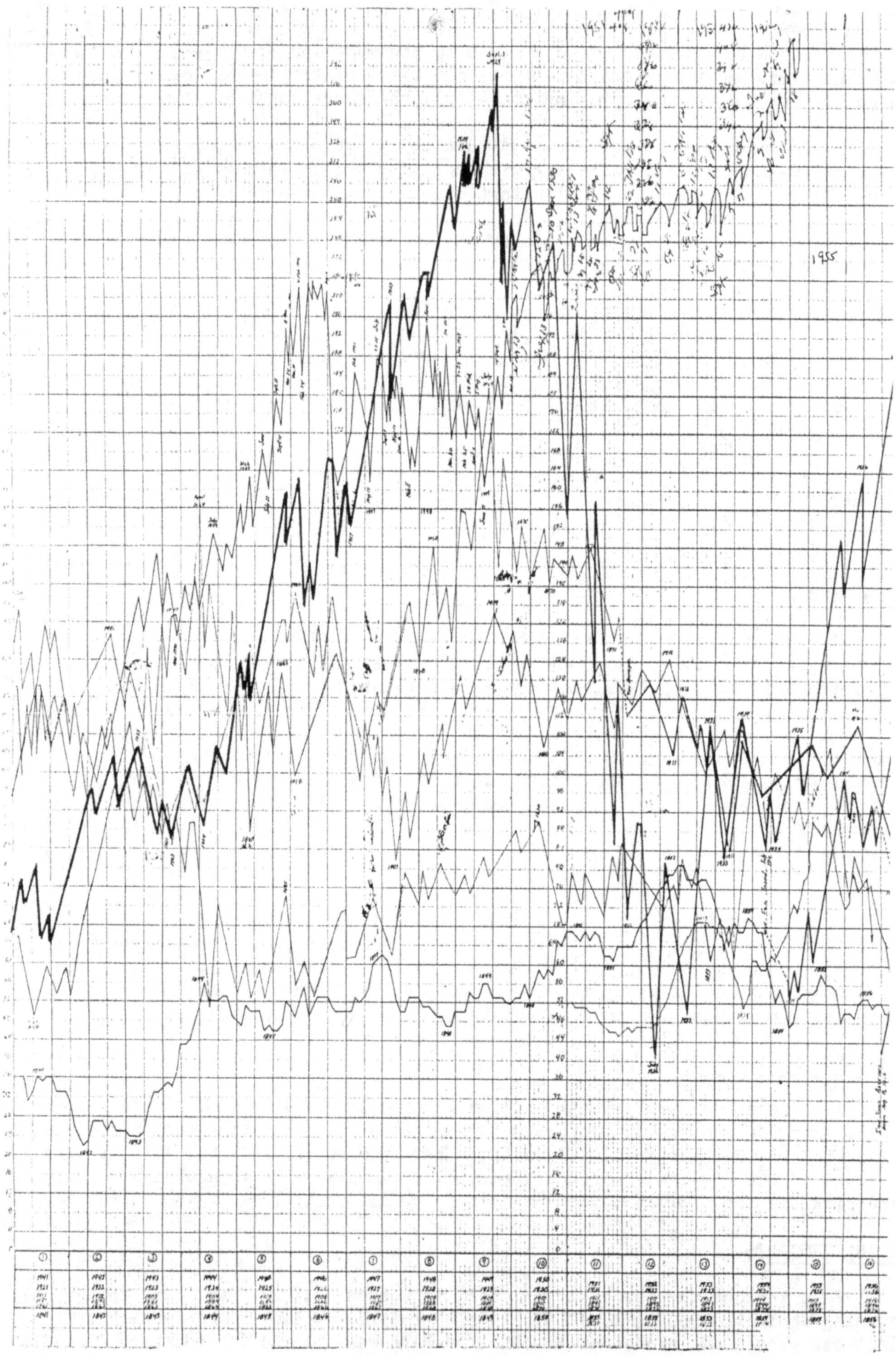
1955

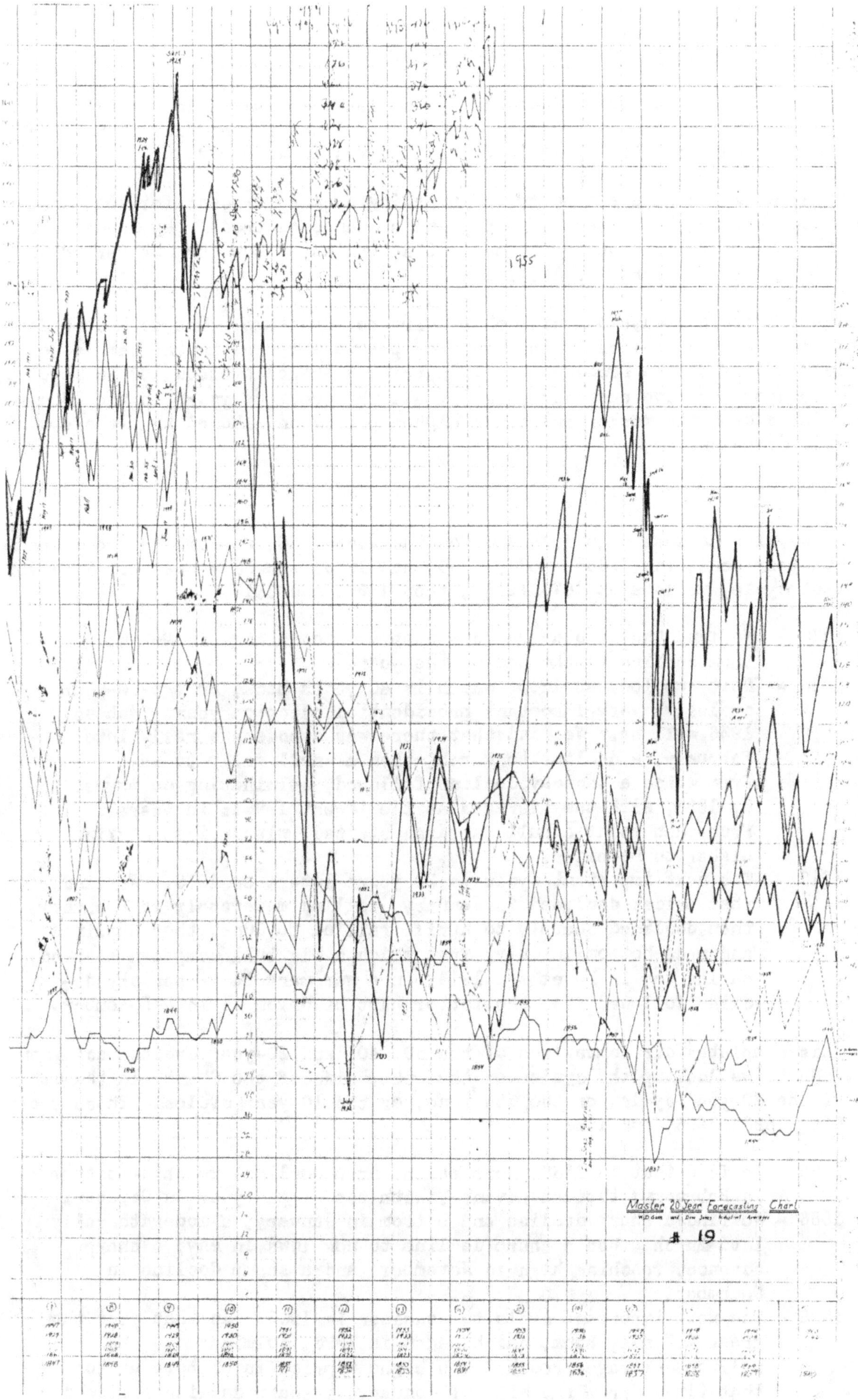
Master 20 Year Forecasting Chart
W.D. Gann and Dow Jones Industrial Averages
19

the high of the year was reached in December.

Then, look back at 1865, 1885, 1905, and 1925, the years in the 5th zone or the 10-year cycles. We find that in 1865 the high was reached in October; in 1905 the high was in October; in 1925 the high was in November.

Then, we would have a good guide in making up the Forecast for 1935 and would know what months to watch for top and a change in trend. My Annual Forecast for 1935, which was made up in October, 1934, indicated top for October 28 and a secondary top for November 15-16, 1935.

There are other ways of using this Chart to advantage. One method of determining the trend is to compare the years of previous cycles in the same zone. For example: After the Dow-Jones 30 Industrial Averages crossed 108 in May, 1935 they were above the average high price of all the previous years in the 15th-year zone. Therefore, the market indicated higher prices and showed that there would be a bull campaign.

1936 FORECAST:

If we wish to make up a forecast for the year 1936, we compare the years in the 16th-year zone, viz. 1856, 1876, 1896, and 1916. As 60 years back is a very important cycle, we look at 1876 first, then 1896, and 1916.

1876 - We find that the averages run up and reach high in March; then decline to the end of the year.

1896 - Next, we look at 1896, which is 40 years back, or two 20-year cycles, a very important presidential election year, just as 1936 will be. We find that there was a moderate rally into February, a decline to March, then a small rally to May, from which a panicky decline followed, culminating on August 8, 1896, with the averages at the lowest levels in years. From that point a bull campaign started, with prices working higher to December.

1916 - The next important cycle is 20 years later, or 1916. We find that prices declined in January, rallied moderately in February, then declined sharply to April, rallied to June, then declined and made bottom in July, from which a big bull campaign started, making top in November, 1916, in a war market. A panicky decline followed from the latter part of November into December.

This completes our comparison of the 60, 40, and 20-year cycles back from 1936. Next, we look up the cycles on the other side of the Chart, in the 6th year of the 20-year cycle, or the 6th zone, or the 10-year cycles. These years are 1866, 1886, 1906, and 1926.

1866 - We find that in 1866 there was a sharp decline, reaching bottom in February; then an advance, with top of the year in October.

1886 - We find a sharp decline and bottom in January, a moderate rally into March, then a sharp decline to new lows in May; a sharp advance, reaching high in November, and a sharp decline in December.

1906 - The next important cycle to consider is 1906. In that year the great McKinley boom, which began in 1896, culminated. The railroad averages reached the highest price in history up to that time. From the high of January, a sharp decline followed to May. Much of this selling was caused by the San Francisco earthquake. Then there was a rally into June, followed by a sharp decline to low in July, with the bottom just slightly higher than the low of May. From this low there was an advance to September, when another top was made, but lower than the top in January; then followed a decline into December and a panic followed in 1907.

1926 - The next important 10-year cycle to consider is 1926, when the great Coolidge bull campaign was under way. From the low in December, 1925, stocks rallied to February, 1926; then had a sharp decline to March, some stocks breaking as much as 100 points. From this bottom there was a sharp advance to new high levels, reaching top in August; then another sharp decline to bottom in October, from which a rally followed to December, but stocks did not get back to the high reached in August that year.

Now, when I get ready to make up my Forecast for 1936, I will consider all of these cycles. I will go back and also check the 7-year cycles, the 14-year and 15-year cycles, which is half of the 30-year cycle. But, at this writing, with my knowledge and experience of the future cycles, I expect the 1896 cycle to repeat in 1936.

1936 is likely to be a very uncertain election year just as it was in 1896, when the Bryan silver scare caused a panicky decline into August. There is a possibility of a three-cornered fight, with two Democratic presidential candidates and one Republican. There certainly is going to be a time during 1936 when the investors are going to get scared and speculators are going to get scared and sell stocks, causing sharp declines.

My opinion, at this writing, is that the first decline will start in the month of January and wind up with a sharp decline. February—The market may drift along in a narrow, trading range with some rallies, but there will be another decline in the month of March, just as there was in 1926. I am confident that there will be another break in the months of May and June, especially in the latter half of May, as this will be running out four years from the 1932 low and 6 years from April, 1930 high, all of which are indications of important changes in trend.

We know that presidential nominations will take place in July, therefore this is a month to watch for uncertainties and declines, unless sharp declines have come before that time. The ending of the cycle from 1896 in August in quite important and regardless of how high or how low stocks are, there are likely to be some sharp declines before the end of August. Again, in the last half of September, uncertain conditions and possibility of sharp declines are indicated. This may mark the last low and an election rally may start if there are indications of a change in Administration by the election of a Republican president, which, I believe, at this writing, will happen.

September, October, and November are all important because these months are 7 years from the top in September, 1929 and 7 years from the panicky decline in October and November, 1929. I would expect a rally to take place after the election in November, which would last anyway until the early part of December. If conditions show signs of improvement and if the people are satisfied with the man elected, then the advance will probably continue into December, with high prices around the end of the year.

This is merely a general outline that I am giving without completing all of my calculations and making up the Annual Forecast in detail.

INDIVIDUAL STOCKS:

I have told you before that you should not depend upon the Averages to forecast the trend of individual stocks. These Averages give you the general trend, and while many stocks will follow this average trend, you should figure out each stock individually and let its position on geometrical angles and time periods determine the different months in the year when the stock is likely to make tops and bottoms.

Take any individual stock and make up a chart like the Master Forecasting Chart, carrying it across 10 years or 20 years, and see how its tops and bottoms come out. I have made up a chart of the 10-year cycles on U. S. Steel and also a chart of the 20-year cycles, and am always glad to furnish these charts to students of my Course on Forecasting so that they may study the individual stocks and be convinced that the theory will work on an individual stock even better than it will work on the Averages.

No man can study the Master 20-year Forecasting Chart and the cycles without being convinced that time cycles do repeat at regular intervals and that it is possible to forecast future market movements. By studying Resistance Levels, Geometrical Angles, and Volume of Sales in connection with the Cycles, you can determine when the trend is changing at the end of campaigns.

FAST MOVES AND CULMINATIONS AT IMPORTANT TIME PERIODS

It is important to go over the monthly chart of Industrial or Railroad averages or any individual stock and look up the months when fast advances and fast declines have occurred and figure the number of months from any important top and bottom.

Watch how bottoms and tops come out on the important Geometrical Angles or proportionate parts of the circle of 360°, which are:

$11\frac{1}{4}$	$56\frac{1}{4}$	*90	$123\frac{3}{4}$	$168\frac{3}{4}$	$213\frac{3}{4}$	$247\frac{1}{2}$	$292\frac{1}{2}$	$326\frac{1}{4}$
$22\frac{1}{2}$	*60	$101\frac{1}{4}$	*135	*180	*225	$258\frac{3}{4}$	*300	$337\frac{1}{2}$
$33\frac{3}{4}$	$67\frac{1}{2}$	$112\frac{1}{2}$	$146\frac{1}{4}$	$191\frac{1}{4}$	$236\frac{1}{4}$	*270	$303\frac{3}{4}$	$348\frac{3}{4}$
*45	$78\frac{3}{4}$	*120	$157\frac{1}{2}$	$202\frac{1}{2}$	*240	$281\frac{1}{4}$	*315	*360

(* very important)

These angles measure the time periods. Always watch what happens around 45, 60, 90, 120, 135, 180, 225, 240, 270, 300, 315 and 360 months from any important top or bottom, as all of these angles are very strong and important, just the same as the 45° angle, and indicate strong culmination points.

REVIEW OF DOW-JONES INDUSTRIAL STOCKS FROM 1896:

Go back to the extreme low of August, 1896—

1897 - A secondary low was recorded in April, 1897. We find that there was a fast advance in the 11th to 13th months from August, 1896 low.

1898 - A fast advance occurred in the 16th and 24th months from the bottoms of 1897 and 1896, and a fast decline in the 17th and 25th months.

1899 - A bull year. Fast advance occurred in the 29th to 32nd months from 1896 and in the 21st to 24th months from 1897 bottom. Fast declines occurred in the 40th and 32nd months from these bottoms.

1900 - Fast advance 42nd to 44th months from 1897 and 50th to 52nd months from 1896 bottom.

1901 - A fast decline on the 49th month from 1897 and 57th month from 1896 low. Top reached in June.

1903 - A bear year. 22nd to 28th month from 1901 top, a fast decline- also 72nd to 78th months from 1897 bottom and 80th to 86th months from 1896 bottom. Bottom reached in October and November, 1903.

1904 - Fast advance, 12 to 14 months from 1903 bottom.

1905 - Fast move up in the 16th to 18th months; fast decline in the 19th month, and a fast advance in the 25th to 27th months from 1903 bottom.

1906 - Top of campaign reached in January. Fast decline in the 30th month from 1903 bottom.

1907 - Fast decline in the 14th month from 1906 top and in the 19th to 22nd months. Extreme low reached in November, 1907, in the 135th month from 1896 bottom, 127 months from 1897 low, and 22 months from 1906 top.

1909 - Top of campaign reached in October, 45 months from 1906 top and 23 months from 1907 bottom, 158 months from 1896.

1914 - July, a fast decline in the 57th month from 1909 top, 21 months from 1912 top. Extreme low of campaign in December, 107 months from 1906 top, 26 months from 1912 top, 220 months from 1896 low, 84 months or 7 years from 1907 bottom, and 134 months from 1903 bottom.

1915 - This was a war year. March and April—Fast advance on the 3rd and 4th months from the 1914 bottom. May—A sharp, severe decline, 90 months from November, 1907 bottom and 225 months from 1896 bottom. Note these fast moves on a 90° angle and 225° angle, which is equal to a 45° angle, or 180 plus 45.

1916 - April—A sharp decline, 16 months from the 1914 bottom, 123 months from 1906 top, and 236 months from 1896 low. September—Fast advance, 21 months from 1914 low, and 240 months from 1896 low, the end of the 20-year cycle, indicating an important change in trend. November—Top of a fast advance; Dow-Jones Industrial Averages at the highest price in history up to that time. This was 23 months from 1914 bottom and 243 months from 1896 bottom. December—A sharp decline, 24 months from 1914 bottom.

1917 - August to December—A fast decline, 9 to 13 months from November, 1916 top, 32 to 36 months from the 1914 bottom, 117 to 121 months from the 1907 bottom, and 252 to 256 months from 1896 low.

1919 - A fast advance started in February and lasted until July. This was 27 to

32 months from the 1916 top, and 50 to 55 months from 1914 low. February, 1919 was 135 months from the 1907 low and 270 months from 1896 bottom. The 135th and 270th months, being 3/8 and 3/4 of the circle, were very important for changes in trend and starting of moves. October and early November—Final top, 36 months from 1916 top. November—A panicky decline, 23 months from 1917 low, 59 months from 1914 bottom (end of a 5-year cycle), and 279 months from 1896 bottom.

1920 - November and December—A fast decline, 12 to 13 months from 1919 top, 35 to 36 months from 1917 low, 72 months from 1914 bottom, 157 months from 1907 bottom, and 291 to 292 months from 1896 bottom.

1921 - August—Low of bear campaign, 21 months from 1919 top, 80 months from 1914 bottom, 165 months from 1907 bottom, and 300 months from 1896 bottom.

1924 - May—The last low was made, from which a fast advance started one of the greatest bull campaigns in history, ending in 1929. This was 54 months from the 1919 top, 33 months from 1921 low, 113 months from 1914 low, and 333 months from 1896 low.

1926 - March—A big decline, with some stocks declining 100 points. This was 23 months from May, 1924 low, 29 months from 1923 low, 55 months from 1921 low, 135 months from 1914 low, and 355 months from 1896 low.
August—Stocks reached the highest price up to that time, the Dow-Jones Industrial Averages selling at 166. This was 27 months from May, 1924 low, 34 months from October, 1923 low, 60 months from 1921 bottom, 225 months from 1907 low, and 360 months or 30 years from 1896 low. Then a 20-point decline followed to October, which was 2 months in a new 30-year cycle from the bottom of 1896.

1928 and 1929 were years of some of the fastest moves in history.

1929 - May to September—One of the fastest moves, advancing nearly 100 points on Averages. Final high in September. This was:

118 months from 1919 top,
240 months from 1909 top,
42 months from March, 1926 low,
64 months from May 1924 bottom,
71 months from October, 1923 low,
97 months from August, 1921 low,
177 months from 1914 low,
262 months from 1907 low,
37 months in the second cycle of 30 years from 1896 low.

Note the strong time angles on the Monthly Chart running out in October and November, 1929, which are 32, 40, 45, 67½, 75, 120, 180.

1930 - April—Last top before another big decline. This was 49 months from March, 1926 low, 71 months from 1924 low, and 78 months from 1923 low.
May—A sharp, severe decline. This was 270 months from 1907 low and 45 months in the second cycle from 1896 low. Then there were fast declines to 1931.

1931 - September—A decline of 46 points on the Dow-Jones Averages. This was 24 months from the 1929 top, 95 and 86 months from 1923 and 1924 lows, 121 months or the beginning of a new 10-year cycle from 1921 low, 201 months from 1914 low, and 61 months in the new cycle from 1896.

1932 - July 8th—Extreme low of the bear campaign was reached. This was 71 months in the new cycle from 1896 low, 131 months from 1921 low, 105 and 96 months from 1923 and 1924 lows, 27 months from April, 1930 top, and 34 months from

1929 top. August and September—A sharp, fast advance in stocks. This was 35 and 36 months from 1929 top, 28 and 29 months from April, 1930 top, 72 and 73 months in the new cycle from 1896 low, and 132 to 133 months from 1921 low.

1933 - April to July—A fast advance. This was 43 to 46 months from 1929 top. Always watch for culminations around the 45th month and multiples of 45. It was also 36 to 39 months from the 1930 top, 9 to 12 months from 1932 low, and 80 to 83 months in the new cycle from 1896, or running out a 7-year cycle in the new 30-year cycle. October, 1933—Low of reaction, 42 months from April, 1930 top, 49 months from 1929 top, and 15 months from 1932 low.

1934 - February—Top. This was 46 months from 1930 high, 53 months from 1929 high, 12 months from 1933 low, 19 months from 1932 low, and most important of all, 90 months in the new 30-year cycle from August, 1926. From this top a sharp decline followed. July—This marked the last low before a big bull campaign started. This was 58 months from 1929 top, 51 months from 1930 top, 24 months from 1932 low, and 95 months or the ending of the 8th year in the new cycle from 1896. Going into the 9th year of this cycle, the market indicated a big bull campaign to follow in 1935, as explained before.

Go over individual stocks and work out their cycles in the same way. Look up the months when extreme highs and lows have been made and note the months from each bottom and top when fast advances and fast declines have taken place. By keeping up the time periods from important tops and bottoms, you will know when important time periods are running out and when a change in trend is likely to take place. Also watch the seasonal changes in trend around March to April, September to October, and November to December.

All of this will help you to pick the stocks that are going to have the greatest advances and the ones that are going to have the greatest declines. The more you work and study, the more you will learn and the greater profits you will make.

NEW YORK STOCK EXCHANGE PERMANENT CHART

This Master Chart is a square of 20, or 20 up and 20 over, making a total of 400, which can be used to measure days, weeks, months or years, and to determine when tops and bottoms will be made against strong angles as indicated on this Permanent Chart. This chart works out the 20-year cycles remarkably well because it is the square of 20. For example:

The New York Stock Exchange was incorporated on May 17, 1792. Therefore, we begin at "0" on May 17, 1792. 1793 ends on "1", when the Stock Exchange was one year old. 1812 will come out on 20, 1832 on 40, 1852 on 60, 1872 on 80, 1892 on 100, 1912 on 120, and 1932 on 140. Note that 140, or 7 times 20, in 1932 is equal to 90° angle and is at the top of the 7th zone or the 7th space over, which indicated that 1932 was the ending of a bear campaign and great cycle and the starting of a bull market. We would watch for a culmination around May to July, 1932, as the cycle ended May 17, 1792.

You will notice that the numbers which divide the square into equal parts, run across 10, 30, 50, 70, 90, 110, etc., and that the year 1802 comes out on 10 the year 1822 on 30, the year 1842 on 50, the year 1862 on 70. Note that the year 1861, when the Civil War broke out, was on the number 69, which is on a 45° angle. Then note that 1882 ended in May on the 90° angle and at the 1/2-point, 180° angle, running horizontally across.

Again in 1902 it was at 110, the 1/2-point, and in 1903 and 1904 hit the 45° angle. Note that the years 1920 and 1921 hit the 45° angle on No. 129, and 1922—the first year of the bull market—was at 130 at the 1/2-point.

Note that 1929 was on the 137th number, or 137 month, and hit an angle of 45°, and that the year 1930 was at the 1/2-point on the 4th square, a strong Resistance Point, which indicated a sharp, severe decline.

1933 was on 141 or the beginning of the 8th Zone and at the center or half-way point of the 2nd quarter of the Square of 20, indicating activity and fast advances and fast declines.

The years 1934 and 1935, ending in May, were on 142 and 143, and 1935 comes out on the 45° angle at the grand-center in the 8th Zone and at the half-way point of the 2nd square, going to 1/2 of the total square, which indicated great activity.

You can also use this chart from October 12, 1492, when Columbus discovered America. 1892 was end of 400 years or Square of 20. 1932 was 40 years in the n Square of 20.

You can use this Square of 20 for time periods on individual stocks and for price resistance levels.

If you will study the weeks, months, as well as the years, and apply them t these important points and angles, you will see how they have determined the important tops and bottoms in the past campaigns.

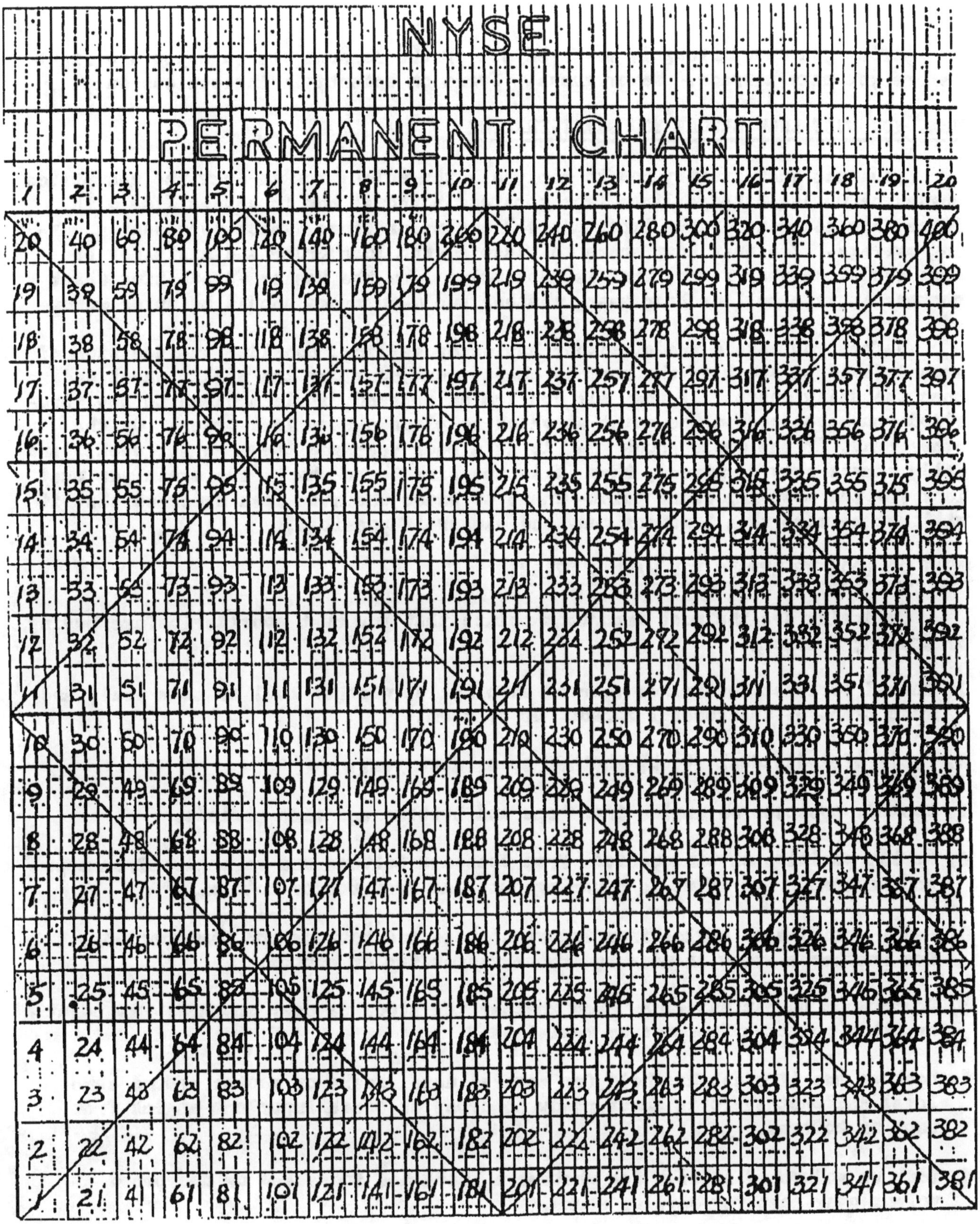
NYSE
PERMANENT CHART

HOW TO TRADE

::: :: :::::

After you have thoroughly mastered all of the lessons, be sure you are right before you make a trade. Never guess. Trade on scientific indications only.

WHAT YOU MUST KNOW BEFORE YOU START TRADING:

You must know exactly how to apply all the rules; how to draw the geometrical angles or moving-average lines from tops and bottoms; how to square Time with Price; how to bring in the important 45° angles or lines, which represent a moving average. You must know where to place a stop loss order and must look up what cycle the year is in, that is, determine from the Master Forecasting Chart whether it is a bull or bear year, whether the main trend should be up or down.

Before you make a trade, either buying or selling, consider the position of each individual stock on the monthly chart; next consider the weekly chart and then the daily chart. If they all confirm an uptrend, it is a cinch to buy, provided you have located the point at which to place a stop loss order. On the other hand, if the cycle shows that it is a bear year and the monthly, weekly and daily charts show downtrend, then it is the time to go short, but again you must look for the most important point--where to place the stop loss order so that it will not be more than 3 points away and closer if possible.

WHAT TO LOOK UP BEFORE YOU MAKE A TRADE:

Following are the most important points that you must consider before buying or selling a stock:

1. Annual Forecast determines year of Time Cycle, whether bull or bear year, and main trend of the general market, up or down.

2. Cycle of individual stock, whether up or down year.

3. Monthly position on angles from tops and bottoms and time periods.

4. Weekly position on time periods from tops and bottoms and on angles from tops and bottoms. See if it is squaring out Time from top or bottom.

5. Daily position on angles from important tops and bottoms and time periods. See whether a stock is near square of recent top or bottom.

6. Resistance Levels on price. See whether the stock is near any half-way point or other points of support or resistance.

7. Look to see if stock has held for several days, weeks or months around same level and whether it is about ready to cross or break important angles from tops or bottoms.

8. Look up volume of sales. See whether a stock has increased or decreased volume over past few days or weeks.

9. Look up space or price movement, up or down, for past movements. Find out what was the greatest advance or decline for past few weeks or months. For example: If a stock has reacted 5 points several times and at the time you

look it up, you find it is 3 points down from the last top and the trend is up on monthly, weekly and daily with the price near a support angle, you could buy with a stop loss order 2 to 3 points away; then if the stock broke back over 5 points, the previous reaction limit, it would show a change in trend and you should be out of it.

10. Remember, the most important factor to depend on to determine the position of a stock is Geometrical Angles. Be sure to bring up the angles from "O" from recent tops and bottoms.

11. Never overlook the fact that you must have a definite indication before making a trade.

12. Most important of all—Always locate the point at which to place a stop loss order to limit risk.

PRACTICE TRADING ON PAPER:

After you feel sure that you have mastered all the rules and know exactly how to determine the trend of a stock and the place to begin trading, then to make yourself doubly sure and establish confidence, practice trading on paper until you thoroughly understand how to use the rules and when to use them. If you make mistakes trading on paper, then you would make mistakes at that time in actual trading and you are not ready to begin trading. When you feel that you are competent to start trading, apply all of the rules and trade only on definite indications. If you are not sure of the trend or the buying and selling price and not sure where to place a stop loss order, then wait until you get a definite indication. You can always make money by waiting for opportunities. There is no use getting in partly on guesswork and losing.

WHEN TO CLOSE A TRADE:

After you start actual trading, when you make a trade, don't close it or take profits until you have a definite indication according to the rules that it is time to sell out or buy in or to move up the stop loss order and wait until it is caught. The way to make a success is to follow the trend always and not get out or close a trade until the trend changes.

WHEN TO WAIT AND NOT TRADE:

It is just as important to know when not to enter the market as it is to know when to enter it. The time not to make a trade is when you find a stock has been holding in a narrow trading range for some time, say, a 5-point or a 3-point range, but has not broken under bottoms previously made or crossed tops previously made. A stock may stay for weeks or months or even years in a trading range and will not indicate any big move or change in trend until it crosses a previous top or breaks a previous bottom. If a stock is inactive in this positie it is no time to start trading in it.

Another time not to make a trade is when a stock has narrowed down between two important angles—has not broken under one or crossed the other. Wait until it gets out in the clear and gives a definite indication before you trade.

After a prolonged decline stocks nearly always narrow down and hold in a trading range for some time. Then you should wait until the angles from the bottom are broken or the angles from the top are crossed and the stock breaks ov-

or an old top before you make a trade. In other words, at all times trade when you have a definite, well-defined trend.

CAPITAL REQUIRED FOR TRADING

Before you do any trading, you must know the amount of capital required to make a success trading and the exact amount that you must risk on any one trade in order to always have capital left to trade with.

You can begin trading in 10 shares, 100 shares, 1000 shares or any other amount, but the main point is to divide your capital properly and to distribute the risks equally to protect your capital.

Whatever amount of capital you use to trade with, follow this rule: Divide your capital into 10 equal parts and never risk more than 10% of your capital on any one trade. Should you lose three consecutive times, then reduce your trading unit and only risk 10% of your remaining capital. If you follow this rule, your success is sure.

As a general rule, I have always considered it advisable to use at least $3,000 capital for every 100 shares of stock traded in and to limit risks to 3 points or less on every trade. In this way you will be able to make 10 trades on your capital and the market would have to beat you 10 consecutive times to wipe out your capital, which it will not do. You should try to make trades at a price where it will only be necessary to use one to two-point stop loss orders, which will cut down the risk.

If you want to start trading in small units of stock, use a capital of $300 for each 10 shares and never risk more than 3 points on the initial trade. Try to make the first trade, if possible, where your stop loss order will not be more than one or two points.

ALWAYS FOLLOW RULES: Decide this important point before you start trading. If you do not intend to follow the rules strictly, do not begin trading. Never allow guesswork or the human element to enter into your trading. Stick to the "Capital" rule and under no condition risk more than one-tenth of your capital on any one trade. Follow the mathemtical rules and you will make a success.

PYRAMIDING

You should only pyramid or increase your trading in active markets where volume is above normal. The position on angles and volume of activity will show you when to pyramid. You should never begin pyramiding until a stock has gotten into a strong position on angles or into a weak position on angles, or until it has broken out of a trading range by crossing old tops or breaking old bottoms.

HOW TO PYRAMID:

If you are trading in 100 shares, after you have made your first trade with a risk limited to 3 points or 10% of your capital, then do not pyramid, or buy or sell a second lot, until the market has moved at least 5 points in your favor; then when you buy or sell a second lot, use a stop loss order not more than 3 points away on both trades.

Example: We will assume that after buying the second lot, the trend reverses and the stop loss orders on both trades are caught 3 points away from where you bought the last lot. This will give you a loss of 3 points on the last trade and a profit of 2 points on the first trade, or a net loss of only one point. On the other hand, if the market continues to move in your favor, your profits will be twice as much after buying the second lot.

Whe the market has moved 5 points more in your favor, you buy a third lot, moving up the stop loss orders on the first and second lots and placing a stop on the entire lot of three trades not more than 3 points away and closer, if possible.

Continue to pyramid as long as the market moves 5 points in your favor, always following up with stop loss orders. When a stock selling between 5 and 75 a share has moved 15 to 25 points in your favor, you should begin to watch for a change in trend and be careful about buying or selling another lot on which you may have to take a loss.

THE RUN OR PYRAMIDING MOVE:

The big money in pyramiding is made in the run between accumulation and distribution, that is, after a stock passes out of the zone of accumulation. Pyramids should be started after double or triple tops are crossed and the stock clears the zone of accumulation. Then, when you get into this run, buy every 5 points up, protecting with a stop loss order not more than 3 points away from the last trade.

Reverse this rule in a declining market: After double or triple bottoms are broken and the stock clears the zone of distribution, sell every 5 points down, protecting with stop loss orders not more than 3 points above the last trade.

FAST MARKETS AND WIDE FLUCTUATIONS:

When stocks are very active and moving very fast, selling above $100, then you will find it best to make trades 7 to 10 points apart. The angles and price Resistance Points as well as old tops and bottoms will determine points to place stop loss orders with safety.

In fast-moving markets, like the panic of October and November, 1929, when you pyramid on active stocks and have very large profits, you should follow down, with a stop loss order about 10 points away from the market. Then, after a severe decline reduce stop loss orders, placing them about 5 points above the low level. When a market is moving as fast as this, you should not wait for the stock to get into a strong position on angles. Reverse this rule in an advancing market.

SAFEST PYRAMIDING RULE:

One of the safest rules to use for pyramiding when stocks are selling at extremely high levels or extremely low levels is to start with 100 shares and when the market moves 5 points in your favor, buy another 50 shares; then when it move 5 points more, buy or sell 30 shares; then on the next 5-point move in your favor buy or sell 20 shares, and continue to follow the market up or down with this amount until there is a change in the main trend.

WHEN NOT TO PYRAMID:

Safety is the first consideration in starting or continuing a pyramiding campaign in a stock. Mistakes are made by buying or selling a second lot too near the accumulation or the distribution point. After a big move up or down, you must always wait for a definite change in trend before starting a pyramid.

Never buy a second lot for a pyramid when a stock is near a double top or sell a second lot when a stock is near a double bottom.

A stock often holds several days or weeks in a range of 10 to 12 points, moving up and down, not crossing the highest top or breaking the last bottom made. As long as it remains in this range, you should not pyramid. When it gets out of this range, crossing the highest top or breaking the lowest bottom, then it will indicate a bigger move and you should start to pyramid.

Always check and double check, follow all the rules, study the major and minor time cycles for forecasting, the angles from tops and bottoms, the Resistance Points of Price between tops and bottoms. If you ignore one important point, it may get you wrong. Remember, the whole can never exceed all of its parts, and all of the parts make up the whole. If you leave out one of the parts or one of the rules, you do not have a complete trend indicator.

W. D. Gann

November, 1935

Chapter 6

Enhanced Master Charts

W. D. GANN
78 WALL STREET
NEW YORK

SCIENTIFIC ADVICE
AND ANALYTICAL REPORTS
ON STOCKS AND COMMODITIES
AUTHOR "TRUTH OF THE STOCK TAPE"
"THE TUNNEL THRU THE AIR"

MEMBER
AMERICAN ECONOMIC ASSN
ROYAL ECONOMIC SOCIETY
CABLE ADDRESS
"GANWADE NEW YORK"

MASTER CHARTS

The Master Charts are permanent and represent natural angles and permanent resistance points for either price, time or volume. These points do not change and you should study them carefully on each different Master Chart and learn how to apply them.

MASTER "12" CHART

The MASTER CHART is the Square of "12" or 12 x 12, making the first square end at 144. The Second Square of "12" ends at 288, the Third Square of "12" at 432, and the Fourth Square at 576, which will cover most anything that you want, but you can make up as many more squares as you need.

This chart may be used and applied to anything-- TIME, SPACE, PRICE OR VOLUME, the number of points up or down; days, weeks, months and years.

On Square No. 1, which runs from 1 to 144, I have drawn the finer angles to show the grand-center or strongest resistance point in each minor square. The minor centers, which are the strongest for minor tops and bottoms are 14, 17, 20, 23, 50, 53, 56, 59, 86, 89, 92, 95, 122, 125, 128, 131.

The major center is where the strongest resistance is met. These numbers are 66, 67, 78 and 79. Stocks going up or coming down to these prices will meet with stubborn resistance. The next strong angle is the 45°, and the numbers of greatest resistance on it are 14, 27, 40, 53, 66, 79, 92, 105, 118, 131 and 144. The other diagonal 45° angle from 12 is equally strong. The numbers are 12, 23, 34, 45, 56, 67, 78, 89, 100, 111, 122 and 133.

The numbers which are cut by the 45° angles thru the center of each of the 1/4 squares are next in strength. These numbers are 7, 20, 33, 46, 59, 72, 61, 50, 39, 28, 17 and 6, and on the other side of the square, after you pass the half-way point, these numbers are 73, 86, 99, 112, 125, 138, 139, 128, 117, 106, 95 and 84.

The numbers at the tops and bottoms of the squares are important prices for important tops and bottoms to be made because they are opposition numbers and are equal to the half-way point. These numbers for Square No. 1 are 1, 13, 25, 37, 49, 61, 73, 85, 97, 109, 121, 133. The top numbers are 12, 24, 36, 48, 60, 72, 84, 96, 108, 120, 132, and 144. These are very important to measure time in days, weeks, months and years.

The opposition angle, which runs thru the center of the Square, from east to west, equally dividing it, is one of the very strong angles because it equals one-half. Any stock moving up or down and reaching these prices will meet with any resistance and make tops or bottoms. These numbers are 6, 7, 18, 19, 30, 31, 42, 43, 54, 55, 66, 67, 78, 79, 90, 91, 102, 103, 114, 115, 126, 127, 138, 139.

Remember, when anything has moved three sections over from the beginning, it reaches the square of its own place, which is the first strong resistance. When it has moved six sections over, it reaches the opposition, or what equals the half-way point of its own place and meets still stronger resistance. Moving over nine places or sections from its own place, it reaches the 3/4 point, another square. The 8th and 9th sections are the strongest and hardest points to pass because this is the "death" zone. The next and still stronger is the 12th section or column which ends at 144. Anything getting into this section meets the strongest resistance but once it moves out of this square and gets as much as 3 points into Square #2, that is, making 147, will indicate much higher. But after reaching this, it should not drop back to 141 or 3 points into Square #1.

When a stock gets into the Second Square of "12", it has faster moves, and when the time or number of months from any bottom or top moves into the Second Square, it is an indication of faster moves, both up and down.

Apply the same rule to the 3rd, 4th, 5th and 6th Squares. In the 3rd and 4th squares of the Master "12", you will find that most of the big bull and bear campaigns culminate, when measured by months, which determines the division, according to time. All of the other rules given you to apply to Space movements, angles and time, can be used with the Master "12" tables.

SQUARE OF NINE

You have already had the MASTER SQUARE OF TWELVE explained, which represents days, weeks, months and years, and the measurements of TIME in the Square of Twelve or the square of the Circle; also used to measure price movements and resistance levels.

The SQUARE OF NINE is very important because nine digits are used in measuring everything. We cannot go beyond 9 without starting to repeat and using the 0. If we divide 360° by 9, we get 40, which measures 40°, 40 months, 40 days, 40 weeks or 40 months, and shows why bottoms and tops often come out on these angles measured by one-ninth of the circle. This is why the children of Israel were 40 years in the wilderness.

If we divide our 20-year period, or 240 months, by 9, we get 26-2/3 months, making an important angle of 26-2/3°, months, days or weeks. Nine times 9 equals 81, which completes the First Square of Nine. Note the angles and how they run from the main center. The Second Square of Nine is completed at 162. Note how this is in opposition to the main center. The Third square of Nine is completed at 243, which would equal 243 months or 3 months over our 20-year period and accounts for the time which often elapses before the change in the Cycle, sometimes running over 3 months or more. The Fourth Square of Nine ends at 324. Note the angles of 45° cross at 325, indicating a change in cycles here. To complete the 360° requires Four Squares of Nine and 36 over. Note that 361 equals a Square of 19 times 19, thus proving the great value of the Square of Nine in working out the important angles and proving up discrepancies.

Beginning with "1" at the center, note how 7, 21, 43, 73, 111, 157, 211, 273 and 343 all fall on a 45° angle. Going the other way, note that 3, 13, 31, 57, 91, 133, 183, 241, and 307 fall on an angle of 45°. Remember there are always four ways you can travel from a center following an angle of 45°, or an angle of 180° or an angle of 90°, which all equal about the same when measured on a flat surface. Note that 8, 23, 46, 77, 116, 163, 218, 281 and 352 are all on an angle from the main center; also note that 4, 15, 34, 61, 96, 139, 190, 249, and 316 are on an angle from the main center, all of these being great resistance points and measuring out important time factors and angles.

Study the SQUARE OF NINE very carefully in connection with the MASTER TWELVE and 360° CIRCLE CHART.

SIX SQUARES OF NINE

You will receive six Permanent Charts, each containing 81 numbers. The First Square of Nine runs from 1 to 81. Everything must have a bottom, top, and four sides to be a square or cube. The first Square running up to 81 is the bottom, base, floor or beginning point. Squares #2, 3, 4, and 5 are the four sides, which are equal and contain 81 numbers. The Sixth Square of Nine is the top and means that it is times times as referred to in the Bible, or a thing reproducting itself by being multipled by itself. Nine times nine equals 81 and six times 81 equals 486. We can also use 9 times 81, which would equal 729.

The number 5 is the most important number of the digits because it is the balance or main center. There are four numbers on each side of it. Note how it is shown as the balancing or center number in the Square of Nine.

We square the Circle by beginning at 1 in the center and going around until we reach 360. Note that the Square of Nine comes out at 361. The reason for this is: It is 19 times 19, and the 1 to begin with and 1 over 360 represent the beginning and ending points. 361 is a transition point and begins the next circle. Should we leave the first space blank or make it "0", then we would come out at 360. Everything in mathematics must prove. You can begin at the center and work out, or begin at the outer rim and work in to the center. Begin at the left and work right to the center or to the outer rim or square.

Note the Square of Nine or the Square of the Circle, where we begin with 1 and run up the side of the column to 19, then continue to go across until we have made 19 columns, again the square of 19 by 19. Note how this proves up the circle. One-half of the circle is 180°. Note that in the grand-center, where all angles from the four corners and from the East, West, North and South reach gravity center, number 181 appears, showing that at this point we are crossing the Equater or Gravity center and are starting on the other half of the circle.

We have astronimical and mathematical proof of the whys and wherefores and the cause of the workings of geometrical angles. When you have made progress, proved yourself worthy, I will give you the Master Number and also the Master Word.

THE HEXAGON CHART

Since everything moves in a circle and nothing moves in straight lines, this chart is to show you how the angles influence stocks at very low levels and very high levels and why stocks move faster the higher they get, because they have moved out to where the distance between the angles of 45° are so far apart that there is nothing to stop them and their moves are naturally rapid up and down.

We begin with a circle of "1" in the center and while this only contains 1, yet the circle is 360° just the same. We then place a circle of circles around this circle and six circles complete the second circle, making a gain of 6 over the first one, ending the second circle at 7, making 7 on this angle a very important month, year, and week as well as day, the seventh day being sacred and a day of rest. The third circle is completed at 19. The fourth circle around is completed at 37, a gain of 18 over the previous circle. The fifth circle is completed at 61, a gain of 24 over the previous circle. The sixth circle is completed at 91, a gain of 30 over the previous circle, and the seventh circle at 127, a gain of 36 over the last circle. Note that from the first the gain is 6 each time we go around. In other words, when we have traveled six times around we have gained 36. Note that this completes the first Hexagon and as this equals 127 months, shows why some campaigns will run 10 years and seven months, or until they reach a square of the Hexagon, or the important last angle of 45°.

The eighth circle around is completed at 169, a gain of 42 over the first. This is a very important angle and an important time factor for more reasons than one. It is 14 years and one month, or double our Cycle of 7 years. Important tops and bottoms culminate at this angle as you will see by going over your charts.

The ninth circle is completed at 217, a gain of 48 over the previous circle. The tenth circle is completed at 271, a gain of 54. Note that 271 is the 9th circle from the first, or is the third 90° angle or 270°, three-fourths of a circle, a very strong point. All this is confirmed by the Master Twelve Chart, by the four seasons and by the Square of Nine Chart, and also confirmed by the Hexagon Chart, showing that mathematical proof is always exact no matter how many ways or from what directions you figure it.

The eleventh circle is completed at 331, a gain of 60 over the last circle. The twelfth circle is completed at 397, which completes the Hexagon, making a gain in 11 circles of 66 from the beginning. 66 months, or 5 years and six months, marks the culmination of major campaigns in stocks. Note how often they culminate on the 60th month, then have a reaction, and make a second top or bottom in the 66th month. Note the number 66 on the Master Twelve Chart. Note it on the Square of Nine and see that 66 occurs on an angle of 180° on the Hexagon Chart, all of which confirms the strong angle at this point.

We have an angle of 66°, one of 67½, and one of 68, confirming this point to be doubly strong for tops and bottoms or space movements up or down.

Note the number 360 on the Hexagon Chart. It completes a circle of 360°. From our beginning point this occurs at an angle of 150° on the Hexagon Chart going around, but measuring from the center, it would equal an angle of 90° or 180°, making this a strong point, hard and difficult to pass, and the ending of one campaign and the beginning of another.

Again with the center of the Hexagon Chart at "1" notice that 7, 9, 37, 61, 91, 127, 169, 217, 271, 331, and 397 are all on this direct angle and are important points in time measurement. Beginning with "1" and following the other angle, note that 2, 9, 22, 41, 66, 97, 134, 177, 226, 281, and 342 are all on the same angle of 90°, or an angle of 60° and 240° as measured by the Hexagon Chart.

Go over this Chart and the important angles each way and you will see why resistance is met either on days, weeks, months, or years, and why stocks stop and make tops and bottoms at these strong important points according to time and price.

When any stock has passed out above 120° or especially above 127° or 127 points and gone out of the square of the first Hexagon, its fluctuations will be more rapid and it will move faster up and down. Notice near the center that in traveling from 6 to 7 it strikes the angle of 180° or 90°, but when the stock gets out to 162, it can travel up to 169 before striking another strong angle. That is why fast moves occur up and down as stocks get higher and as they move from a center in time.

Remember that everything seeks the center of gravity and important tops and bottoms are formed according to centers and measurements of time from a center, base or beginning point, either top or bottom. The angles formed going straight up and across, may form just the same going across as the stock travels over for days, weeks, months or years. Thus, a stock going up to 22½ would strike an angle of 22½°. If it moves over 22½ days, 22½ weeks, or 22½ months, it would also strike an angle of 22½°, and the higher it is when these angles are struck and the angle it hits going up, the greater the resistance to be met. Reverse the rule going down.

Market movements are made just the same as any other thing which is constructed. It is just the same as constructing a building. First the foundation has to be laid and then the four sides have to be completed and last, but not least of all, the top has to be put on. The cube or hexagon proves exactly the law which works because of time and space in the market. When a building is put up it is built according to a square or hexagon. It has four walls or four sides, a bottom and a top; therefore, it is a cube.

In working out the 20-year Cycle in the stock market, the first 60°, or 5 years, from the beginning forms the bottom of the cube. The second 60°, running to 120, completes the first angle or the first side and runs out the 10-year Cycle. The third 60°, or the second side, ends 15 years or 180°. It is very important because we have the building half completed and must meet the strongest resistance at this point. The fourth 60°, or the end of 20 years or 240 months, completes the third side. We are now two-thirds around the building, a very strong point which culminates and completes our 20-year Cycle. The fifth 60°, or 300° point, days, weeks, or months, completes 25 years, a repetition of the first 5 years, but it completes the fourth side of our building and is a very important angle. The 6th 60° or 360°, completing the circle and ending 30 years as measured by our Time Factor, which runs 1° per month on an angle of 45°, completes the top. This is a complete cube and we begin over again.

Study this in connection with the Hexagon Chart. It will help you.

W. D. Gann

W. D. GANN
91 WALL STREET
NEW YORK

Scientific Advice and Analytical Reports [S]tocks and Commodities
[Aut]hor of "Truth of the Stock Tape" [an]d "The Tunnel Thru the Air"

Member American Economic Ass'n Royal Economic Society
Cable Address "Ganwade New York"

MASTER CHARTS (continued)

THE MASTER CHART OF 360°.

This chart begins at "0" and runs around the circle to "360". We first divide by two and get 180°; then divide 180 by 2 and we get 90°; then divide 90 by 2 and we get 45°; then divide 45 by 2 and we get 22½°; then 22½ by 2 and we get 11¼°; then divide 11¼ by 2 and we get 5-5/8°, - all of which form the important angles around the circle.

I have only shown all the important angles from 3-3/4 to 360°. All the angles drawn in red because they are the important square angles.

After dividing the circle by 2, the next important number to divide by is 3. Dividing by 3, we get 120°, 240° and 360°, making the important triangle points. We then divide 120 by 2 and get the angles of 60°, 150°, 210°, 300° and 330°. We divide 60 by 2 and get the angles of 30° and their proportionate parts around. Then divide 30 by 2 and get the angles of 15° and their proportionate angles around the circle. Then divide 15 by 2 and we get the angles at 7½° around the circle.

24 hours in a day divided into the circle equals 15° for each hour. There are 48 divisions of the circle of 7½°, which are important in measuring day, weekly and monthly time periods.

Study the Major Chart of 360° carefully and you will see why cycles repeat. When anything has traveled up 180°, it starts to go down to the opposite point and each angle up to 180° is the opposite on the other side of the circle. That is why tops and bottoms come out at each one of these degrees. For instance, top coming out at 90° or 90 months at one time will occur 90° or 90 months apart and there will be similar tops causing rapid fluctuations and fast moves up and down because this angle is so acute that stocks can not remain long before starting in the opposite direction.

Note the culminations that occur every 14 and 15 years, 180 months, or when an 180° angle or an angle straight up and down is reached. How rapid the moves are when they near this angle and how fast they move up and down and how quickly reverse. It is the same with the 45°, the 135°, the 225° and the 315° angle. Note how this proves the important campaigns when tops and bottoms work out in regularity an equal number of months apart. Note the 22½° and then follow the next important angle, the 30° angle, then the 45°, then note the 60 and 67½° are close together but both very strong angles. Note also 112½° and 120°, both strong angles and close together, indicating important tops and bottoms. Also note 150° and 157½°, strong angles close together, indicating important tops and bottoms, and so on all the way around.

When the circle is divided by 2 and 3 and redivided, we get the following important angles and measurements of time, space and volume around the circle of 360°:-

5-5/8, 7-1/2, 11-1/4, 15, 16-7/8, 22-1/2, 27-7/8, 30, 33-3/4, 37-1/2, 39-3/8, 45, 50-5/8, 56-1/4, 60, 61-7/8, 67-1/2, 73-1/8, 75, 78-3/4, 82-1/2, 84-3/8, 90, 95-5/8, 101-1/4, 105, 106-7/8, 112-1/2, 118-1/8, 120, 123-3/4, 129-3/8, 135, 140-5/8, 146-1/4, 150, 152-7/8, 157-1/2, 163-1/8, 168-3/4, 174-3/8, 180, 185-5/8, 191-1/4, 196-7/8, 202-1/2, 208-1/8, 210, 213-3/4, 219-3/8, 225, 230-5/8, 236-1/4, 240, 241-7/8, 247-1/2, 253-1/8, 258-3/4, 264-3/8, 270, 275-5/8, 281-1/4, 286-7/8, 292-1/2, 298-1/8, 300, 303-3/4, 309-3/8, 315, 320-5/8, 326-1/4, 330, 331-7/8, 337-1/2, 343-1/8, 348-3/4, 354-3/8, 360, which completes the circle.

These points are all made by a division of angles and are measurements of one-half, one-third, one-fourth, one-eight, one-sixteenth, one-thirty-second and one-sixty-fourth.

Compare these points with your Master Twelve Chart, your Square of Nine Chart, your Hexagon Chart and your Major Chart of 360°. You will see how they all confirm the important angles and time factors.

The number "7" being so important in determining the culmination in weeks, days, months and years, we must divide the circle by 7 to get the important points, or the one-seventh points in the circle, which are vital and important angles.

The first one-seventh of 360 equals 51-3/7, the second equals 102-6/7, the third equals 154-2/7, the fourth equals 205-5/7, the fifth equals 257-1/7, the sixth equals 308-4/7 and the seventh completes the circle, equalling 360 degrees, days, weeks, months or years. If you divide each of these points by 2, you will also get other important and valuable angles which will confirm and correspond to the other angles in the other charts.

One-seventh of a year or one-seventh of a circle shows why so many fast market movements culminate in the 49th day or the 52nd day and why the 7th week is so very important in culminations and also the 7th month as well as the 7th year.

1½ times 51-3/7 equals 77-1/8 and shows why the angles are so very strong around that point and why the 77th day, 77th week and 77th month are so important for culminations.

MASTER 360° CIRCLE CHART SQUARED

The Master 360 Circle Chart when squared is 90 x 90, and contains 8,100 cells, zones or spaces. Therefore, the square of 360 will contain 32,400 spaces. This shows you why a stock fluctuates up and down so many times over the same territory, because it is working out the number of cells or vibrations of each space in a square. For example:-

1/8 of 90 equals 1,012-1/2
1/4 of 90 equals 2,025
1/2 of 90 equals 4,050
3/4 of 90 equals 6,075
1/3 of 90 equals 2,700
2/3 of 90 equals 5,400

The square of 360, or 360 times 360, equals 32,400.

1/4 of 360 equals 8,100
1/3 of 360 equals 10,860
1/2 of 360 equals 16,200
2/3 of 360 equals 21,600
3/4 of 360 equals 24,300
7/8 of 360 equals 28,350

These points are very important to use for volums of sales as well as time and price measurements.

Suppose you want to know the number of days required to fill or work out the square of 90. There are 365 days in a year. 20 years will give you 7,300 days, and in counting the leap years will run a little over this. Therefore, about 22 years, 2 months and 10 days are required to work out each vibration in the square of 90.

THE SPIRAL CHART

The Spiral Chart represents the correct position, time and space of anything that begins at zero and begins to move round and round. It shows just exactly how the numbers increase as the spiral moves round and round, and why stocks move faster as they grow older, or swing so much more rapidly as the price reaches higher levels. At center, beginning point or zero, it requires 45° to represent one point. When the stock traveled seven times around from the center, it then required seven points to strike a 45° angle. When it has traveled around the spiral twelve times, it will then require a space of ten points before striking a 45° angle. It would also mean that the stock could move in one direction ten months without striking anything to cause any very great reaction. On this chart, we have only shown the 45, 60, 90, 120, 135, 180, 225, 240, 270, 300, 315 and 360 degree angles. This shows the division of the circle by 2, 4 and 8, and also shows the one-third point and the two-thirds point; being the vital and most important angles, we place them so you can see how space or time makes rapid fluctuations.

NEW YORK STOCK EXCHANGE PERMANENT CHART.

This Chart is a square of 20, or 20 up and 20 over, making a total of 400, which can be used to measure days, weeks, months or years, and to determine when tops and bottoms will be made against strong angles, as indicated on this Permanent Chart.

For example:- The New York Stock Exchange was incorporated May 17th, 1792. Therefore, we begin at "0" on May 17, 1792. 1793 ends on 1, when the Stock Exchange was 1 year old. 1812 will come out on 20;

1832 on 40	1892 on 100
1852 on 60	1912 on 120
1872 on 80	1932 on 140

Note that 139, or 1931, strikes the 45° angle, running from 20 down, and that this is in the 7th zone, or the 7th space over, which indicates that 1931 is the ending of a bear campaign, and the starting of a bull market. But we must watch out for a break around May and June, 1931, when this angle is hit at the end of the 139th year.

You will notice that the numbers which divide the square into equal parts, run across 10, 30, 50, 70, 90, 110, etc., and that the year 1802 comes out on 10, the year 1822 on 30, the year 1842 on 50, the year 1862 on 70. Note that the year 1861, when the Civil War broke out, was on the number 69, which is a 45° angle. Then note that 1882 ended in May on the 90° angle, and at the 1/2 point, 180° angle, running horizontally across.

Again in 1902, it was at 110, the 1/2 point, and in 1903 and 1904, hit the 45° angle.

Note that the years 1920 and 1921 hit the 45° angle on No. 129 and 1922, the first year of the bull market, was at 130 at the 1/2 point.

Note that 1929 was on the 137th number, or 137th month, and hit an angle of 45°, and that the year 1930 was at the 1/2 point on the 4th square, a strong Resistance Point, which indicated a sharp, severe decline.

Again, 138 is at the 1/2 point on the Master 12 Chart.

1933 will be on 141, in the 8th Zone, and at the center or 1/2 point of the 2nd quarter of the Square of 20.

The years 1934 and 1935, ending in May, will be on 142 and 143, and 1935 will come out on the 45° angle at the grand center in the 8th Zone and at the 1/2 point of the 2nd square, going to 1/2 of the total square, which will indicate a decline and bottom for an advance to run up in 1936, with 1937 striking at 145, which is 1/4th of the column on the way up in the square.

If you will study the weeks, months, as well as the years, and apply them to these important points and angles, you will see how they have determined the important tops and bottoms in the past campaigns.

UNITED STATES STEEL NAME CHART

The name, United States Steel, contains 17 letters. Therefore, to make up a Permanent Square for United States Steel according to its name, will require 17 x 17, or a square of 289. Therefore, 17, which is really 2½ times the lowest price at which Steel ever sold is an important point.

The prices 34, 51, 68, 85, 102, 119, 136, 153, 170, 187, 204, 221, 238, 255, 272 are all important because they strike important vibrations on the name and angles of U. S. Steel.

The basic number or low point, for example 9, the lowest digit on U. S. Steel, and its vibrations according to its name, all cause slight variations at times from other stocks, because each stock works according to its own base, beginning point, numbers and name.

U. S. Steel works good to the natural angles and Master Chart, because its digit is 9 and comes out on exact 9 vibrations all the way through, finishing at 261, which was 28 nines from its beginning point, or lowest level.

A study of all these various tables will help you to understand Resistance Levels.

UNITED STATES PERMANENT MASTER CHART

We use the square of 7 for the United States because the name of America contains 7 letters, and this square is 49, a very important and fatal number.

We begin the United States Chart on October 12th, 1492. Make up these Squares of 7 and put on the years. You will note how this indicates the panic years in the United States and the years of prosperity.

You can also make up a square of 21 x 21, which is the number of letters in the name of United States of America. These angles and important points will all come out about the same as when we use America, because three times 7 is 21. However, you will get some stronger angles and more important points if you make up the square of 21 x 21, which will run out to 441, with the 1/2 point at 220-1/2.

The more you study these Permanent Charts, the more you will appreciate their great value, and will see that numbers do determine everything in the future, and that geometrical angles and mathematical points measure every Resistance Level, time, price, space or volume.

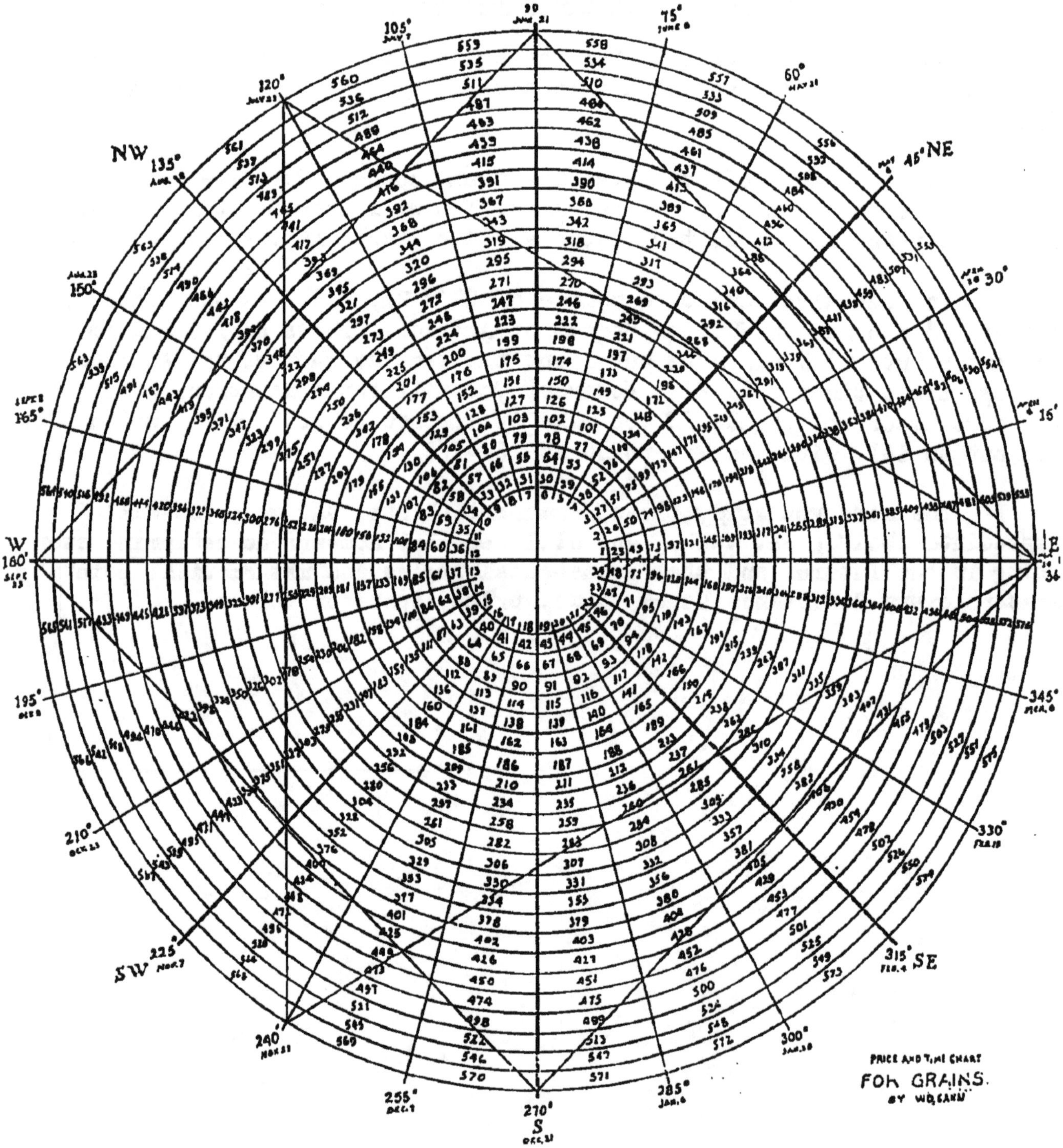

PRICE AND TIME CHART
FOR GRAINS
BY W.D. GANN

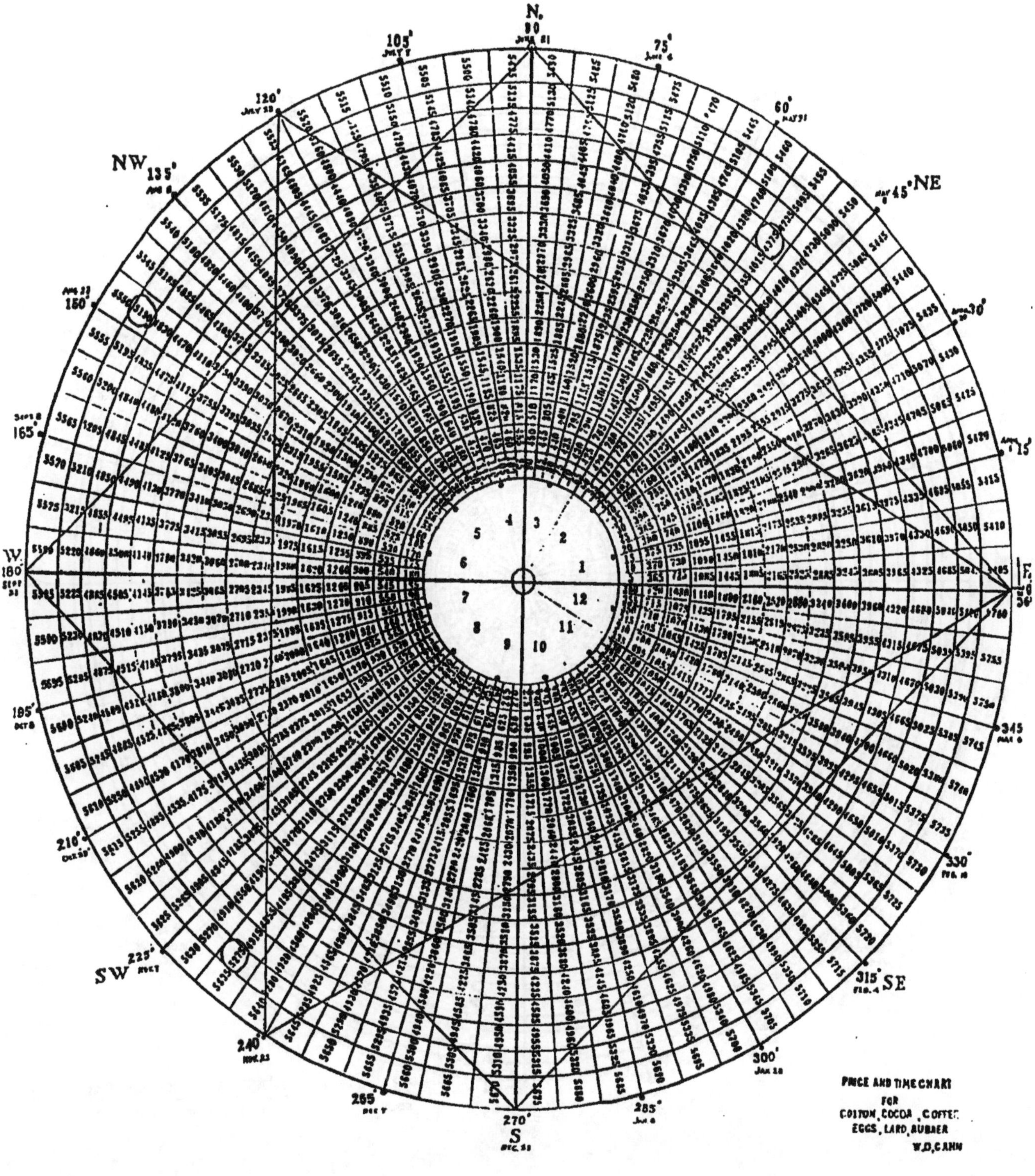

PRICE AND TIME CHART
FOR
COTTON, COCOA, COFFEE,
EGGS, LARD, RUBBER
W.D. GANN

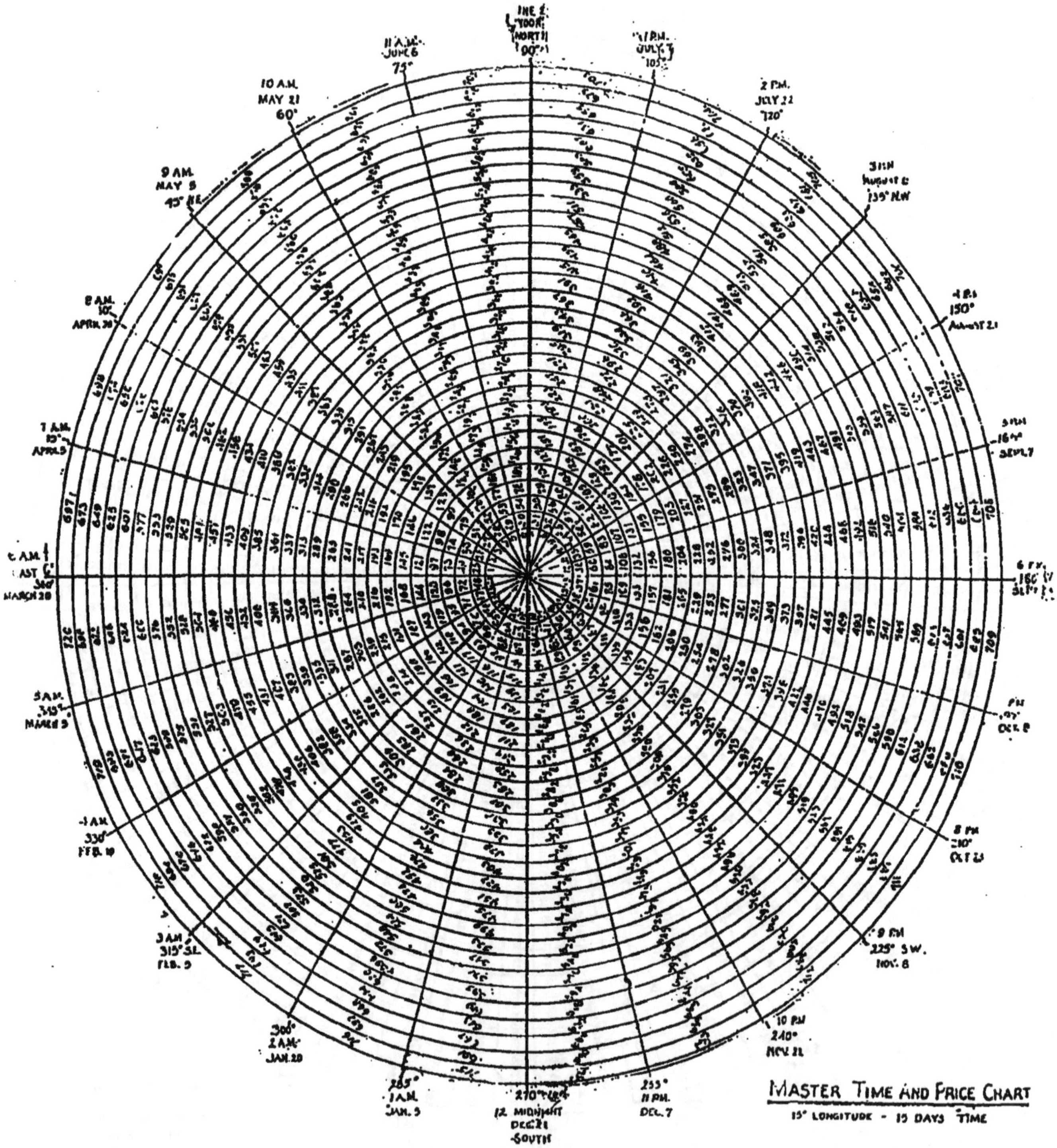

MASTER TIME AND PRICE CHART

15° LONGITUDE - 15 DAYS TIME

MASTER 360° CHART

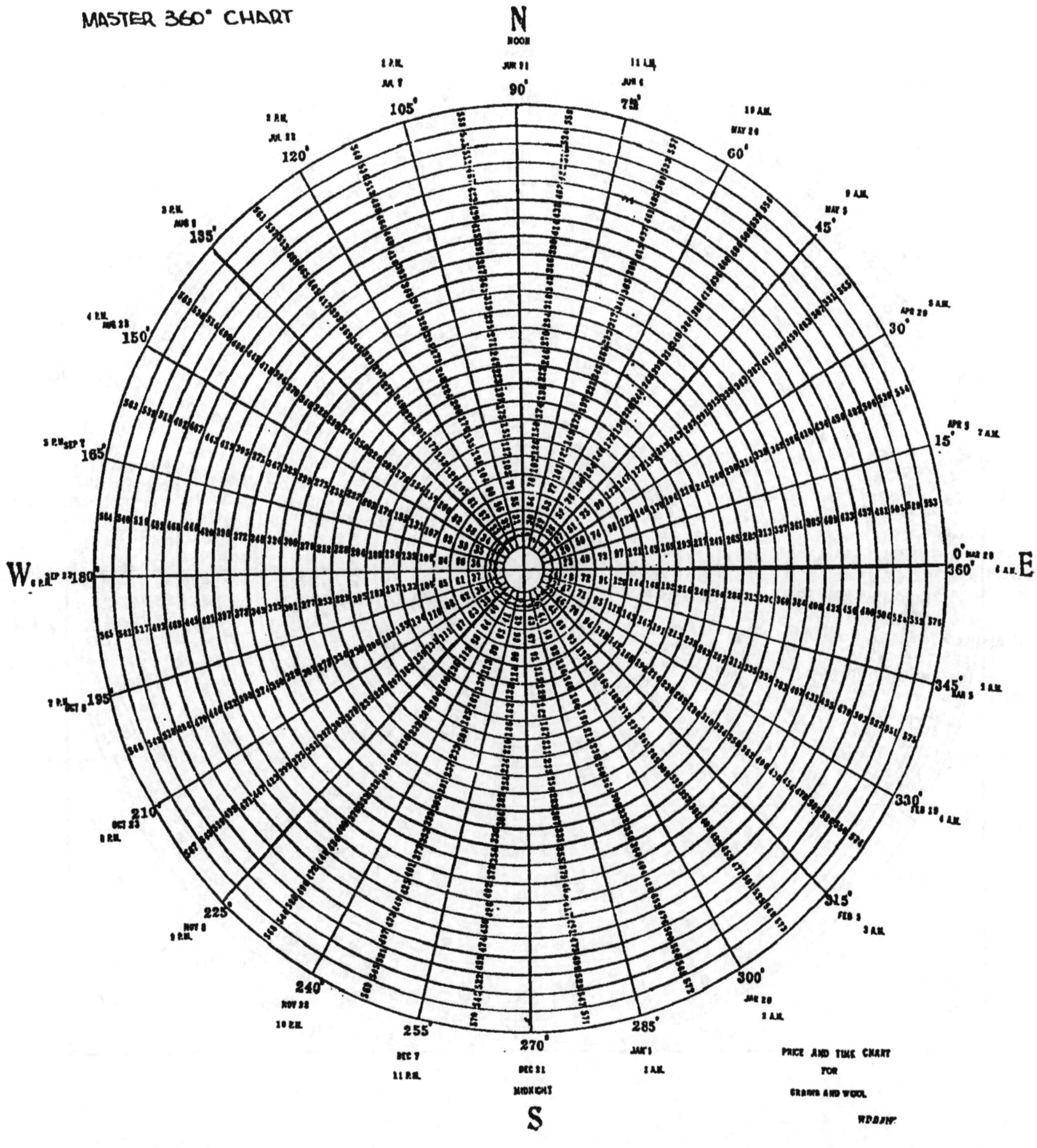

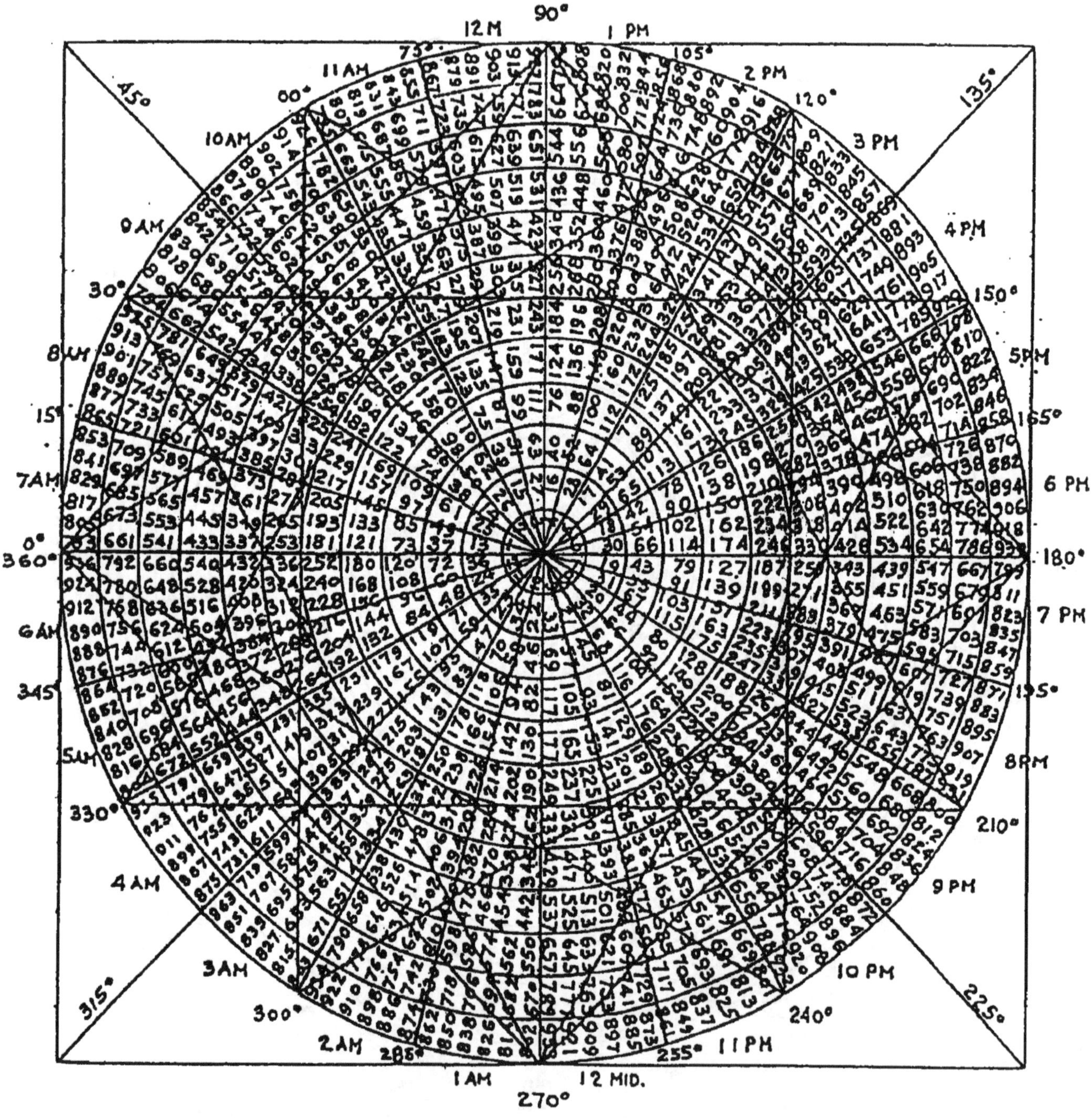

90°
12 M
1 PM
105°
11 AM
2 PM
120°
135°
45°
10 AM
3 PM
9 AM
4 PM
30°
150°
8 AM
5 PM
15°
165°
7 AM
6 PM
0°
360°
180°
6 AM
7 PM
345°
195°
5 AM
8 PM
330°
210°
4 AM
9 PM
3 AM
10 PM
315°
225°
300°
240°
2 AM
285°
255°
11 PM
1 AM
12 MID.
270°

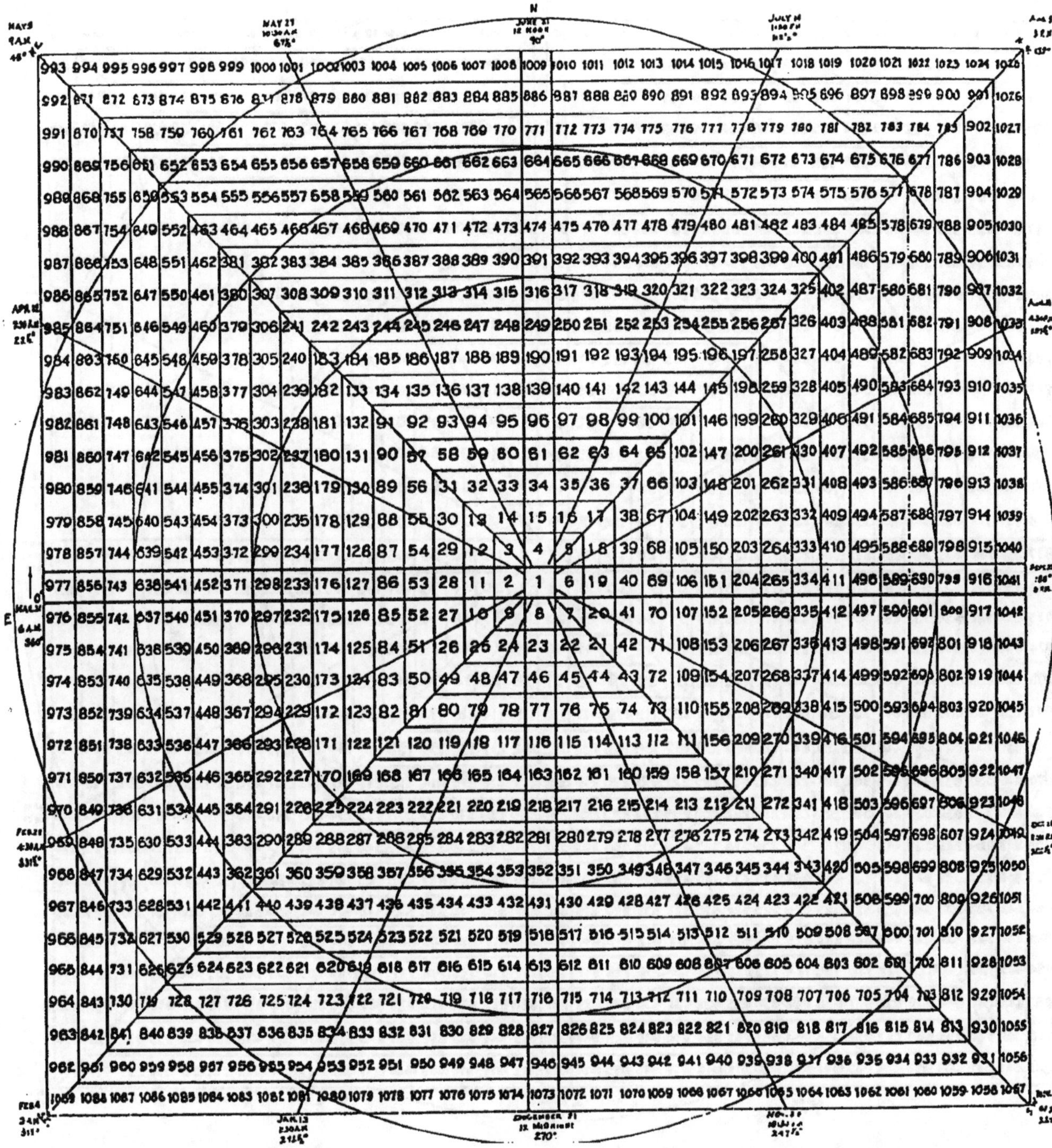
N
E
W

MASTER TIME & PRICE CHART

[illegible] OPPOSIT POINTS

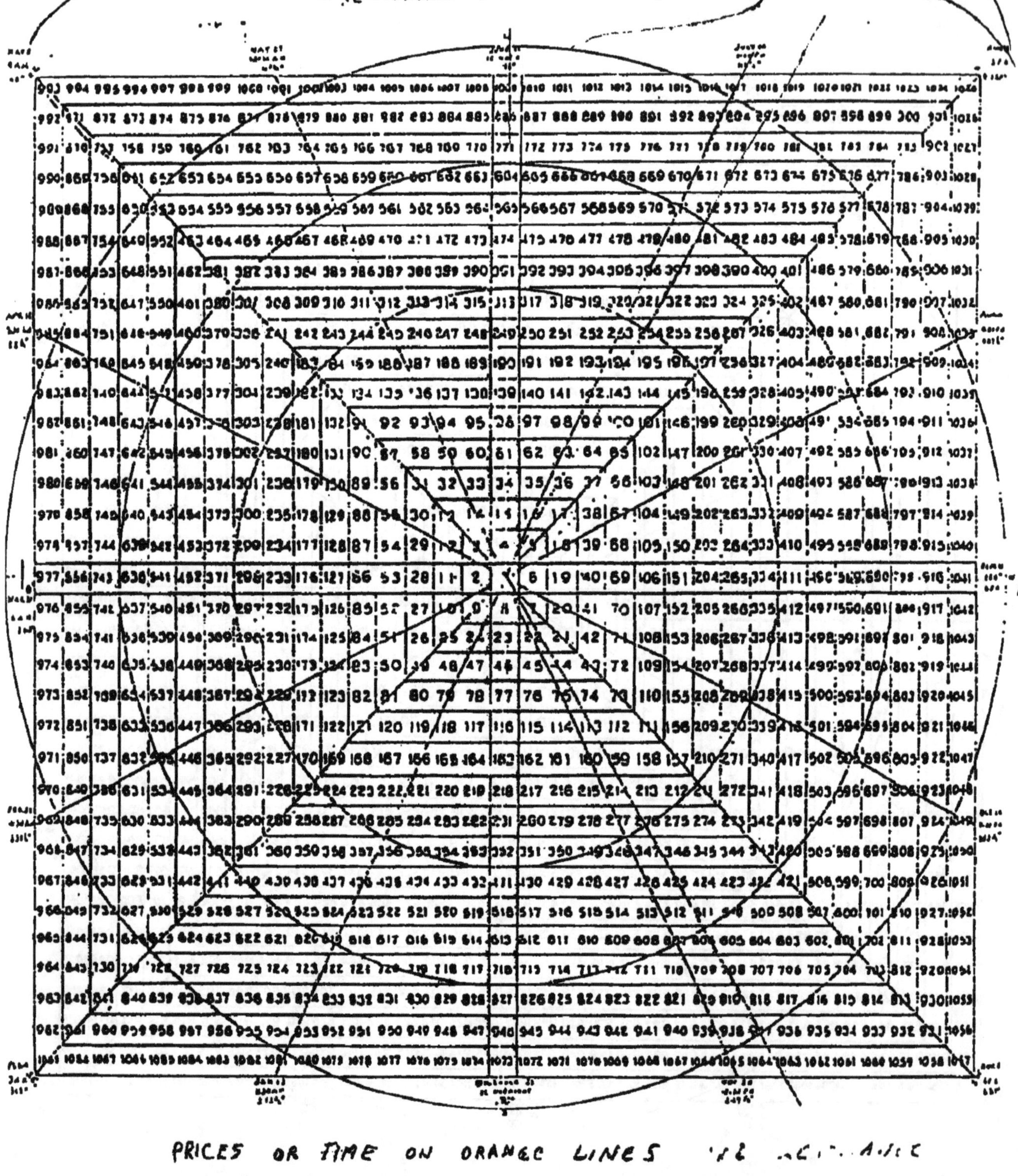

PRICES OR TIME ON ORANGE LINES [illegible]

OR [illegible] PRICES [illegible]

TIME ON [illegible] ARE TURNING POINTS-

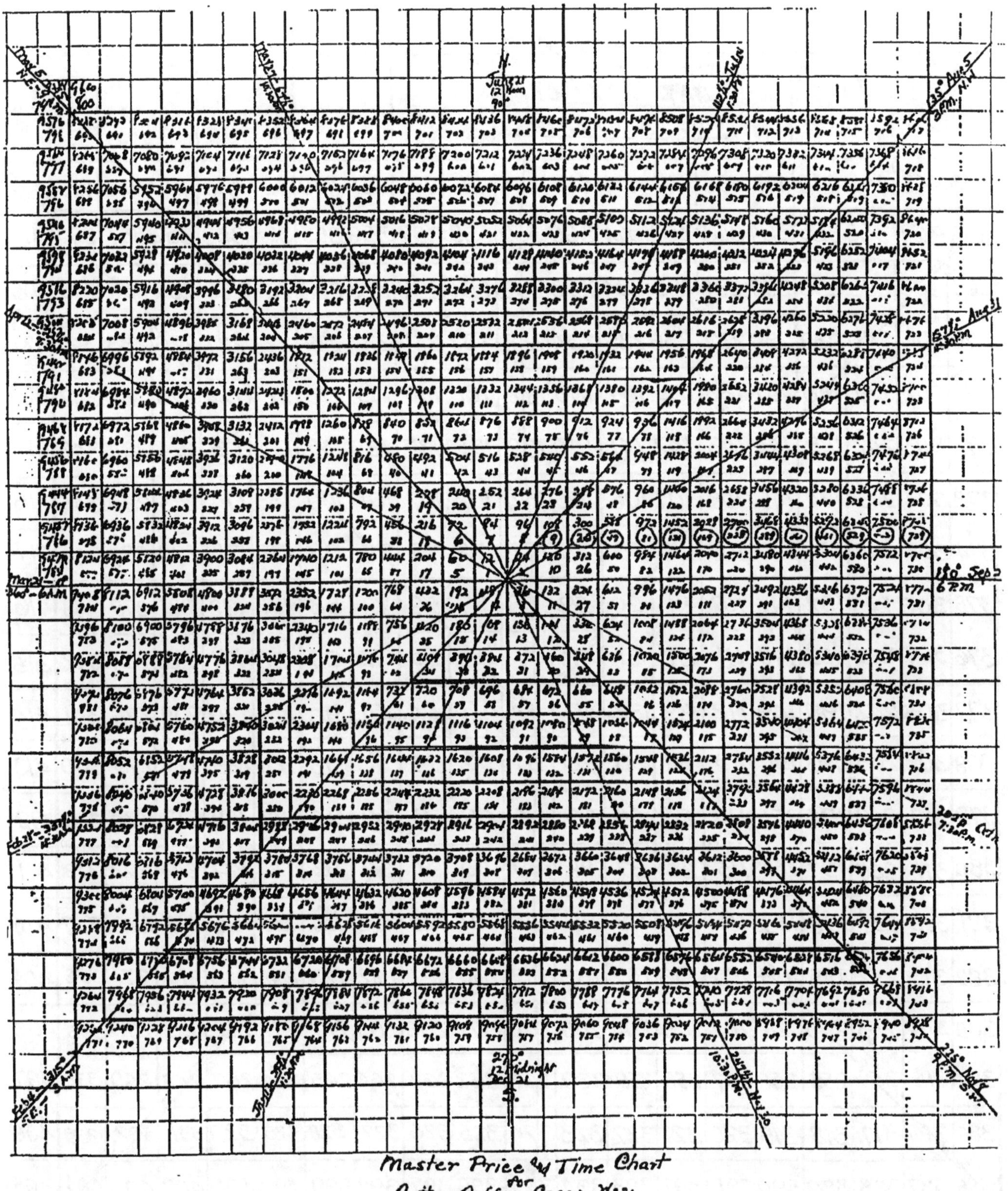

Master Price & Time Chart for Cotton, Coffee, Cocoa, Hogs, and Grains

MASTER CHART

MAY SOY BEANS
PRICE & TIME

4	443	442	441	440	439	438	437	436	435	434	433	432	431	430	429	428	427	426	425	424
	368	367	366	365	364	363	362	361	360	359	358	357	356	355	354	353	352	351	350	423
	369	300	299	298	297	296	295	294	293	292	291	290	289	288	287	286	285	284	349	422
	370	301	240	239	238	237	236	235	234	233	232	231	230	229	228	227	226	283	348	421
	371	302	241	188	187	186	185	184	183	182	181	180	179	178	177	176	225	282	347	420
	372	303	242	189	144	143	142	141	140	139	138	137	136	135	134	175	224	281	346	419
	373	304	243	190	145	108	107	106	105	104	103	102	101	100	133	174	223	280	345	418
	374	305	244	191	146	109	80	79	78	77	76	75	74	99	132	173	222	279	344	417
	375	306	245	192	147	110	81	60	59	58	57	56	73	98	131	172	221	278	343	416
	376	307	246	193	148	111	82	61	48	47	46	55	72	97	130	171	220	277	342	415
	377	308	247	194	149	112	83	62	49	44	45	54	71	96	129	170	219	276	341	414
	378	309	248	195	150	113	84	63	50	51	52	53	70	95	128	169	218	275	340	413
	379	310	249	196	151	114	85	64	65	66	67	68	69	94	127	168	217	274	339	412
	380	311	250	197	152	115	86	87	88	89	90	91	92	93	126	167	216	273	338	411
	381	310	251	198	153	116	117	118	119	120	121	122	123	124	125	166	215	272	337	410
	382	313	252	199	154	155	156	157	158	159	160	161	162	163	164	165	214	271	336	409
	383	314	253	200	201	202	203	204	205	206	207	208	209	210	211	212	213	270	335	408
	384	315	254	255	256	257	258	259	260	261	262	263	264	265	266	267	268	269	334	407
	385	316	317	318	319	320	321	322	323	324	325	326	327	328	329	330	331	332	333	406
	386	387	388	389	390	391	392	393	394	395	396	397	398	399	400	401	402	403	404	405

Coffee Rio [illegible] Oct 2 1936

9300 9330 9310 9350 9420 [illegible] 9480 9510 9540 9570 9600 9630

8410 [illegible] 8670 8700 8730 [illegible] 8770 [illegible] 8850 8880 [illegible] [illegible] 8970 9000 9030 9060 [illegible] 9120 9150 9180 9210 9240 9270

7590 7550 7550 8010 8040 8070 8100 8130 8160 8150 8190 8760 8750 8810 8840 8370 8440 [illegible] 8460 8490 8520 8550 [illegible]

7320 7360 7390 7350 7380 7410 7440 7470 7500 7550 7560 [illegible] 7620 7650 7650 7710 [illegible] 7770 7800 7830 7860 7890

6630 6660 6690 [illegible] [illegible] 6750 6810 6840 6870 6900 6930 6960 6990 7020 7050 7080 7110 7140 7170 7200 7230

6000 6030 6090 6120 6150 6180 6210 6240 6270 6300 6330 6360 6390 6420 6450 6480 6510 6540 6570 6600

5460 5490 5520 5550 5580 5610 5640 5670 5700 5730 5760 5790 5970 5850 5880 5510 5940 5970 6000

4970 4950 4990 5020 5050 5080 5140 5180 5150 5150 5220 5250 5280 5310 5340 5370 5400 5430

4410 4440 4470 4500 4500 4560 4550 4620 4650 4680 4710 4740 4770 4800 4830 4860 4890

3930 3960 3990 4020 4050 4080 4110 4140 4170 4200 4230 4260 4290 4320 4350 4380

3480 3510 3540 3570 3600 3630 3660 3690 3720 3750 3780 3810 3840 3870 3900

3060 3090 3120 3150 3180 3210 3240 3270 3300 3330 3360 3390 3420 3450

2670 2700 2730 2760 2790 2770 2850 2880 2910 2940 2970 3000 3030

2310 2340 2370 2400 2430 2460 2490 2520 2550 2580 2610 2640

1980 2010 2040 2070 2100 2130 2160 2190 2220 2250 2280

1680 1710 1740 1770 1800 1830 1860 1890 1920 1950

1410 1440 1470 1500 1530 1560 1590 1620 1650

1170 1200 1230 1260 1290 1320 1350 1380

960 990 1020 1050 1080 1110 1140

780 810 840 870 900 930

600 660 690 720 750

510 540 570 600

390 420 450

360 390

330

Jan 300

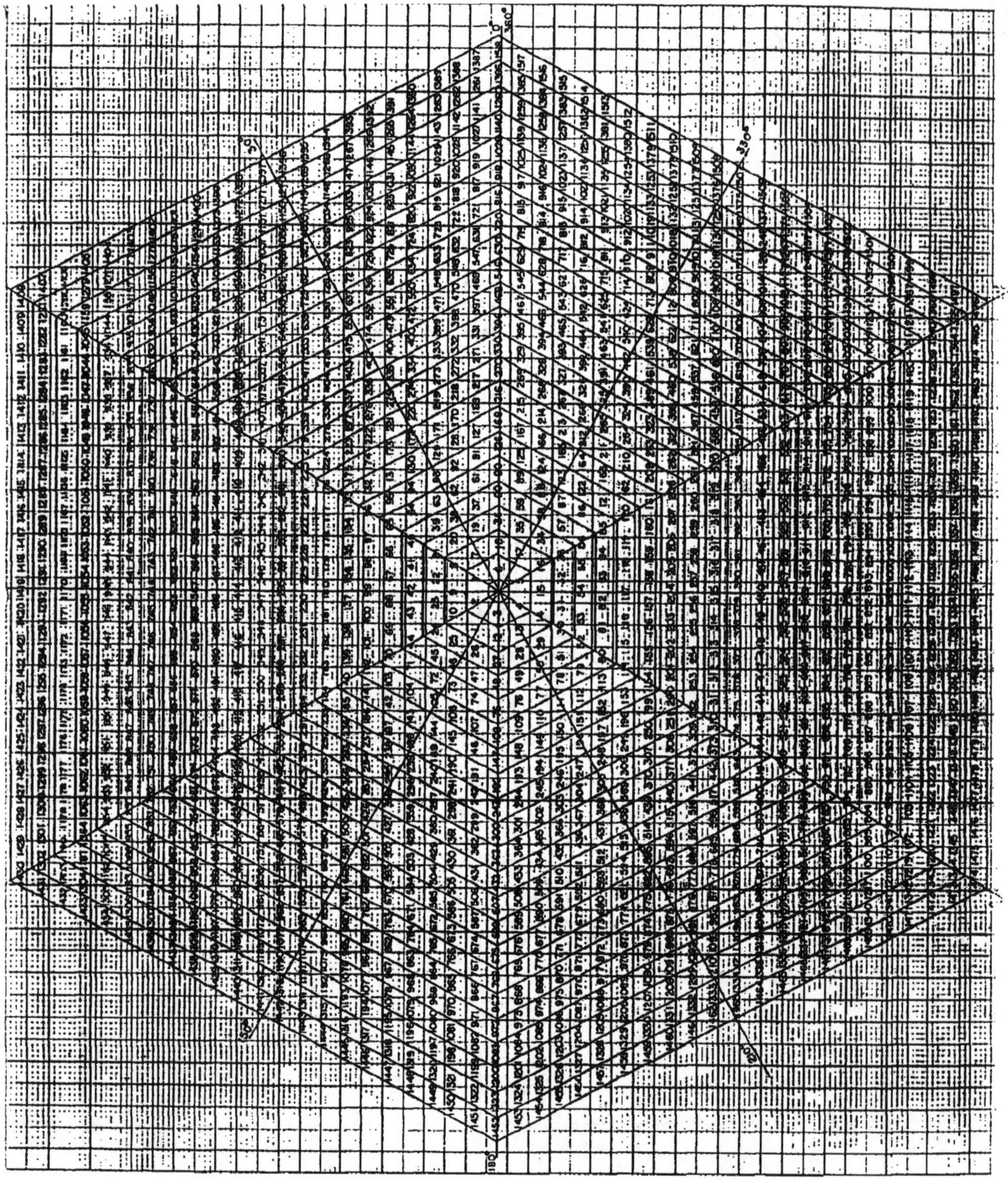

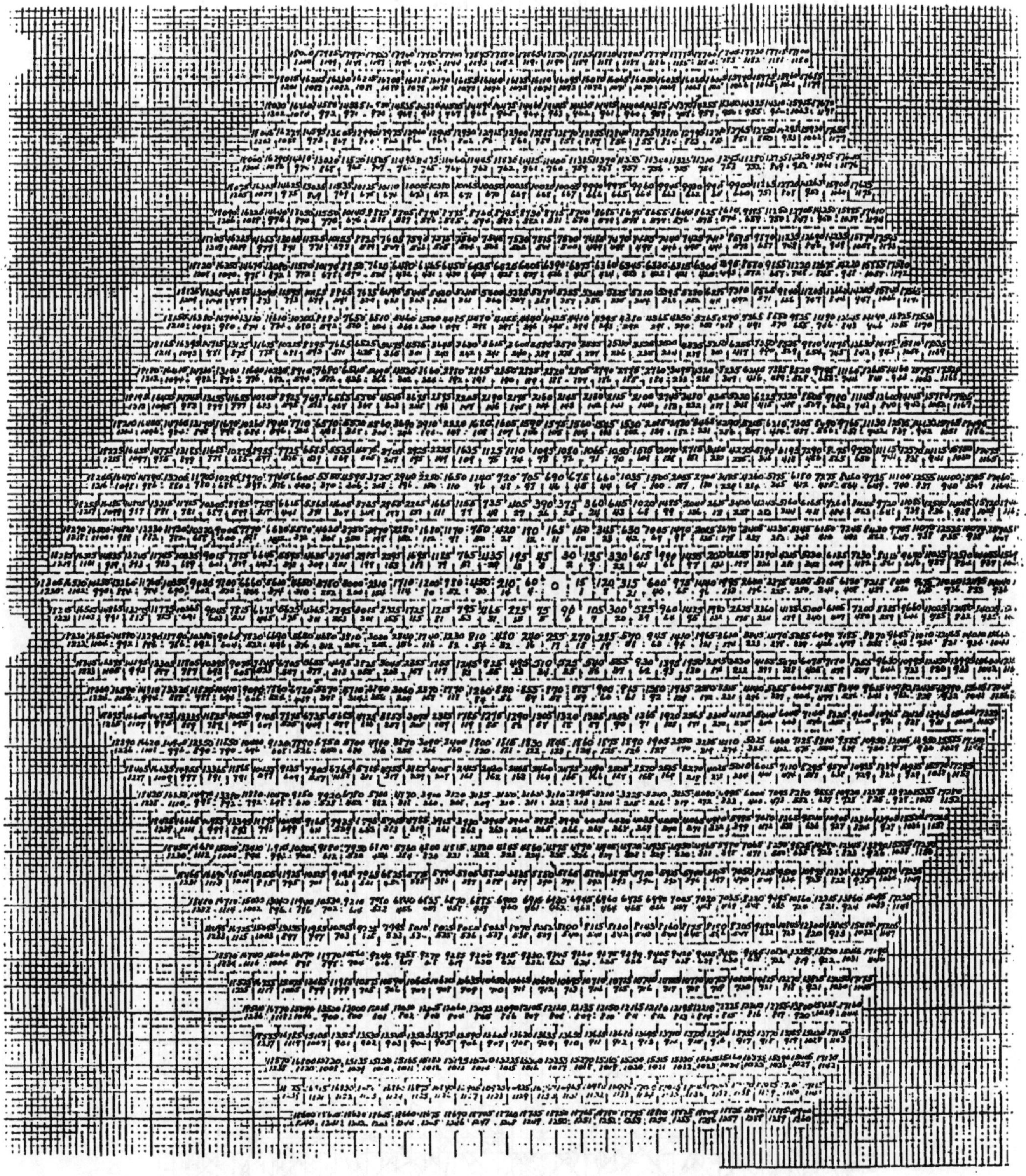

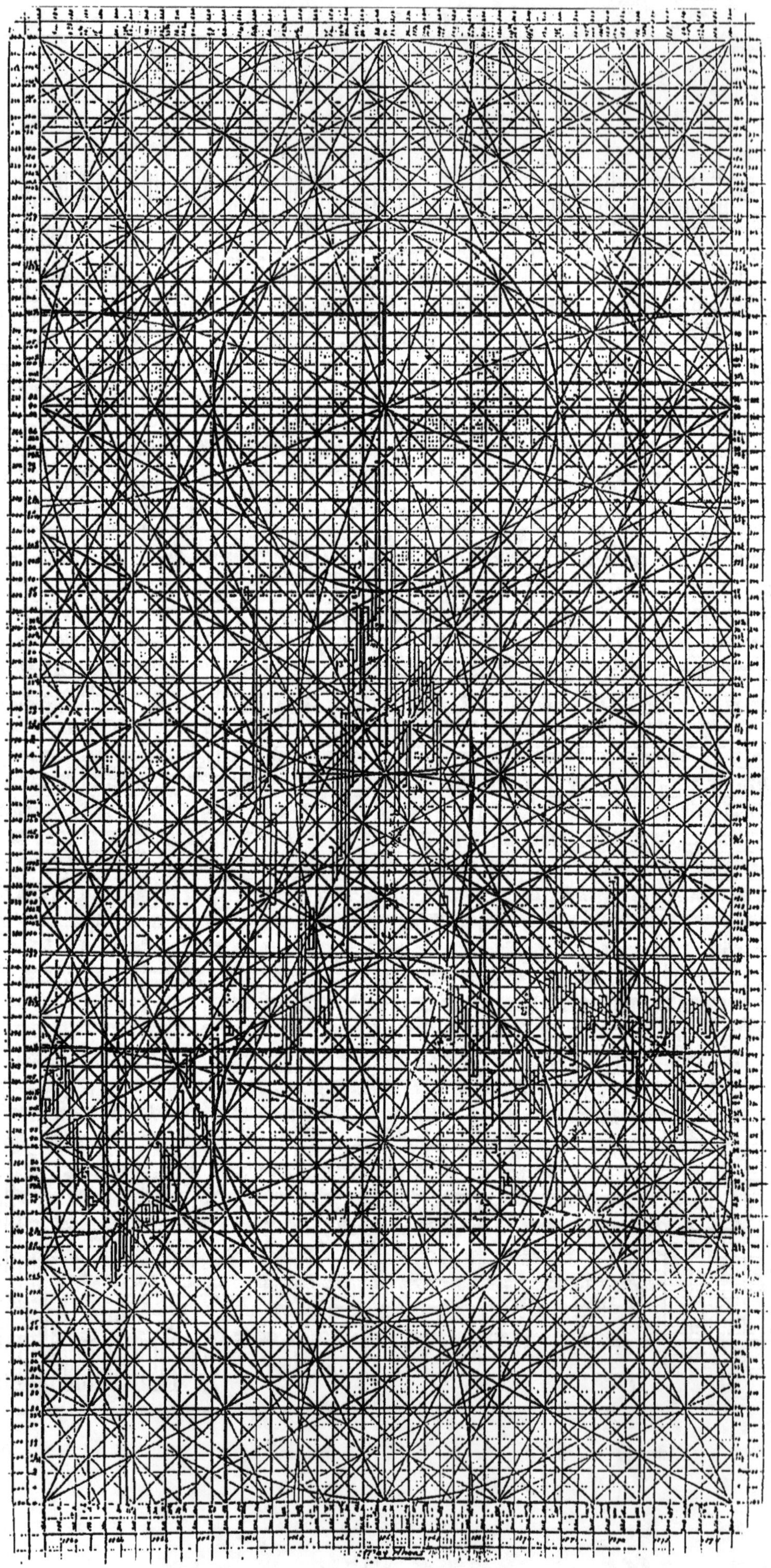

WEEKLY TIME PERIODS 7 DAYS FROM HIGHS OR LOWS. THE YEAR IS DIVIDED INTO 1/8s AND 1/3s.

CASH AND MAY SOY BEANS

		1	2	3	4	5	6	7	8	9	10	11	12	13	14	15	16	17	18	19	20	21	22	23	24	25	26	27	28	29	30	31	32	33	34	35	36
High and low prices		105	44	120	202½	60¼	67	89	202	194	203½	164	334	436 3/4	320½	428	239	278 3/8	201½	210	220½	224	323½	232½	344½	268½	309 3/4	281	314 3/4	279 3/4	309	259½	422	361	306 3/4	265 3/4	299
Dates		1920	1932	1936	1937	1938	1939	1940	1941	1941	1942	1942	1947	1948	1948	1948	1948	1948	1949	1949	1949	1949	1950	1950	1951	1951	1951	1952	1952	1953	1953	1953	1954	1954	1954	1954	1954
Mar 20		Feb 13	Dec 28	Oct 5	Apr 10	Oct 20	July 27	Aug 10	Sept 13	Oct 17	Jan 27	Oct 28	Oct 28	Jan 15	Feb 14	May 20	Oct 9	Nov 26	Feb 9	Mar 24	Nov 16	Dec 28	May 8	Oct 16	Feb 8	Jul 9	Dec 10	Apr 21	Aug 14	Feb 13	Apr 16	Aug 20	Apr 27	May 10	Jul 27	Sept 27	Nov 4
May 5	1/8	Mar 31	Feb 11	Nov 16	Mar 27	Dec 4	Sept 3	Sept 27	Oct 30	Dec 1	Mar 12	Dec 12	Dec 12	Mar 1	Mar 30	Jul 7	Nov 23	Jan 9	Mar 25	May 9	Dec 29	Feb 11	Apr 28	Nov 30	Mar 24	Aug 28	Jan 23	June 7	Oct 1	Mar 20	June 3	Oct 7	June 13	Jul 5	Sept 12	Nov 12	Dec 17
June 21	1/4	May 17	Mar 24	Jan 30	Jul 13	Jan 18	Oct 28	Nov 22	Dec 12	Jan 15	Apr 27	Jan 26	Jan 26	Apr 12	May 16	Aug 23	Jan 7	Feb 24	May 11	June 24	Feb 14	Mar 27	June 25	Jan 14	Mar 10	Oct 10	Mar 16	Jul 24	Nov 13	May 16	Jul 16	Nov 21	July 31	Aug 12	Oct 26	Dec 26	Feb 2
July 23	1/3	June 17	Apr 27	Feb 1	Aug 13	Feb 16	Nov 27	Dec 10	Jan 1	Feb 15	May 26	Feb 24	Feb 24	May 16	June 16	Sept 23	Feb 4	Mar 25	June 11	Jul 27	Mar 15	Apr 27	Aug 11	Feb 12	June 10	Nov 9	Apr 8	Aug 24	Dec 14	June 15	Aug 19	Dec 20	Aug 31	Sept 21	Nov 27	Jan 25	Mar 1
Aug 8	3/8	Jul 3	May 15	Feb 16	Aug 29	Mar 3	Dec 11	Dec 25	Jan 26	Feb 28	June 12	Mar 11	Mar 11	May 30	Jul 2	Nov 8	Feb 20	Apr 9	June 27	Aug 9	Mar 20	May 13	Sept 11	Feb 27	June 26	Nov 24	Apr 22	Sept 5	Dec 29	Jul 1	Sept 17	Jan 4	Sept 15	Nov 6	Dec 11	Feb 9	Mar 18
Sept 22	1/2	Aug 19	June 29	Apr 2	Oct 14	Apr 17	Jan 25	Feb 8	Mar 11	Apr 14	Jul 31	Apr 25	Apr 25	Jul 19	Aug 18	Nov 22	Apr 9	May 24	Aug 13	Sept 26	May 24	June 29	Nov 10	Apr 13	Aug 12	Mar 17	June 7	Oct 26	Feb 19	Aug 17	Oct 20	Feb 18	Oct 31	Nov 30	Jan 25	Mar 26	May 9
Nov 8	5/8	Oct 4	Aug 15	May 18	Nov 28	June 12	Mar 9	Mar 23	Apr 25	May 29	Sept 14	June 10	June 10	Sept 2	Oct 3	Jan 6	May 22	Jul 9	Oct 28	Nov 12	June 29	Aug 15	Dec 25	May 28	Sept 24	Feb 12	Jul 23	Dec 9	Mar 27	Oct 2	Dec 4	Apr 3	Dec 15	Jan 4	Mar 14	May 10	June 17
Nov 22	2/3	Oct 19	Aug 31	June 3	Dec 12	June 18	Mar 24	Apr 8	May 12	June 15	Sept 30	June 26	June 26	Sept 16	Oct 16	Jan 20	June 7	Jul 21	Oct 13	Nov 26	Jul 11	Aug 31	Jan 8	June 14	Oct 30	Mar 6	Aug 4	Dec 23	Apr 12	Oct 19	Dec 16	Apr 18	Dec 30	Jan 28	Mar 24	May 26	June 30
Dec 21	3/4	Nov 16	Sept 30	Jul 4	Jan 11	Jan 19	Apr 24	May 9	June 12	Jul 10	Oct 30	Jul 27	Jul 27	Oct 10	Nov 17	Feb 19	Jul 8	Aug 28	Nov 12	Dec 25	Aug 18	Sept 30	Feb 7	Jul 15	Nov 11	Apr 6	Sept 5	Mar 22	May 13	Nov 14	Jan 17	May 10	Jan 28	Feb 17	Apr 24	June 26	Aug 12
Feb 4	7/8	Jan 2	Nov 14	Aug 20	Feb 24	Sept 4	June 10	June 24	Jul 28	Sept 1	Dec 14	Sept 12	Sept 12	Dec 2	Jan 1	Apr 4	Aug 24	Oct 9	Dec 26	Feb 8	Sept 20	Nov 14	Mar 23	Aug 31	Dec 26	May 23	Oct 23	Mar 17	June 28	Dec 31	Mar 2	Jul 4	Mar 13	Apr 2	June 10	Aug 11	Sept 17
Mar 20	1 yr 52	Feb 15	Dec 26	Oct 5	Apr 10	Oct 20	July 27	Aug 10	Sept 13	Oct 17	Jan 27	Oct 28	Oct 28	Jan 15	Feb 14	May 20	Oct 9	Nov 26	Feb 9	Mar 24	Nov 16	Dec 28	May 8	Oct 16	Feb 8	Jul 9	Dec 10	Apr 21	Aug 14	Feb 13	Apr 16	Aug 20	Apr 27	May 18	Jul 27	Sept 27	Nov 4

TIME AND PRICE PERIODS IN 7 DAYS, 1 to 40 years.

DAYS	YEAR	1	2	3	4	5	6	7	8	9	10	11	12	13	14	15	16	17	18	19	20	21	22	23	24	25	26	27	28	29	30	31	32	33	34	35	36	37	38	39	40
46	1/8	6½	58½	110½	162½	214½	266½	318½	370½	422½	474½	526½	578½	630½	682½	734½	786½	838½	890½	942½	994½	1046½	1098½	1150½	1202½	1254½	1306½	1358½	1410½	1462½	1514½	1566½	1618½	1670½	1722½	1774½	1826½	1878½	1930½	1982½	2034½
91	1/4	13	65	117	169	221	273	325	377	429	481	533	585	637	689	741	793	845	897	949	1001	1053	1105	1157	1209	1261	1313	1365	1417	1469	1521	1573	1625	1677	1729	1781	1833	1885	1937	1989	2041
121	1/3	17	69	121	173	225	277	329	381	433	485	537	589	641	693	745	797	849	901	953	1005	1057	1109	1161	1213	1265	1317	1369	1421	1473	1525	1577	1629	1681	1733	1785	1837	1889	1941	1993	2045
136	3/8	19½	71½	123½	175½	227½	279½	331½	383½	435½	487½	539½	591½	643½	695½	747½	799½	851½	903½	955½	1007½	1059½	1111½	1163½	1215½	1267½	1319½	1371½	1423½	1475½	1527½	1579½	1631½	1683½	1735½	1787½	1839½	1891½	1943½	1995½	2047½
182	1/2	26	78	130	182	234	286	338	390	442	494	546	598	650	702	754	806	858	910	962	1014	1066	1118	1170	1222	1274	1326	1378	1430	1482	1534	1586	1638	1690	1742	1794	1846	1898	1950	2002	2054
227	5/8	32½	84½	136½	188½	240½	292½	344½	396½	448½	500½	552½	604½	656½	708½	760½	812½	864½	916½	968½	1020½	1072½	1124½	1176½	1228½	1280½	1332½	1384½	1436½	1488½	1540½	1592½	1644½	1696½	1748½	1800½	1852½	1904½	1956½	2008½	2060½
242	2/3	35	87	139	191	243	295	347	399	451	503	555	607	659	711	763	815	867	919	971	1023	1075	1127	1179	1231	1283	1335	1387	1439	1491	1543	1595	1647	1699	1751	1803	1855	1907	1959	2011	2063
273	3/4	39	91	143	195	247	299	351	403	455	507	559	611	663	715	767	819	871	923	975	1027	1079	1131	1183	1235	1287	1339	1391	1443	1495	1547	1599	1651	1703	1755	1807	1859	1911	1963	2015	2067
319	7/8	45½	97½	149½	201½	253½	305½	357½	409½	461½	513½	565½	617½	669½	721½	773½	825½	877½	929½	981½	1033½	1085½	1137½	1189½	1241½	1293½	1345½	1397½	1449½	1501½	1553½	1605½	1657½	1709½	1761½	1813½	1865½	1917½	1969½	2021½	2073½
365	1 yr	52	104	156	208	260	312	364	416	468	520	572	624	676	728	780	832	884	936	988	1040	1092	1144	1196	1248	1300	1352	1404	1456	1508	1560	1612	1664	1716	1768	1820	1872	1924	1976	2028	2080

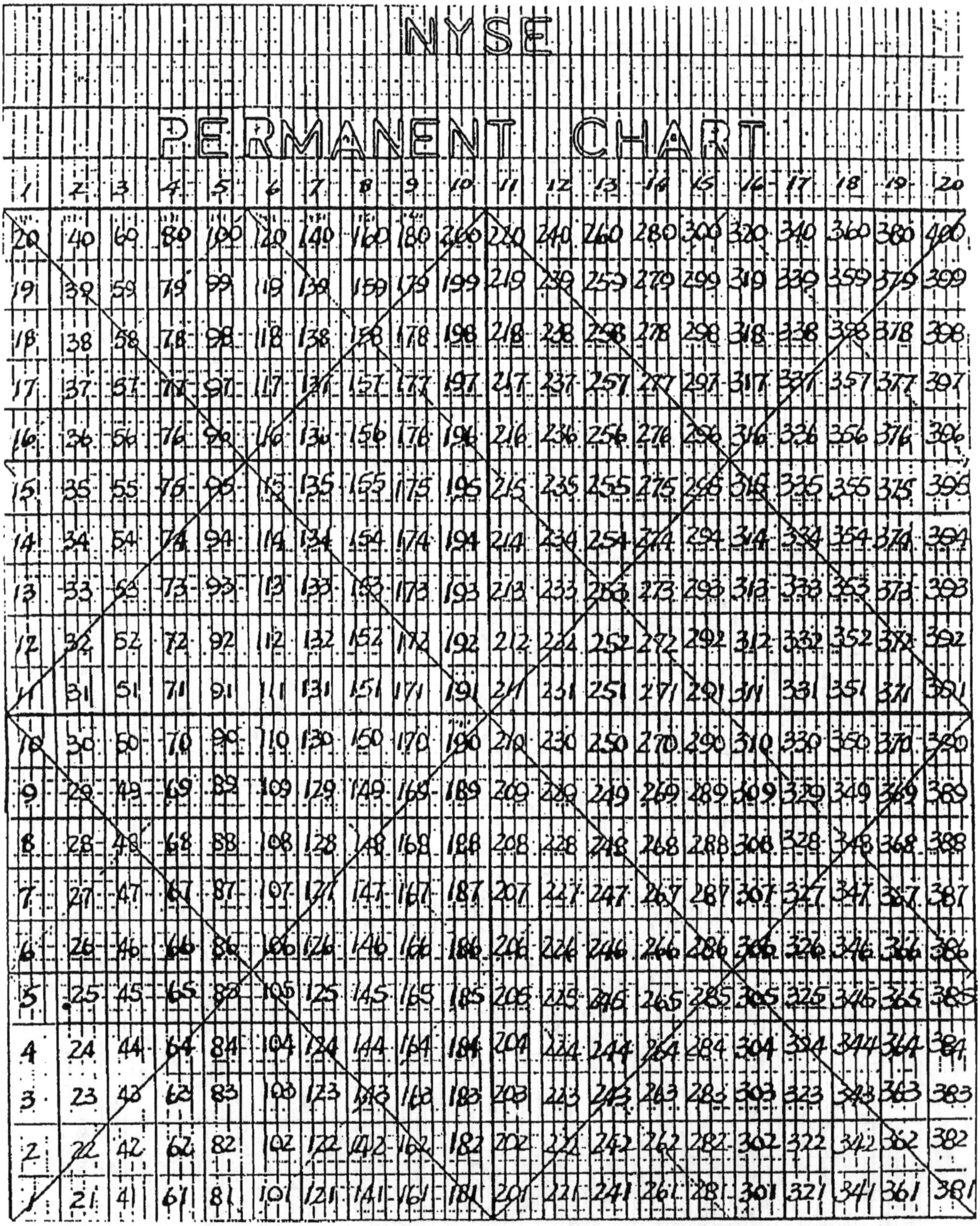
NYSE
PERMANENT CHART

Master 360° Circle Chart

		1	2	3	4	5	6	7	8	9	10	11	12	1	2	3	4	5
12	24	360	720	1080	1440	1800	2160	2520	2880	3240	3600	3960	4320	4680	5040	5400	5760	6120
	23	345	705	1065	1425	1785	2145	2505	2866	3225	3585	3946	4305	4665	5025	5385	5745	6105
11	22	330	690	1050	1410	1770	2130	2490	2850	3210	3570	3930	4290	4650	5010	5370	5730	6090
7/8	21	315	675	1035	1395	1755	2115	2475	2835	3195	3555	3915	4275	4635	4995	5365	5715	6075
10	20	300	660	1020	1380	1740	2100	2460	2820	3180	3540	3900	4260	4620	4980	5340	5700	6060
	19	285	645	1005	1365	1725	2085	2445	2805	3165	3525	3885	4245	4605	4965	5325	5685	6045
9 3/4	18	270	630	990	1350	1710	2070	2430	2790	3150	3510	3870	4230	4590	4950	5310	5670	6030
	17	255	615	975	1335	1695	2055	2415	2775	3135	3495	3855	4215	4575	4935	5295	5655	6015
8 2/3	16	240	600	960	1320	1680	2040	2400	2760	3120	3480	3840	4200	4560	4920	5280	5640	6000
5/6	15	225	585	945	1305	1665	2025	2385	2745	3105	3465	3825	4185	4545	4905	5265	6625	5985
7	14	210	570	930	1290	1650	2010	2370	2730	3090	3450	3810	4170	4530	4890	5250	5610	5970
	13	195	555	915	1275	1635	1995	2355	2715	3075	3435	3795	4155	4515	4875	5235	5595	5955
6 1/2	12	180	540	900	1260	1620	1980	2340	2700	3060	3420	3780	4140	4500	4860	5220	5580	5940
	11	165	525	885	1245	1605	1965	2325	2685	3045	3405	3765	4125	4485	4845	5205	5565	5925
5	10	150	510	870	1230	1590	1950	2310	2670	3030	3390	3750	4110	4470	4830	5190	5550	5910
	9	135	495	855	1215	1575	1935	2295	2655	3015	3375	3735	4095	4455	4816	5175	5535	5896
4 1/3	8	120	480	840	1200	1560	1920	2280	2640	3000	3360	3720	4080	4440	4800	5160	5520	5880
	7	105	465	825	1185	1516	1905	2265	2625	2985	3345	3705	4065	4425	4785	5145	5505	5865
3 1/4	6	90	450	810	1170	1530	1890	2250	2610	2970	3330	3690	4050	4410	4770	5130	5490	5850
	5	75	435	795	1155	1515	1875	2235	2595	2955	3315	3675	4035	4395	4755	5115	5475	5835
2 1/6	4	60	420	780	1140	1500	1860	2220	2580	2940	3300	3660	4020	4380	4740	5100	5460	5820
1/8	3	45	405	765	1125	1485	1845	2205	2565	2925	3285	3645	4005	4365	4725	5086	5445	5805
1	2	30	390	750	1110	1470	1830	2190	2550	2910	3270	3630	3990	4350	4710	5070	5430	5790
	1	15	375	735	1095	1455	1815	2175	2535	2895	3255	3615	3975	4335	4695	5055	5415	5775
		30° 1/12	60° 1/6	90° 1/4	120° 1/3	150° 5/12	180° 1/2	210° 7/12	240° 2/3	270° 3/4	300° 5/6	330° 11/12	360° 0	30° 1/12	60° 1/6	90° 1/4	120° 1/3	150° 5/12

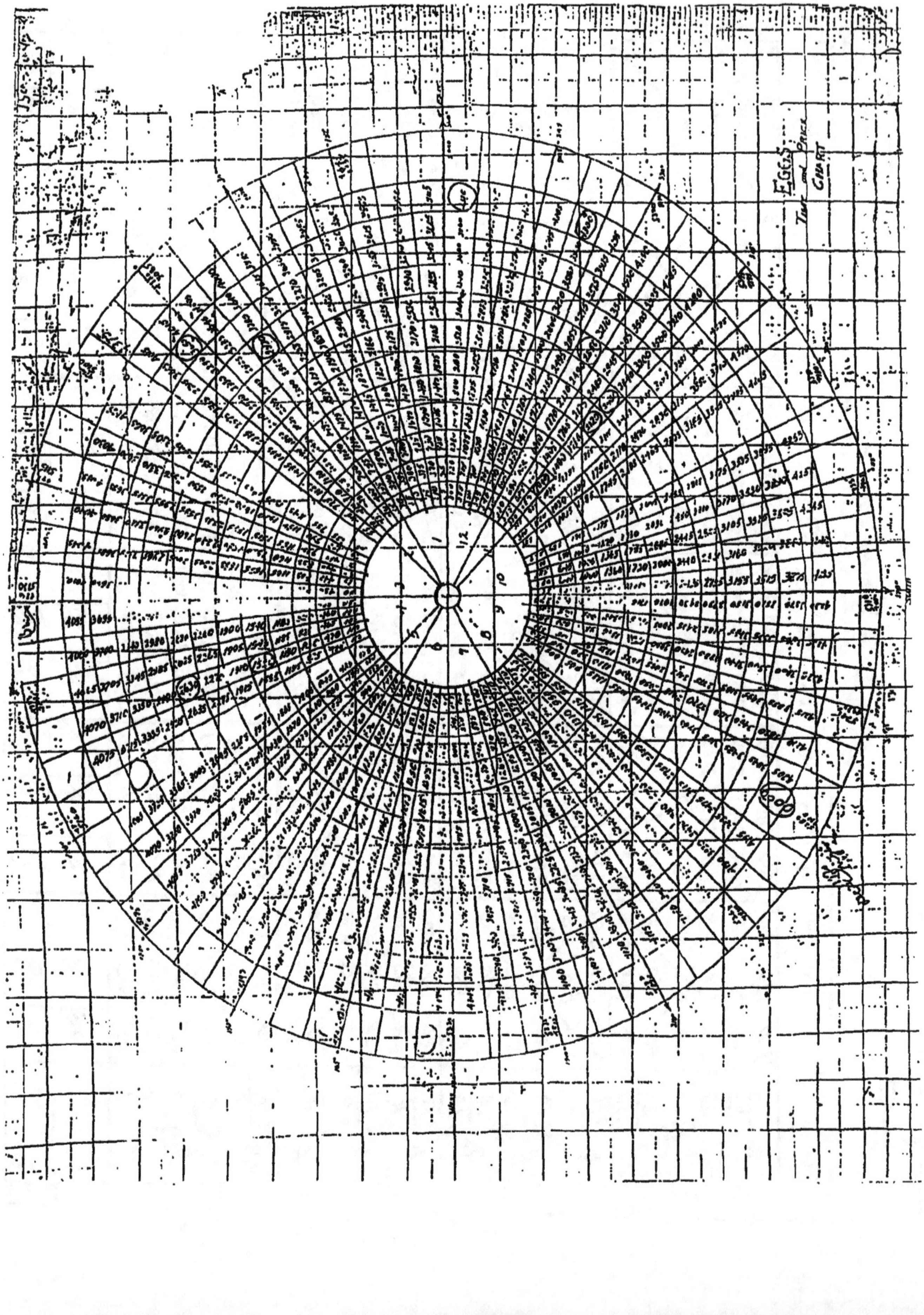
EGGS
Time and Price
Chart

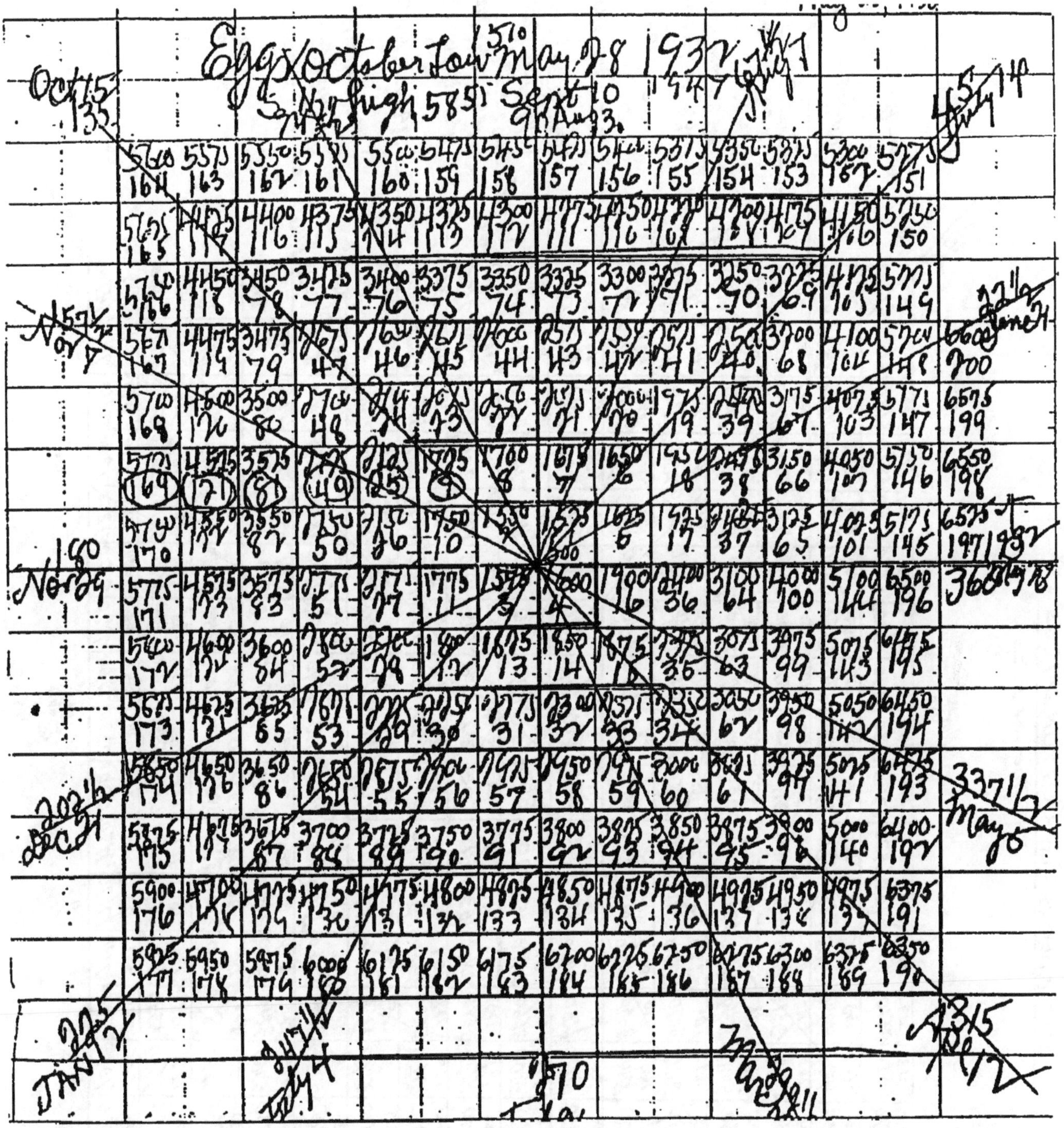
Eggs October Low May 28 1932

Even Squares for Cotton & Eggs

Time and Price

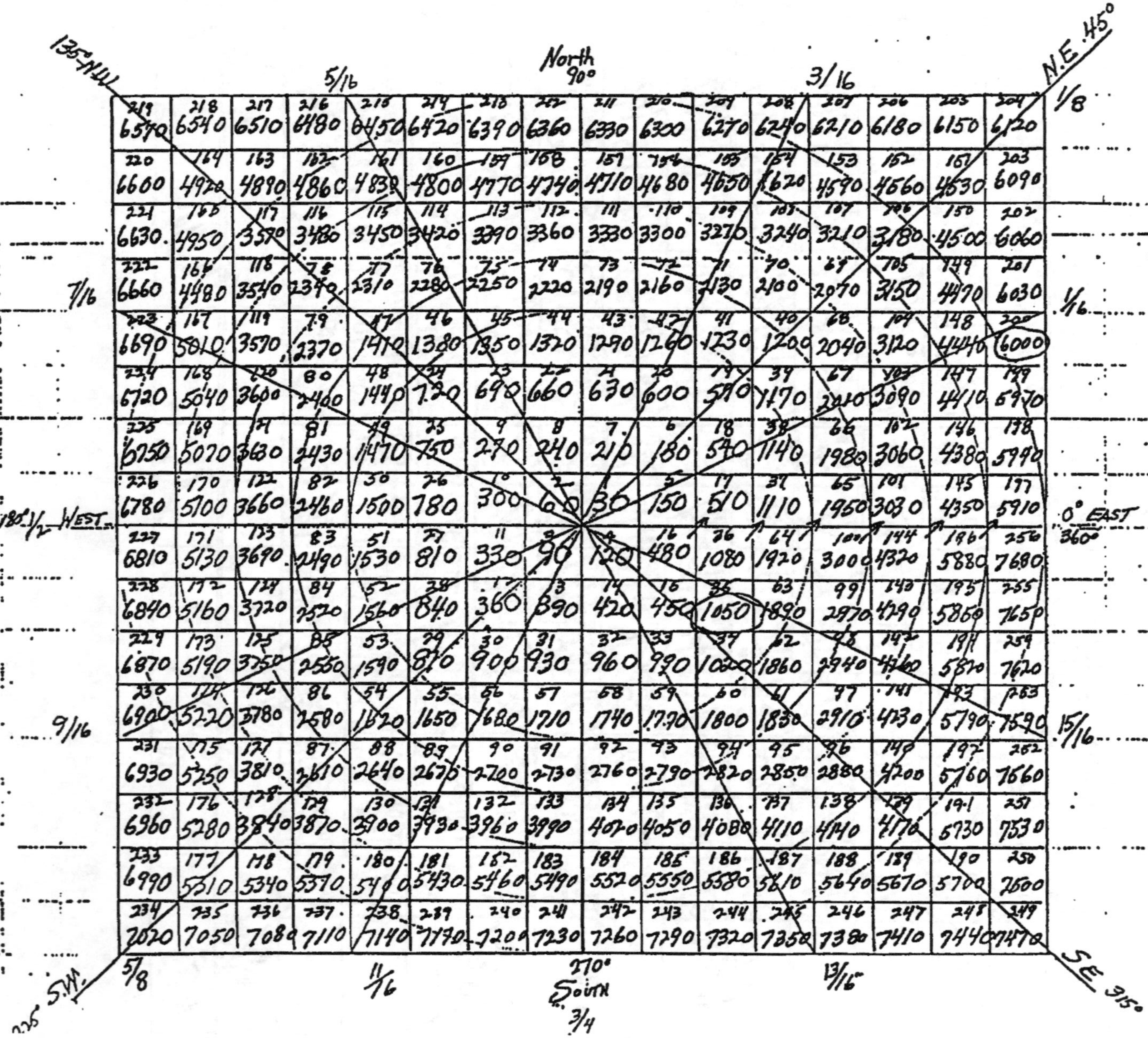

DEC-28-1920
DEC-28 1948 = 336 Months
April 28-1949 - 4 "
340 "
J 4/28-1949 = 343 "
7X49 = 343 "

DEC 28-1920 - High 60¢
MAY 2. 1949 = 1481 weeks

Square of 38 = 1444
" " 39 = 1521
" " 40 = 1600

From □ 38 to 39
1/4 = 19 1/4 Weeks
1/2 = 38 1/2 "
1481 + 38 1/2 = 1482 1/2
... MAY 13-1949 = 1482 1/2

1440 = 4 X 360

MAY 30, 1949 = 45 Weeks
In New 360 cycle.

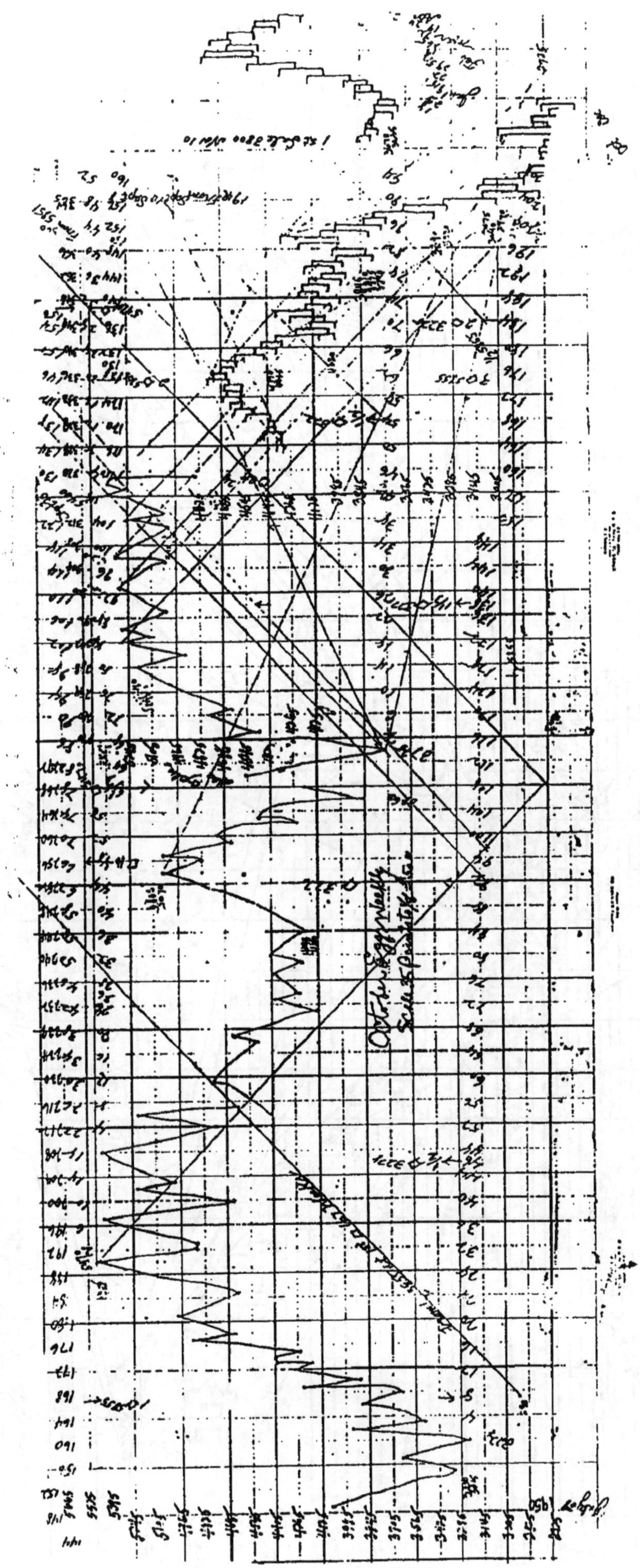

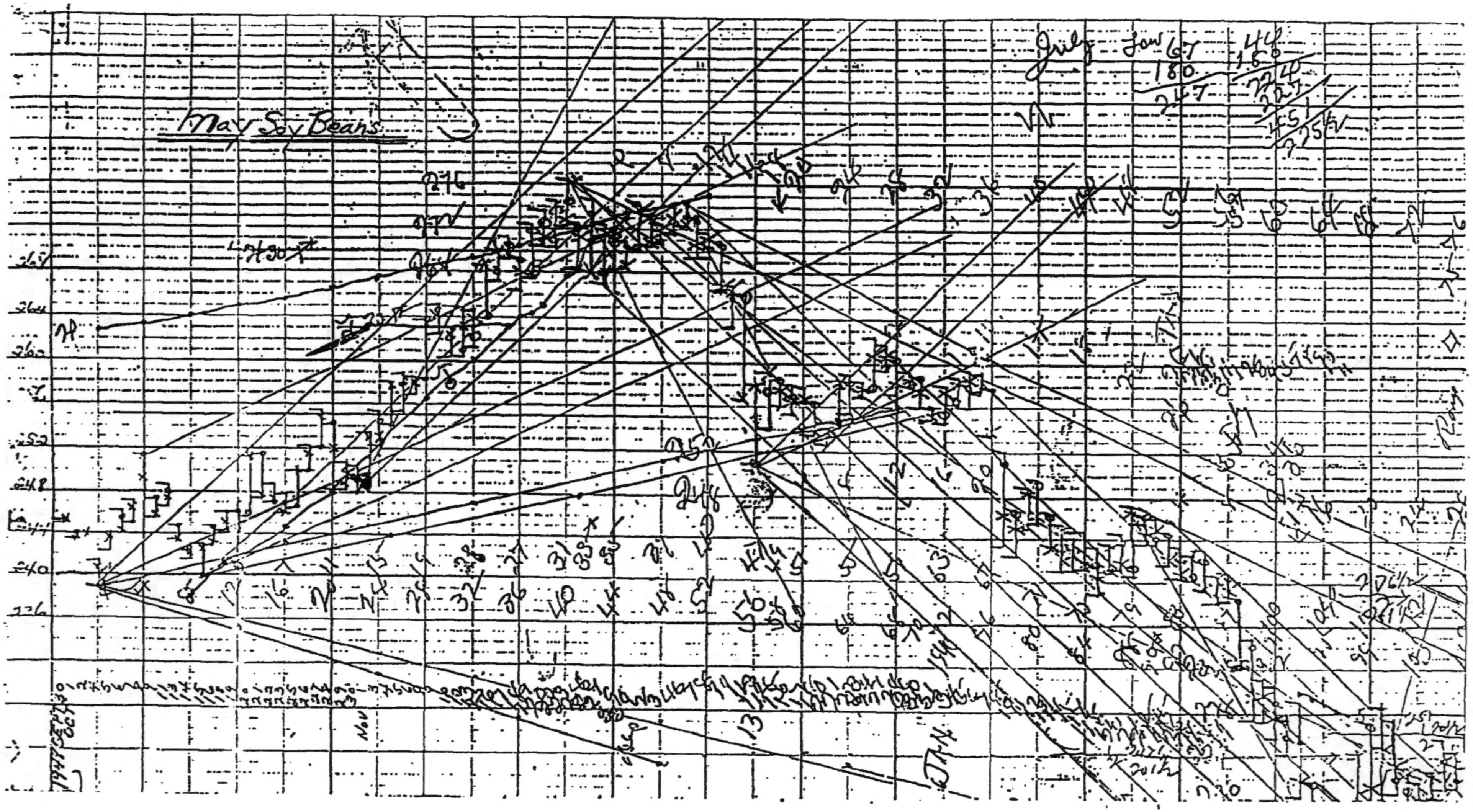
May Soy Beans
July Low
NOV

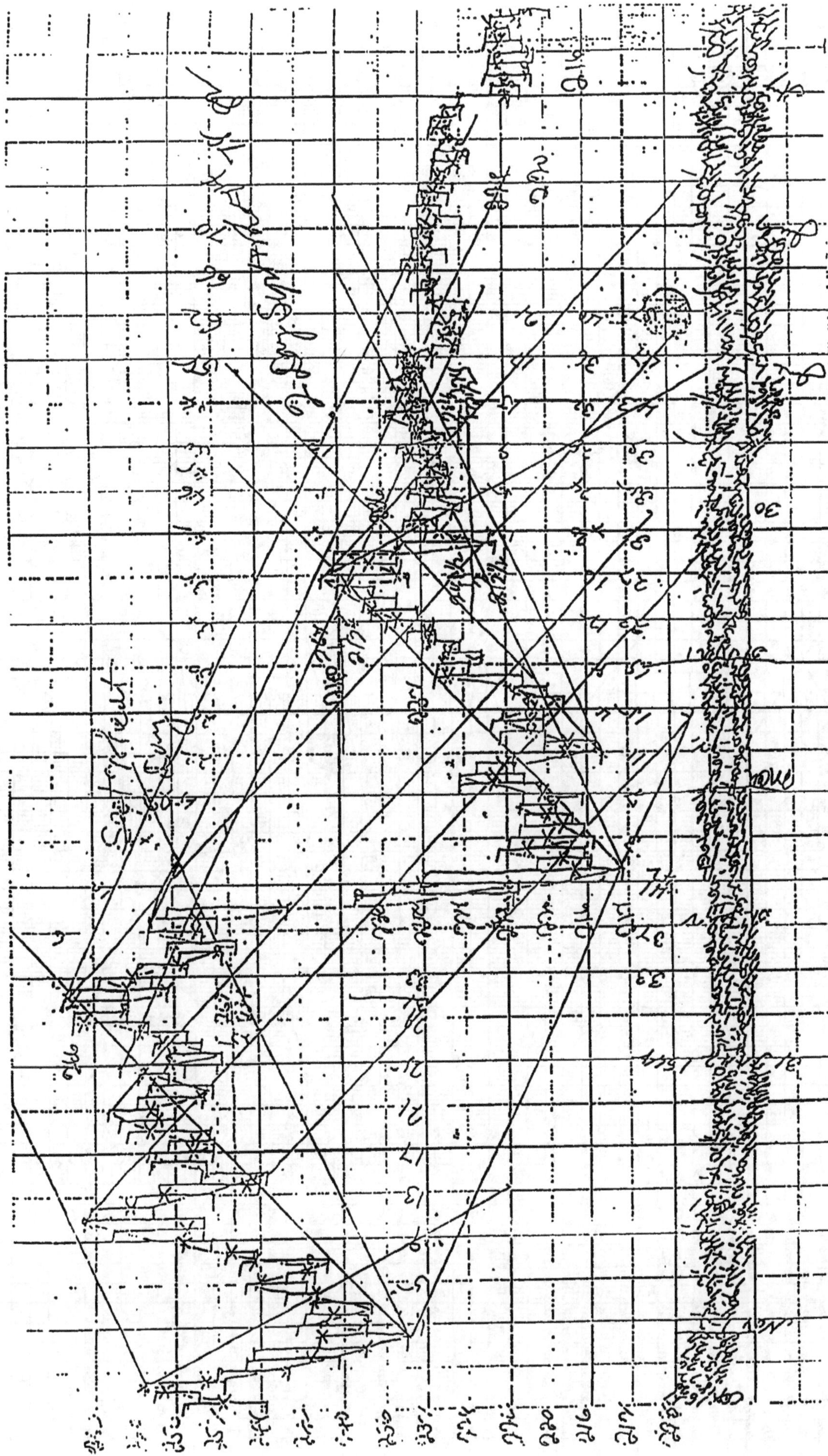

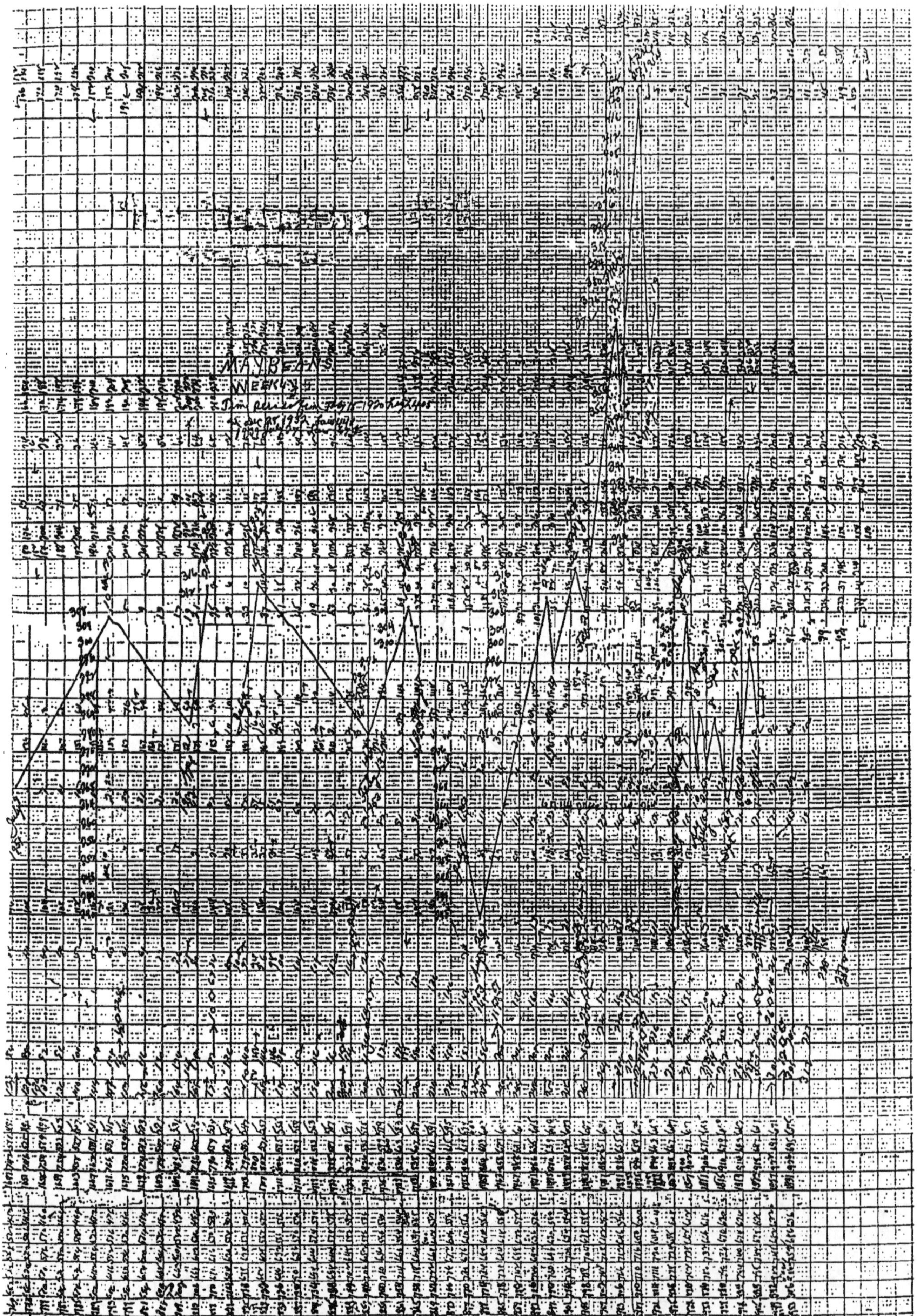
MAY BEANS
WEEKLY

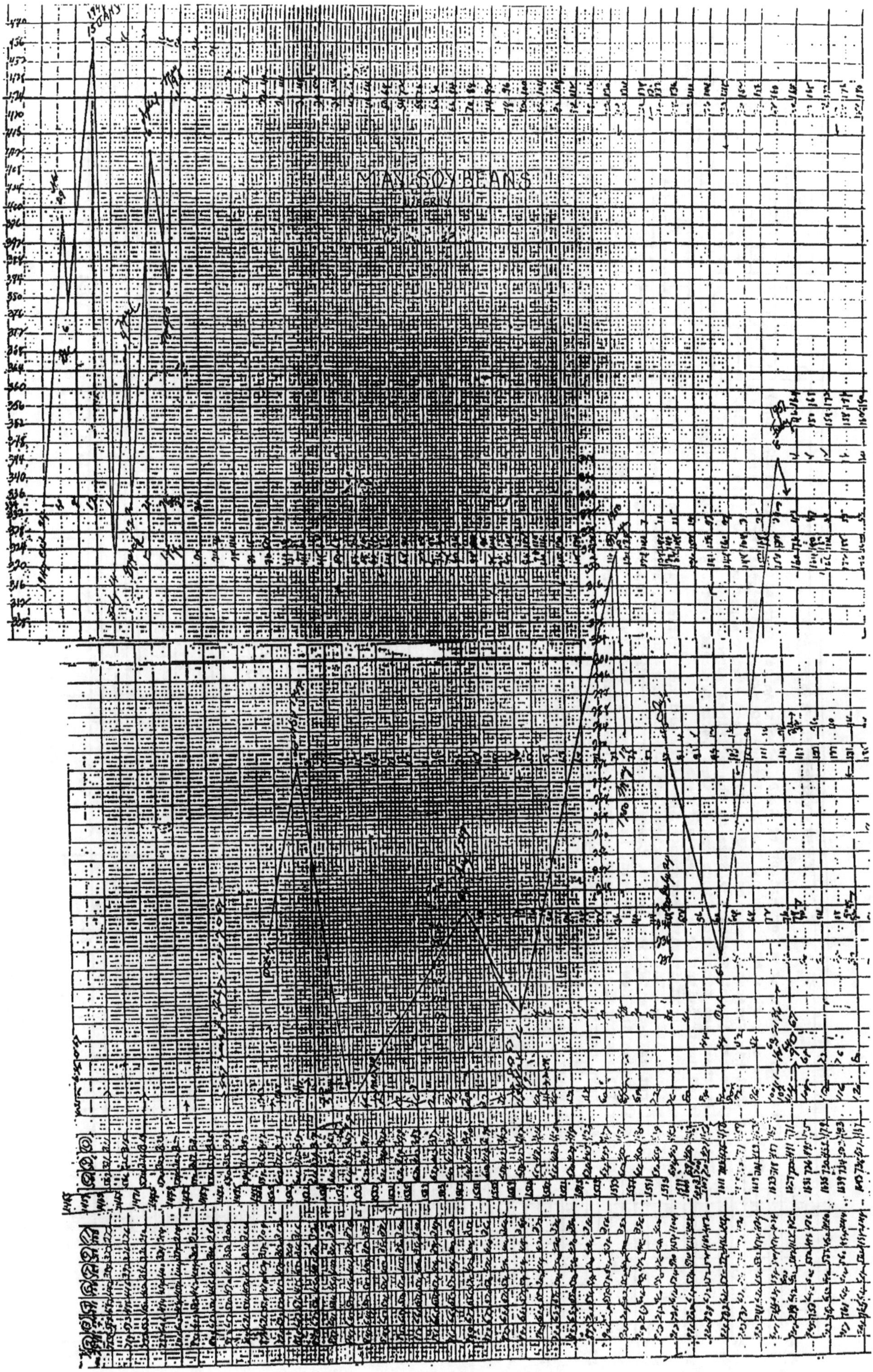
MAY SOYBEANS

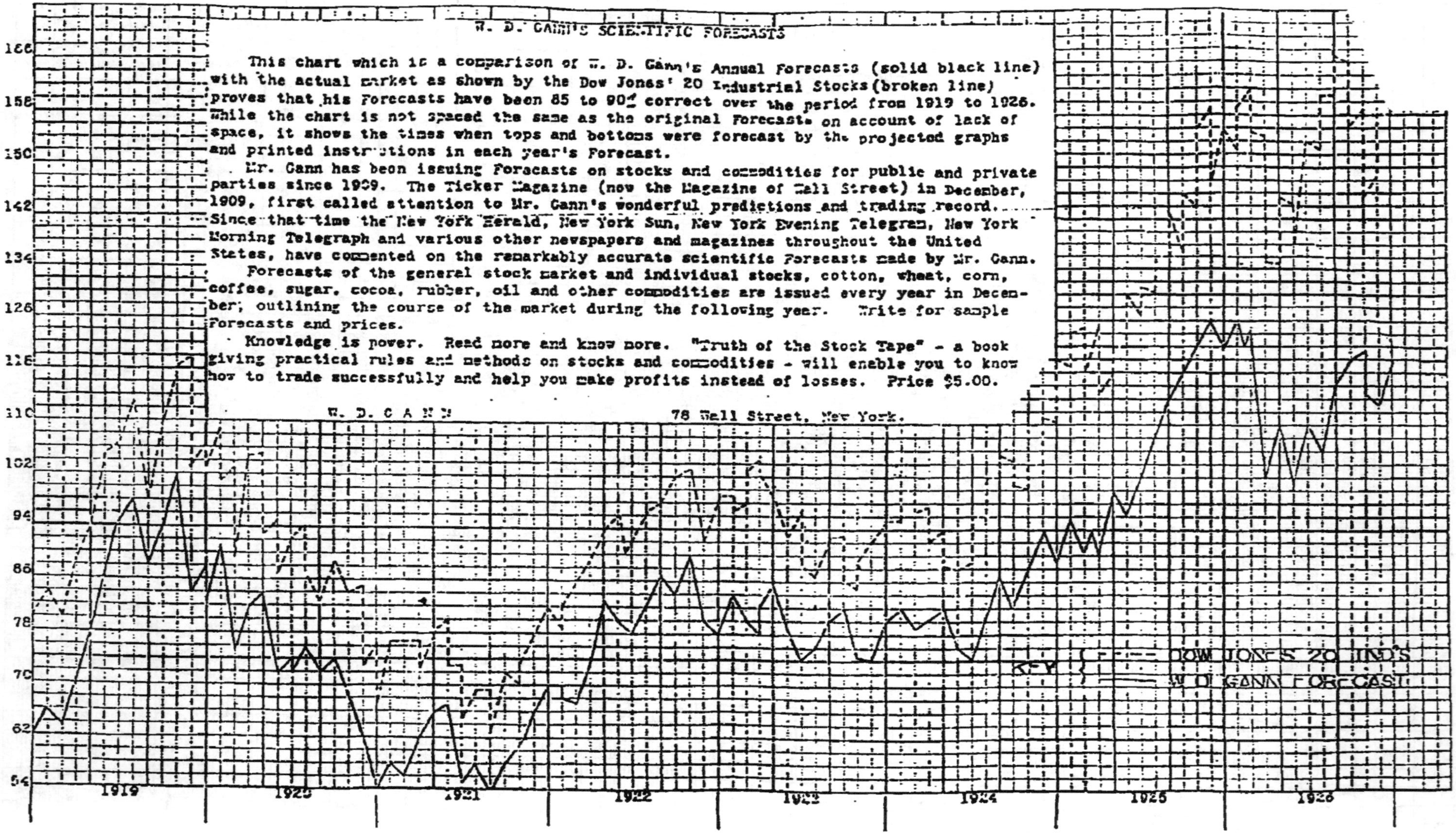

W. D. GANN'S SCIENTIFIC FORECASTS

This chart which is a comparison of W. D. Gann's Annual Forecasts (solid black line) with the actual market as shown by the Dow Jones' 20 Industrial Stocks (broken line) proves that his Forecasts have been 85 to 90% correct over the period from 1919 to 1926. While the chart is not spaced the same as the original Forecasts on account of lack of space, it shows the times when tops and bottoms were forecast by the projected graphs and printed instructions in each year's Forecast.

Mr. Gann has been issuing Forecasts on stocks and commodities for public and private parties since 1909. The Ticker Magazine (now the Magazine of Wall Street) in December, 1909, first called attention to Mr. Gann's wonderful predictions and trading record. Since that time the New York Herald, New York Sun, New York Evening Telegram, New York Morning Telegraph and various other newspapers and magazines throughout the United States, have commented on the remarkably accurate scientific Forecasts made by Mr. Gann.

Forecasts of the general stock market and individual stocks, cotton, wheat, corn, coffee, sugar, cocoa, rubber, oil and other commodities are issued every year in December, outlining the course of the market during the following year. Write for sample Forecasts and prices.

Knowledge is power. Read more and know more. "Truth of the Stock Tape" - a book giving practical rules and methods on stocks and commodities - will enable you to know how to trade successfully and help you make profits instead of losses. Price $5.00.

W. D. GANN   78 Wall Street, New York.

CHAPTER 7

METHOD FOR FORECASTING THE STOCK MARKET

W. D. GANN
78 WALL STREET
NEW YORK

Scientific Advice
and Analytical Reports
on Stocks and Commodities
…thor of "Truth of the Stock Tape"
and "The Tunnel Thru the Air"

Member
American Economic As…
Royal Economic Soci…
Cable Address
"Ganwade NewYork"

METHOD FOR FORECASTING THE STOCK MARKET

KIND OF CHARTS

You should keep a yearly, monthly, weekly and overnight chart. You will find on the weekly chart that stocks will often reverse the minor trend and run up two or three weeks, but the third week it will not make a higher top or a higher bottom; yet at other times it will hold for several weeks without advancing above the level made in the first two weeks' rally. In cases of this kind, it is always safe to buy or sell with a stop 3 points above or below the two weeks' reverse move. If the market is going higher, it should continue up the third week, or down, as the case may be. The rules apply in a bear market as in a bull market.

The Overnight Chart, in order to show a reversal in trend, must go 3 points above the last top or bottom. The Overnight Chart is based on Bottoms. As long as higher bottoms are made, it continues upward. As long as lower bottoms are made, it continues downward. The basis of all movements are calculated from bottoms. For a market to advance, bottoms must be progressive or increasing, and if a market declines, bottoms must decrease.

HOW TO FORECAST

Every movement in the market is the result of a natural law and of a Cause which exists long before the Effect takes place and can be determined years in advance. The future is but a repetition of the past, as the Bible plainly states: "The thing that hath been, it is that which shall be; and that which is done is that which shall be done, and there is no new thing under the sun." -Eccl. 1:9.

Everything has a major and a minor, and in order to be accurate in forecasting the future, you must know the major cycle, as the most money is made when extreme fluctuations occur.

The major cycle of stocks occurs every 49 to 50 years. A period of "jubilee" years of extreme high or low prices, lasting from 5 to 7 years occur at the end of the 50-year cycle.

"7" is a fatal number referred to many times in the Bible and it is ruled by the planet Saturn, which brings about contractions, depression, and panics. Seven times "7" equals 49, which is shown as the fatal evil year, causing extreme fluctuations.

The most important Time cycle is the 20-year cycle, or 240 months and most stocks and averages work closer to this cycle than any other. Five years is one-quarter of twenty and ten years is one-half of twenty and very important because it is 120 months. Fifteen years is three-quarters of twenty years and important because it is 180 months, just the same as 7 1/2 years is 90 months, because 84 5/8 is 15/16 of 90.

The next important major cycle is 30 years, which is caused by the planet Saturn. This planet makes one revolution around the sun every 30 years. Saturn rules the products of the earth and causes extreme high or low prices in products of the earth at the end of each 30-year cycle, and this makes Stocks high or low. The most important cycle of all is the 20-year cycle.

The next important major cycle is the 10-year cycle, which produces fluctuations of the same nature and extreme high or low every 10 years. Stocks come out remarkably close on each even 10-year cycle. The minor cycles are 3 years and 6 years. The smallest cycle is 1 year, which will often show a change in the 10th or 11th month.

In rapid markets a move will run 6 to 7 weeks and have some kind of a minor reversal in trend, but often markets will continue for several months, only reacting two weeks, then resting possibly two or three weeks and resuming the main trend. Often they move right on up or down in the third week. This same rule applies to daily movements. Fast markets will only move two days in the opposite direction to the main trend and on the third day they will resume their upward or downward course in harmony with the main trend.

In all movements use the angles and also calculate the 1/3, 2/3, 1/4, and 3/4 points of the major or minor move. One-half is the most important as it equals the 45° angle, which is the strongest and most fatal. The next in importance is 2/3, which would equal a triangle, or 120°.

All rules based on Natural Law are applied the same to Time, Space and Volume charts.

It never pays to guess. Always consider the main time swing of a market; then watch your weekly and Overnight charts until they show a reversal or time has expired. All markets move in three to four sections. The third or fourth movement up or down marks the culmination. A reverse signal is always given before time expires and then the market may make two or three swings up or down into the same territory, going a little higher or a little lower than the tops or bottoms from which the warning signal was given. When this is taking place the market is either being accumulated or distributed.

TIME RULES FOR FORECASTING STOCKS

The stock market moves in 10-year cycles, which is worked out in 5-year cycles -- a 5-year cycle up and a 5-year cycle down.

Rule 1: Bull or bear campaigns do not run more than 3 to 3½ years up or down without a move of 3 to 6 months or one year in the opposite direction. Many campaigns culminate in the 23rd month, not running out the full two years. Watch the weekly and monthly charts to determine whether the culmination will occur in the 23rd or 24th month of the move, or in the 34 to 35, 41 to 42, 49 to 60, 67 to 72, or 84 to 90th months.

Rule 2: A Bull campaign runs five years; -2 years up, 1 year down, and 2 years up, completing a 5-year cycle. The end of a 5-year campaign comes in the 59th or 60th months. Always watch for the change in the 59th month.

Rule 3: A Bear cycle runs five years down. First move 2 years down, then 1 year up and 2 years down - completing the 5-year down swing.

Rule 4: Add ten years to any top and it will give you another top of a 10 year cycle with about the same average fluctuations.

Rule 5: Add ten years to any bottom and it will give you the next bottom of the 10-year cycle and of the same kind of a year and about the same average fluctuations.

Rule 6: Bear campaigns run out in 7-year cycles, or 3 years and 4 years from any complete bottom. From any complete bottom of a cycle first add 3 years to get the next bottom; then add 4 years to get bottom of 7-year cycle.

Rule 7: From any complete top add three years to get the next top; then add three years to the first top, which will give the second top. Add four years to the second top to get the third and final top of a 10-year cycle.

Rule 8: Add five years to any top, will give the next bottom of a five-year cycle with about the same average fluctuations. In order to get tops of a 5-year cycle, add five years to any bottom and it will give the next top with the same average fluctuations. 1917 bottom of a big bear campaign - add five years gives 1922 top of a minor bull campaign. Why do I say "Top of a Minor Bull Campaign"? 1919 was top - add five years to 1919, gives 1924 as bottom of a 5-year Bear cycle. Refer to Rule 2 and 3, which will tell you that a Bull or Bear campaign never runs more than two years in the same direction.

The Bear campaign from 1919 was down two years - 1920 and 1921: therefore, we can only get a 1-year rally in 1922; then two years down - 1923 and 1924, which completes the 5-year Bear cycle. Now, look back to 1913 and 1914 and you will see that 1923 and 1924 must be Bear years to complete the 10-year cycle from the bottoms of 1913 and 1914. Then note 1917 bottom of a Bear year. add seven years and it gives 1924 also as bottom of a Bear cycle.

Rule 9: How to make up Annual Forecasts for any year. Take ten years back and the future year will run very close to the last 10-year cycle. For instance - 1932 will run like 1902, 1912, and 1922.

There is a major cycle of 30 years, which runs out three ten-year cycles. The 10-year cycle back from the present and the 20-year cycle have the most effect on the future. But in completing the 30-year cycle, it is best to have 30 years past records to check up to make up a future forecast. For instance: In order to make up my 1922 Forecast, I check 1892, 1902, and 1912, and watch for minor variations in monthly moves. But I know that 1922 will run closest to 1912. However, some stocks will run close to the fluctuations of 1892 and 1902. Remember each stock works from its own base or from its own tops and bottoms, and not always according to Average tops and bottoms. Therefore, judge each stock individually and keep up weekly and monthly charts on them.

Rule 10: Extreme Great Cycles. There must always be a major and a minor, a lesser and a greater, a positive and a negative; that is why stocks have three important moves in a 10-year cycle, two tops three years apart and the next one four years. This works again the five years moves, 2 years up and 1 year down, then 2 years up - two major and one minor move. The smallest complete cycle or workout in a market is five years, and 10 is a complete cycle. Five times ten equals 50, which is the greatest cycle. At the end of a Great Cycle of 50 years, extreme high and low prices occur. Go back over past records and you can verify this.

The number "7" is the basis of time, and a panick occurs and depression in the stock market every seven years, which is extreme and greater than the three-year decline. Note 1907, 1917, etc. Seven times seven is fatal, which makes 49 years, and causes extreme fluctuations in the 49th to 50th year. Remember that you must begin with bottoms or tops to figure all cycles, whether major or minor. Extreme fluctuations also occur at the end of a 30-year cycle as you can see by going back 30 to 50 years.

Rule 11: Monthly moves can be determined by the same rule as yearly; i. e., add three months to a bottom, then add four, making seven, to get minor bottoms and reaction points. But remember in a Bull market a reaction may only last two or three weeks; then the advance is resumed. In this way, a market may continue up for twelve months without breaking a monthly bottom. In Big up

SWING A reaction will not last over two months, the third month being up, the same rule as in yearly cycle - two down and the third up. This same rule applies in Bear markets - rallies not lasting more than two months. Most moves run out in six to seven weeks. Seven days in a week, and seven times seven making 49 days, a fatal turning point. Always watch your annual trend and consider whether you are in a bear or Bull market. Many times when in a Bull year, with the monthly chart showing up, a stock will react two or three weeks, then rest three or four weeks, going into new territory and advancing six to seven weeks more. Always consider whether or not your big time limit has run out before judging a reverse move, and do not fail to consider your indications on time both from main tops and bottoms.

Rule 12: Daily Charts: The daily swing runs on the same rules as yearly and monthly cycles, but of course it is only a minor part of them. Important daily changes occur every seven and ten days. During a month natural changes in trend occur around the 6th to 7th, 9th to 10th, 14th to 15th, 19th to 20th, 23rd to 24th, 29th to 31st. These minor moves occur in accordance with tops and bottoms of individual stocks. Watch for a change in Trend 30 days from the last top or bottom. This is very important. Then watch for changes 60 90, 120 days from tops or bottoms. 180 days, or six months, is very important and sometimes marks changes for greater moves. Also the 9th and 11th months from tops or bottoms should be watched for important minor and often major changes.

A daily chart gives the first short change, which may run for seven or ten days, the Weekly the next important changes in trend, and the monthly the strongest. Remember weekly moves run three to seven weeks; monthly moves 2 to 3 months or more, according to the yearly cycle, before reversing.

It is important to note whether a stock is making higher or lower bottoms each year. For instance, if a stock has made a higher bottom each year for five years, then makes a lower than previous year, it is a sign of a reversal and may mark a long down cycle. The same rule applies in stocks that are making lower tops for a number of years in a Bear market.

Study all the instructions and rules I have given you. Read them over several times, as each time they will become clearer to you. Study the charts and work out the rules in actual practice, as well as on past performances. In this way you will make progress and will realize and appreciate the value of my method of forecasting.

INSTRUCTIONS FOR FORECASTING THE STOCK MARKET

First, remember time is the most important of all factors and not until sufficient time has expired does any big move up or down start. The time factor will overbalance both space and volume. When time is up, space movement will start and big volume will begin either up or down, Time rules. Always consider your annual Forecast.

Second, consider each individual stock and determine its trend from its position according to distance in time from bottom or top. Each stock works out its 5, 10, 20, 30, 50 and 60 year cycles from its own bottoms and tops, regardless of the movements of other stocks, even those in the same group.

Third, monthly reversals or changes in trend often occur after two to three months. The change starts in the third month, according to the main time factor you are working in.

Fourth, weekly time rules. A stock will run down two to three weeks and sometimes four, but as a rule a reversal or change will occur in the third week and will only run three weeks against the main trend. In a Bull market two weeks' decline, or possible three, and in the middle of the third week the trend will turn up and close higher at the end of the third week. In some cases the change in trend will not come until the fourth week. Then the reversal will come and it will close higher at the end of the fourth week. All of these rules are reversed in a bear market.

Fifth, rapid advances or declines on big volume will run about seven weeks. These are culmination moves up or down. Watch for bottom or top around the 49th to 52nd day, although at times the bottom or top will come on the 42nd to 45th day and a change in trend will start.

Remember that at the end of any big movement, either monthly, weekly, or daily move, sometime must be consumed for accumulation or distribution. So, you must allow for this. Watch your angles and time periods. After a market has declined seven weeks, it may have two or three short weeks on the side and then turn up, which agrees with the monthly rule for a change in the third month.

In regard to daily time rules, the daily chart gives the first change but remember it may only run from seven to ten days, then follow the main trend. The weekly chart will give the next important change in trend but remember it may not run more than three to four weeks or in extreme cases not more than six to seven weeks, then reverse and follow the main trend.

The monthly chart may reverse and run down three to four months, then reverse and follow the main trend again, or run up three to four months in a bear market, then reverse and follow the main trend, although as a general rule, in a bear market stocks never rally more than two months. They start breaking in the third month and follow the main trend down.

Never decide that the main trend has changes one way or the other without consulting your angles from top or bottom and without considering the position you are in in the cycle of each individual stock. When extreme advances or declines occur, the first time that the market reverses over one-fourth or one-half of the distance traveled, in the last section, you can consider that the trend has turned up or down at least for the present.

It is important to watch space movements because when time is running out one way or the other, space movements will show a reversal by breaking back over 1/4, 1/3, or 1/2 of the distance of the last move, which indicates the main trend has changed.

HOW TO USE ANGLES FROM TOPS AND BOTTOMS

The angles to be used from a bottom of a stock up start from the point marked "O" and those starting down from the top of the chart marked "T" are the way they are put on from the top running down. Remember, the first thing to do when you want to put angles on from bottom to top is to draw the angle of 45°, then draw next the angle of 2 x 1 on each side of the 45° angle. In many cases, you will not have to use any other angles for a long time, then put on the other angles when they are necessary. Of course, if your stock is advancing very rapidly, then keep your 1 x 4 angle on and your 8 x 1. The same applies when it is having a sharp decline--keep your angle of 8 x 1 and 4 x 1 drawn down, using the scale of 1 point to each 1/8 of an inch, as shown on your Pattern Chart.

A stock to keep above the 45° angle must make a gain of one point per month, i. e. it must raise its bottoms one point per month. To keep above the angle of 8 x 1 going up, it must raise its bottoms eight points per month, and to keep above the angle of 4 x 1 it must raise its bottoms four points per month. To keep above the angle of 3 x 1, it must raise its bottoms three points per month, and to keep above the angle of 2 x 3 it must raise its bottoms 1½ points per month or make a gain of 18 points per year. On the left hand side of the angle of 45°, beginning with the angle of 6 x 1, the stock only has to make a gain of 2 points per year. If a stock cannot rise above an angle of this kind, it is in a very weak position and of course on the bear side of the square.

The angle to the left of the angle of 3 x 1 indicates a gain of 3 points per year and the angle of 3 x 1 indicates a gain of 4 points per year. The next angle of 2 x 1 indicates a gain of 6 points per year or 1/2 point per month.

Coming down after having broken the angle of 45° and breaking this angle, a stock is in a very weak position, especially if it is a long ways from the base, and indicates much lower prices.

The angle of 3 x 2 on the left rises at the rate of [illegible] 2 points in 12 months or a gain of 3/4 of a point per month in order to keep above this angle. It is not necessary to draw angles from a long ways back. You can make the calculation and determine where they cross. For example: Suppose in 1900, in the month of January, a stock made bottom at 15, and I want to calculate where the 45° angle will cross 20 years later in January, 1930. The 45° angle rises at the rate of 1 point per month, then 10 years would be 120 months or 120 points added to 15 at the bottom; the 45° angle would cross at 135 in January, 1930. All of the other angles may be calculated in a long way back in the same way.

I have marked on the Pattern Chart the measured degrees of the angles, which you will see are $3\frac{3}{4}°$, $7\frac{1}{2}°$, 15°, $18\frac{3}{4}°$, $26\frac{1}{4}°$, 30°, $33\frac{3}{4}°$, $37\frac{1}{2}°$, 45°, $52\frac{1}{2}°$, $56\frac{1}{4}°$, 60°, $63\frac{3}{4}°$, $71\frac{1}{4}°$, 75°, $82\frac{1}{2}°$, $86\frac{1}{4}°$, and 90°. You do not have to bother about measuring these angles. All you have to do to get the angles correct is to count the spaces and draw your lines or angles accordingly.

You will notice on your Pattern Chart how each angle drawn from the top and from the bottom prove themselves by the point at which they cross. For example: The angle of 8 x 1 drawn from "0" and the angle of 8 x 1 drawn from 90 down both cross at 45, 5-5/8 ints over from "0" counting to the right. Then take the angle of x 1 from "0" and 4 x 1 down from 90 and you will notice that they cross at $11\frac{1}{4}$ on 45, equal distance from the other angle and of course twice the measure.

The reason why these angles prove this way is because the 45° angle or 45 points, degrees, or anything else from "0" to 45 is one-half of 90. Therefore parallel angles beginning at "0" going up and at 90 coming down, must cross on a 45° angle or at the gravity center.

RULES FOR ANGLES FROM BOTTOMS

From any bottom, base or beginning point, two 45° angles can be started, one running up from the vertical angle and one running down from the vertical angle. You can also use a 45° angle or any other angle from any top, running the 45° angle down from the top, which indicates a decline of 1 point per month, week or day, according to your scale of prices; then running the 45° angle up from the top, which would indicate a gain of 1 point or 1 degree per month.

For example: Take the low of U. S. Steel on November 13, 1929, when it sold at 150. Start the 45° angle up and it gains 1 point per month; then start the 45° angle down from 150 and the stock has to decline 1 point per month to rest on the angle of 45°.

November, 1930, was 12 months from November, 1929, and S. Steel made low in November, 1930 at 138, which was on a 45° angle from the bottom at 150.

In December, 1930, U. S. Steel made an extreme low of 134-3/8. This was 2 points under the 45° angle from 150, but rested on the angle of 2 x 1 from the low at 111½, made in January, 1927. In December, 1930, U. S. Steel closed above the 45° angle from the bottom of 150. As long as it stays above this angle, it is in a stronger position, but to regain the strongest position, it will have to cross the angles of 45° from 150 on the up side and stay above this angle.

Remember that when any stock breaks under the 45° angle on the daily, weekly or monthly puts it in a very weak position and indicates a decline to the next angle. However, when a stock can regain the 45° angle, it is in a stronger position. The same rule applies to a 45° angle up from any top. When a stock crosses the angle on the daily, weekly or monthly and stays above the 45° angle, it is in a very strong position.

After a stock once drops below or gets above any important angle and then reverses its position by getting back above the angle or dropping back below it, it changes the trend again.

The angles on the Monthly and Weekly charts are, of course, of greater importance than those on the Daily charts, because the daily trend can change quite often, while only the major changes are shown according to the angles on the monthly high and low and weekly high and low charts.

Always consider the distance a stock is from its base or beginning point when it breaks any important angle or crosses any important angle. The farther away from the base, the important the change in trend, whether this be crossing an angle from the top or breaking under an angle from the bottom.

Each stock works out its own square according to its extreme high and low points or the square of its tops. For example: U. S. Rubber-- 143 was the total high to measure the width; then move over 143 spaces or 143 months to the angle of 90° down and divide up the square, as I have done on the monthly high and low chart. You can see how it worked out to the 1/4 of its square, 1/2, 3/4, 1/3, 2/3, etc. It will require 143 months to pass out of the square, or 11 years and 11 months. This period of time will end in December, 1931, which will be an important point to watch for a change in trend on U. S. Rubber.

WHY GEOMETRICAL ANGLES WORK ON STOCKS

Why is the 90° angle the strongest angle of all? Because it is horizontal or straight up and straight down.

What is the next strongest angle to the 90° angle? The 180° angle because it is square to the 90° angle, being 90° from the 90° angle.

What is the next strongest angle to the 180° angle? 270 because it is in opposition to 90, or 180° from the 90° angle, which equals 1/2 of the circle, the strongest point.

What is the next strongest angle after 270? 360 because it ends the circle and gets back to the beginning point and is opposite 180° or half-way point, or the angle which equals 1/2 of the circle.

What angles are next strongest to 90, 180, 270 and 360? 120° and 240° because they are 1/3 and 2/3 of the circle. 120 is 90 plus 30, which is 1/3 of 90. 240 is 180 plus 1/3 or 60, which makes these strong angles, especially strong for measurements of time.

What angles are next in strength? 45, because it is 1/2 of 90, and 135 because it is 90 from 45, and 225 because it is 45 from 180, and 315 because it is 45 from 270. The angle of 225° is 180 from 45 and the angle of 315° is 180 from 135.

The angles of 90, 180, 270 and 360 form the first important cross, known as the Cardinal Cross. The angles of 45, 135, 225 and 315 form the next important cross, which is known as the Fixed Cross. These angles are very important for the measurements of time and space and volume.

Why is the angle of 22½° stronger than 11¼°. Because it is twice as much, being the same reason that a 45° angle is stronger than a 22½. Again the angle of 67½ is 1½ times 45, therefore quite strong when anything is moving up toward 90°. 78¾ is stronger than 67½ because it is 7/8 of 90 and therefore one of the strongest points before we reach 90 and important to watch both on time, space and volume. Many stocks have important moves and make tops or bottoms around the 78th to 80th week, month or day.

Why are the angles of 1/8 of a circle most important for time and space measurement? Because we divide $1 into 1/4, 1/2, and 1/8 parts. We use 25¢ or one quarter, 50/ or 1/2 dollar, and long years ago we had 12½¢ pieces. But the most important figures of our basis of money are the four quarters, but we do use the 1/8 part or 12¢ in all calculations. Stock fluctuations are based on 1/8, 1/4, 3/8, 1/2, 5/8, 3/4, 7/8 and the whole figure. Therefore, any space measurement, as well as time, will work out closer to these figures when changed into angles of time than 1/3 or 2/3 points for the simple reason that the fluctuations moving in 1/8 proportion must come out closer to these figures. Figuring $100, or par, as a basis for stock prices and changing these prices to degrees, 12½ would equal 45°, 25 would equal 90°, 37½ would equal 135°, 50 would equal 180°, 62½ would equal 225°, 75 would equal 270°, 82½ would equal 315°, and 100 would equal 360°.

For example: When a stock sells at 50 on the 180th day, week or month, it is on the degree of its time angle. On February 1, 1915, U. S. Steel made a low at 38, which is closest to a price of 37½, which is 3/8 of 100 and equals a 135° angle. Steel was 14 years old or 168 months old on February 25, 1915 and hit the angle of 135°

which showed that Steel was behind time, but that it was in a strong position holding at 38 above the angle of 135°, or the price of 37½. Then when Steel crossed 200, it equalled 2 circles of 360°. When it advanced to 261⅝, it was closest to 62½ in the third 100 or nearest the 225° angle. It was the strongest angle after it crossed the half-way point or 180° angle. Steel's half-way point on the third hundred was 250; 262½ would be the next point, or 5/8 point, which equals 225°.

Under the instructions for the Master Timing Angles, you will find how far each timing angle had moved from the time Steel was incorporated up to the time it made extreme top. Study these timing angles and you will see what happens when each of the timing angles reach 24, 36, 48, 60, 72, 84, 90, 120, 135, 157½, 180, 210, 225, 240, 270, 300, 315, 330, 345, and 360 months, the equivalent of 360°. Under the Master Timing Angles we also show you what happens when timing angles #5, 6, 7, 8, and 9 cross the other timing angles, or the place where they were at the time Steel was incorporated. Of course these same rules can be applied to any other stock. You can see what happens when each of these Master Timing Angles returns to the same place it was at the time Steel was incorporated, or to the same place when any extreme high or low price is reached. You will learn when these Master Timing Angles return to the same place or to the same angle or degree from which they started. Therefore you will know the exact measurements of cycles according to moving energy. The instructions on the Master Timing Angles give you the cause of all market movements and they can be worked out ahead as far as the year 2000. The figures which we will use are figures made by the United States Government astronomers and are therefore absolutely accurate. A careful study of all these figures and a comparison of the movements of the various stocks will convince you of their value.

HOW TO USE GEOMETRICAL ANGLES

My Method of operating in the Stock Market is all based on mathematical points or geometrical angles. The Resistance Levels are all geometrical angles because they are 1/8, 1/4, 1/2, 3/4, 1/3, 2/3, etc., which are proportional parts of a circle whether large or small and, therefore, represent geometrical angles.

There are three important factors to consider, price, time and space movements. For example, when the price reaches 45, it meets resistance because it is equal to a 45° angle. Then when the price breaks a 45° angle, regardless of whether the price is at 45, 67, 90, 135, 180 or anywhere else, it weakens the position and equals a resistance angle, but is more important when a long ways from the base. The distance the stock breaks the angle of 45° or any other angle from the base is the most important. For example, many times a stock will rest on the angle of 45° in its early stages when advancing, then later in reaction rests on it again, then have a prolonged advance, react and rest on the 45° angle again, and then hit a higher level, break the 45° angle the fourth time, which places it in an extremely weak position because it is so far away from the base and so much time has elapsed since the stock made low level. Reverse this rule in a bear market or a decline and don't forget to consider that the Monthly and Weekly high and low charts are the most important when angles are broken. Daily charts can break angles and recover them and it is impossible for a daily high and low chart to maintain an angle of 45° for a very long period of time except when the final grand rush comes at the end of big bull campaigns.

Suppose at the time a stock breaks a 45° angle that it is at 135, and on the 135th month. This would be at a strong Resistance Level, breaking a strong angle, and striking and breaking a strong angle according to time. This would be time and space balancing at Resistance Levels, or geometrical angles, and would indicate a big decline to follow. Reverse the same rule at the end of a bear campaign.

After considering the three important factors, Resistance Levels, time and geometrical angles, the fourth and next very important factor is the volume of sales at tops or bottoms. Sales increase near the top and decrease near the bottom, that is, when a bear campaign has run for a long time and liquidation has about run its course, the volume of sales decrease, which is an indication that the market is getting ready to make a change in trend.

VANADIUM STEEL, WEEKLY HIGH & LOW CHART, VOLUME OF SALES.

This chart begins September 29, 1928. For each space 1/8 wide, I have used to represent 25,000 shares. For example, during the week ending September 29, 1928, sales were 26,600 shares and the high was 85 and the low 76 which is represented by 1/8. The same with the following week, when sales were 25,000 shares or less and the stock remained in a narrow trading range but gradually worked up until the week ending October 27th, when the volume of sales was 111,400 shares and the stock advanced to 88½. I made the space 4 wide to represent 100,000 shares. Then note November 10th, or the week ending November 10th, when the stock advanced from 84½ to 108, sales were 238,900 shares. The following week, sales were, 116,400 shares and the price only went 3 points higher. Then the stock broke the angle of 45° and declined to 85. During the week ending December 8th, and the following week, the price was around this same level, holding above the angle of 4 x 1 from the bottom, and failing to get back to the low reached during the week ending December 10th. The volume of sales on this decline was small. For the week ending December 22nd, sales were only 25,000 shares. Then the stock started up again.

During the week ending January 19, 1929, sales were 138,800. The following week sales were 61,200 and the next week with the stock getting only ½ point lower, sales were only 25,000 shares. Then followed a quick rally ending in the week of February 9th, with sales of 175,000 shares. This was top. A quick reation followed with sales of 74,200 shares. In the following week, the bottom was around the same level with sales of 153,000 shares. During the week ending March 2nd, sales were 51,500 shares. Then followed two weeks of small volume, 33,500 shares and 32,200 shares. Here the stock again broke under the angle of 22½, or 2 x 1 from the level of September 29, 1928 and a decline followed. Bottom was reached at 68 on the week ending June 1st, when sales were only 33,700 shares. The following week sales were only 27,000 shares which indicated that liquidation was not heavy and had run its course. The stock rallied to 97 during the week ending July 20th. The volume of sales was only 48,700 shares, not enough volume to indicate that the buying was strong enough to force the stock higher at that time. A decline followed and the volume of sales was small. Bottom was reached during the week ending August 10th at 77⅞. During those weeks the sales run 25,000 or less, getting down to 8,800 during the week ending August 31st which indicated that there was not much stock for sale at this price and that some one was just taking what was offered.

During the week ending September 14th, the stock was rushed up to 100 on sales of 138,400. Note that it failed to cross the top of April 6th, and that both of these tops were under the heavy volume of February 16th and 23rd, which indicated the big distribution that took place between 104 and 115 was by people who did not intend to buy the stock back for a long time and that when the stock approached the level of 100, they sold heavily again.

During the week ending September 28th, a decline followed on small volume, but the angle of 45° was broken and the stock continued to work lower. The volume increased during the week ending October 26th to 56,600 shares. The following week it was 50,600 shares, indicating heavy liquidation at this time. Then during the week ending November 9th and 16th, sales dropped to 17,200 shares and 29,000 shares. Final bottom was reached on November 13th at 37⅞. Then a rally followed up to the week ending December 14th, but the volume of sales was small only getting up to 31,000 shares and on the top week 21,000 shares. A reaction followed but the volume of sales was still smaller, 12,300, 11,300, and 13,800 shares. The bottom was reached during the week ending December 21st, when sales were 19,000 shares, then two narrow weeks on the side with the total volume not exceeding 25,000 shares. This indicated that the stock was thoroughly liquidated and was getting ready to go higher, but the week ending February 1, 1930, when the stock crossed the high of December 14th, volume of sales increased to 92,000 shares. Then during the week of February 8, there was a small reaction, but the volume of sales was only 23,000 shares. The advanced was resumed the following week and sales reached 62,400 shares. The next week the sales were 48,300 shares. Then during the week ending March 1, there was a small reaction but the volume of sales were only 36,500 shares which indicated that the buying was better than the selling, and that there was no heavy selling pressure yet. The advance was resumed and the volume of sales increased every week until the week ending March 29, when the stock sold at 124½ with a volume of sales of 206,000 shares. This was the largest volume of sales of any time since November 1928, a reaction of 20 points followed, but during the week ending April 5th, sales were only 83,600 shares. In the following week the stock made a higher bottom showing that the market had not yet reached top.

During the week ending April 19th, sales were 184,600 shares and during the week ending April 26th, sales were 258,100 shares. With the stock up 105 points from the extreme low, and the volume of sales almost equalling the total amount of stock outstanding, was a plain indication that top was being reached for a big reaction. During the week ending May 3rd a big decline followed sales reached 304,000 shares, an angle of 45° from the low at 103½ was first broken, then the angle of 45° from 37½ was broken and the stock declined to 87 during the week ending May 10th on sales of 310,400 shares, breaking all records up to that time. It got down near the angle of 22½°, or the angle of 2 x 1 from the low of 37½. It was a big reaction for two weeks period of time and came down 57 points. Figuring your low of 37½ to the high of 143¼, gives a half-way point of 90 3/8. The stock declined 3 3/8 points beyond this. This was due to the large volume of sales and the momentum. However, often a stock will go 3 3/4 points beyond the half-way point and then recover, especially if it has had a big decline. The greater the decline in number of points, the more allowance can be made for fluctuations around the main center or half-way point and, of course, Vanadium with a very small volume of floating supply of stock makes faster moves and wider range than a stock of large volume.

During the week ending May 10th, the volume of sales of 242,400 shares and the price crossed the top of the following week and advanced to 118½. The following week it advanced to 120¾ on sales of 248,600 shares, showing that the volume of trading was increasing on the way up but the price was not increasing in proportion.

During the week ending May 31st, the stock reached 124 on volume of sales of 135,700 shares, an indication that the selling was better than the buying and that when the price level approached where distribution started, it showed that there was again the very best of selling.

During the week ending June 7th, the price advanced to 125. Figuring the top of 143½ to the low of 87, the 2/3 points was at 126⅞. Then figuring the total value of the stock 143¼, we find the 7/8 point at 125 3/8. This made 125 a very strong Resistance Level because it was at the 7/8 point, of total value, and close to the 2/3 point on the fluctuating moves. Another reason why 125 was a strong Resistance Level is because 25 is 1/4 of 100.

During the week ending June 7th, Vanadium broke the angle of 45° from the low of 87 on heavy volume, the total sales for the week being 237,100. The price got down to 100 and rested on the angle of 22½°, or the angle of 2 x 1 from 37½. On June 9th, Vanadium broke 100 and, of course, was under the angle of 2 x 1 and declined to 89½, this time getting support around the gravity center, or half-way point, from 37½ to 143½. However, Vanadium is in a weak position on angles according to the volume chart, and in a weak position on angles according to the weekly chart, without volume, and the Monthly high and low chart and nothing but a rally is indicated at this time. However, if it can hold for a while and not break the low of 37 on May 10th, it will indicate a better rally, probably 1/3 to 1/2 of the recent decline.

From the low on November 13, to the high in April, the total volume of sales was 1,672,600 shares figuring 25,000 to each 1/8 space to move over each week would bring this over to the 67th space, which I have marked, and you will see from the volume chart that this runs over which is due to the fact that some weeks volume did not equal 25,000 shares. We have to register the top and bottom and this throws us out a little on balance. In the weeks of May 3rd and 10th, the total volume was 614,000 shares, bringing the grand total up to that time to 2,282,000 which brings it to space 91, on the week ending May 10th and puts our volume chart 6 spaces too far over. Note that the volume of these two weeks was about 1/3 of the total volume from 37½ to 143 3/4 and, of course, wiped out half of the advance. Therefore, it is only natural that a rally should follow because the decline was too fast according to time. Bringing the total number of sales up to the week ending June 7, we have 3,170,800 shares. This would bring us to space 126, marked in red ink, and the way we have the volume chart, it is 8 spaces too far over. Therefore, the volume for the week ending June 7th, with the space movement rested exactly on the angle of 2 x 1 from 37½, and 101 to 100¾ would strike up against this angle on the week beginning June 9th. The price on June 9th was 101¼, and the stock declined to 89½. After a stock gets away from a narrow series of fluctuations with small volume and keep your volume chart exact, so as your angles will work out better.

MONTHLY VOLUME CHARTS ON DOW-JONES THIRTY INDUSTRIALS FROM JUNE 1921 to MAY 1930

A study of this volume chart will prove very interesting and valuable. You can see that in June, July and August, 1921, the volume of sales was down to around, 10,000,000 to 15,000,000 shares per month. In March 1928, sales reached 80,000,000 per month for the first time in history. From this time on the volume of sales was very large, with this group of stocks working higher right along from the reaction in June 1928 when the price was 194 to the top in September 1929 when the price reached 381, there was never more than one month's reaction and at no time did the aver-

again break 10 points under a previous month's bottom. The volume of sales increased enormously in October, 1928, and continued large in November, December, and in fact, right on up until August, 1929, when sales were again over 100,000,000 shares, and the month of September sales were over 100,000,000 shares; see how the picture looks with this enormous volume at the top and then in October, the first time since May, 1929, the price broke under the level of the previous month, showing that the trend had turned down. All records for volume of sales was broken in the month of October, when sales reached 141,000,000. In the final reaction in November, or the last wave of liquidation, sales dropped down to around 80,000,000. Then the price worked up every month, making higher bottoms and higher tops with a fairly large volume, until March, 1930, when the volume of sales reached 90,000,000. In April, the total volume of sales reached 111,000,000 shares, a very small gain in price. In the early part of May the price broke under the bottom of the month of April, which was the first time since the low was reached in November, and a sharp decline followed. The volume of sales for the month of May was heavy, reaching 80,000,000; then continued in June on fairly heavy volume, with the price getting down to 250 on June 9th. This movement on volume from November, 1929 to April, 1930, shows a rally in a bear market.

Note the bottom from January, 1929 to May, 1929, and that the rally in April just brought prices up under this heavy volume of sales where distribution took place in 1929. Note that the scale on this chart is 2 points to each 1/8 of an inch instead of 1, for in considering the angles from the low in August, 1921 and the low in November, 1923, the angles are doubled in value, that is, the angle of 2 x 1 equals the angle of 45° and the angle of 4 x 1 equals the angle of 2 x 1 or 22½°. For example, the angle of 2 x 1 from the low in June, 1928 equals the angle of 45°. Note that the price rested on this angle in May, 1929, and that it was broken for the first time in October, 1929 and the big decline followed. Note that the angle of 4 x 1 from August, 1921, which is the equal of the angle of 22½°, or 2 x 1, fairly in April, 1930, come right up under this angle. Then consider the next angle of 4 x 1 from November, 1923, which is also equal to the angle of 22½°, notice prices in March and April got slightly above this angle, but that when the price opened in May, 1930, it dropped under this angle and then broke the angle of 45° from November, 1929 and the angle of 45° is really the angle of 2 x 1, or 22½°, counting the basis of the chart being at the rate of 2 spaces for one. Then the angle of 2 x 1, from November 1929 is equal to the angle of 45°. This angle crosses at 248 in June 1930, the same place where the angle of 2 x 1, from the corner of the top of October, 1919, angle of 2 x 1, or 45 as it is drawn across there, crosses, making 248 a very important point. Also note that the low in January, 1930, was 246. If this angle is broken and this low of 246, of January, is broken, it will indicate very much lower prices for these averages.

FAST ADVANCES AND FAST DECLINES

Why do stocks that have fast advances, reverse quickly and have sharp, quick declines before breaking the angle of 67½°, or the 45° angle on the monthly and weekly charts?

It is because the large volume of sales moves the prices over until the 45° angle is really broken at a very high level, which can be seen by making the combination time, space and volume chart. The volume chart shows that the angle is broken while the time chart, which only shows one space for each month or week, does not show the angle broken.

For example, make up a volume chart on U. S. Steel weekly from May 31, 1929 to date, and you will see that it broke so sharply after the high in September, 1929, because the volume broke the angle before the angles were broken by the weekly or monthly chart.

We are sending you Vanadium weekly from 1929 to date with volume. This will show you how the stock works when volume of sales is charted with time and space.

Why do stocks take such a long time to recover after a long decline and remain so long at low levels?

Because the volume gets so small near the bottom that it requires a long time to overcome the square of distance. When a stock declines 100 points or more in two or three months, for example, we will say exactly 100 points, then to overcome the square of distance at a low level, it requires 100 months. A stock has to square itself on the weekly, monthly and daily high and low chart. The lower the price crosses the 45° angle, the stronger the position of the stock and the higher the stock is and the greatest distance from the base, or beginning point when the 45° angle is broken or, in fact, any other angle, the weaker the stock is.

Why do stocks often cross the 45° angle on the daily, weekly or monthly high and low chart, then have an advance for a short period of time, decline and rest on the 45° angle?

It is because when they cross the 45° angle the first time, they have crossed it before they have run out or overcome the square of distance. Therefore, on the secondary reaction, when they rest on the 45° angle, it is at a time when they have reached the square of distance, and after that time a greater advance follows. Reverse this rule at the top of a bull market. This accounts for the stocks having a sharp, quick decline from the top and then advancing and making a slightly higher top or a series of slightly lower tops, working over until it overcomes the square of distance at a comparatively high level and breaks the 45° angle, then a fast decline follows.

What rule should be followed when stocks make higher bottoms and lower tops?

As stocks advance and make higher bottoms on the monthly, weekly or daily chart, you should always draw angles from higher bottoms. Then when you reach the last section of a bull market, and those important angles are broken from the last bottom, you know that the trend has turned down, Apply this same rule as a market declines. Draw your angles from each lower top and watch your angles until the stocks again cross the 45° angle from a second, third, or fourth lower top. The second lower top, or second higher bottom is always very important to draw angles from, and to measure time from, as well.

When a stock is in a very weak, or a very strong position, it will always show it by its position on angles, and a volume chart, made up according to the proper spacing with volume, that is, considering the total number of shares, will show when the stock is in a strong or weak position and show whether buying or selling predominates, enabling you to determine whether supply is increasing, or whether demand is decreasing.

WHAT RULE TO USE WHEN IN DOUBT

When you are in doubt about the position of a stock and do not know what its trend is, you should, of course, not trade in it. Wait until it shows by breaking resistance level, or crossing a resistance level, or until it crosses an important angle, or breaks an important angle before deciding which way it is going to move, especially after it has been in a long deadlock, or in a sideways movement, as referred to in "Wall Street Stock Selector." As a general rule, when a change in trend takes place of importance, the volume of sales will show it. The volume of sales usually increases when a stock starts to advance from low levels, or from dullness, and the same after a long period of dullness at a high level, when activity starts on the down side, the volume of sales increases. When a stock starts up and is in a strong position, it will show it on angles by keeping above strong angles from the bottom. The same when it starts to decline. If it is in a very weak position and going very fast, it will show it by the position of angles, that is, dropping below and keeping below strong angles, With the daily, weekly and monthly high and low chart, the important angles cannot be crossed at extreme low levels, until proper time has elapsed, neither can important angles be broken at high levels until sufficient time has elapsed. Therefore, the angles are very important because when broken they usually mean that the time has run out, whether you know it or not, and a change in trend will take place.

MASTER "12" CHART

The MASTER CHART is the Square of "12" or 12 x 12, making the first square end at 144. The Second Square of "12" ends at 288, the Third Square of "12" at 432, and the Fourth Square at 576, which will cover most anything that you want, but you can make up as many more squares as you want.

This chart may be used and applies to anything-- TIME,

SPACE OR VOLUME, the number of points up or down; days, weeks, months and years.

On Square No. 1, which runs from 1 to 144, I have drawn the finer angles to show the grand-center or strongest Resistance Point in each minor square. The minor centers, which are the strongest for minor tops and bottoms are 14, 17, 20, 23, 50, 53, 56, 59, 86, 89, 92, 95, 122, 125, 128, 131.

The major center is where the strongest resistance is met. These numbers are 66, 67, 78, and 79. Stocks going up or coming down to these prices will meet with stubborn resistance. The next strong angle is the 45°, and the numbers of greatest resistance are 14, 27, 40, 53, 66, 79, 92, 105, 118, 131, and 144. The other diagonal 45° angle from 12 is equally strong. The numbers are 12, 23, 34, 45, 67, 78, 89, 100, 111, 122 and 133.

The numbers which are cut by the 45° angles thru the center of each of the 1/4 squares are next in strength. These numbers are 7, 20, 43, 46, 59, 72, 61, 56, 39, 28, 17 and 6, and on the other side of the Square, after you pass the half-way point, these numbers are 75, 86, 99, 112, 125, 138, 139, 128, 117, 106, 95 and 84.

The numbers at the tops and bottoms of the squares are important prices for important tops and bottoms to be made because they are opposition numbers and are equal to the half-way point. These numbers for Square No. 1 are 1, 13, 25, 37, 49, 61, 73, 85, 97, 109, 121, 133. The top numbers are 12, 24, 36, 48, 60, 72, 84, 96, 108, 120, 132 and 144.

The opposition angle, which runs thru the center of the Square, from east to west, equally dividing it, is one of the very strong angles because it equals one-half. Any stock moving up or down and reaching these prices will meet with resistance and make tops or bottoms. These numbers are 6, 7, 18, 19, 30, 31, 42, 43, 54, 55, 66, 67, 78, 79, 90, 91, 102, 103, 114, 115, 126, 127, 138, 139.

Remember, when anything has moved three sections over from the beginning, it reaches the square of its own place, which is the first strong resistance. When it has moved six sections over, it reaches the opposition, or what equals the half-way point of its own place and meets still stronger resistance. Moving over nine places or sections from its own place, it reaches the 3/4 point, another square. The 8th and 9th sections are the strongest and hardest points to pass because this is the "death" zone. The next and still stronger is the 12th section or column which ends at 144. Anything getting into this section meets the strongest resistance but once it moves out of this Square and gets as much as 3 points into Square #2, that is, making 147, will indicate much higher, But after reaching this, it should not drop back 3 points or to 141 in Square #1.

When a stock gets into the Second Square of "12", it has faster moves, and when the time or number of months from any bottom or top moves into the Second Square, it is an indication of faster moves, both up and down.

Apply the same rule to the 3rd, 4th, 5th and 6th Squares, In the 3rd and 4th Squares of the Master "12", you will find that most of the big bull and bear campaigns culminate, when measured by months, which determines the division, according to time. All of the other rules given you to apply to Space movements, angles and time, can be used with the Master "12" tables.

SQUARE OF NINE

You have already had the MASTER SQUARE OF TWELVE explained, which represents days, weeks, months and years, and the measurements of TIME in the Square of Twelve or the Square of the Circle.

The SQUARE OF NINE is very important because nine digits are used in measuring everything, and we cannot go beyond 9 without starting to repeat and using the 0. If we divide 360° by 9, we get 40, which measures 40°, 40 months, 40 days, or 40 weeks, and shows why bottoms and tops often come out on these angles measured by one-ninth of the total circle.

If we divide our 20-year period, or 240 months, by 9, we get 26-2/3 months, making an important angle of 26-2/3°, months, days or weeks. Nine times 9 equals 81, which completes the First Square of Nine. Note the angles and how they run from the main center. The Second Square of Nine is completed at 162. Note how this is in opposition to the main center. The Third Square of Nine is completed at 243, which would equal 243 months or 3 months over our 20-year period and accounts for the time which often elapses before the change in the Cycle, sometimes running over 3 months or more. The Fourth Square of Nine ends at 324. Note the angles of 45° cross at 325, indicating a change in cycles here. To complete the 360° requires Four Squares of Nine and 36 over. Note that 361 equals a Square of 19 times 19, thus proving the great value of the Square of Nine in working out the important angles and proving up discrepancies.

Beginning with "1" at the center, note how 7, 21, 43, 75, 111, 157, 211, 273 and 343 all fall on a 45° angle. Going the other way, note that 3, 13, 31, 57, 91, 133, 183, 241 and 307 fall on an angle of 45°. Remember there are always four ways you can travel from a center following an angle of 45°, or an angle of 180° or an angle of 90°, which all equal about the same when measured on a flat surface. Note that 8, 23, 46, 77, 116 163, 218, 281 and 353 are all on an angle from the main center also note that 4, 15, 34, 61, 96, 139, 190, 249 and 316 are on an angle from the main center, all of these being great resistance points and measuring out important time factors and angles.

Study the SQUARE OF NINE very carefully in connection with the MASTER TWELVE and 360° CIRCLE CHART.

SIX SQUARES OF NINE

We are sending you six Permanent Charts, each containing 81 numbers. The First Square of Nine runs from 1 to 81. Everything must have a bottom, top, and four sides to be a square or cube. The First Square running up to 81 is the bottom, base, floor or beginning point. Squares #2, 3, 4 and 5 are the four sides, which are equal and contain 81 numbers. The Sixth Square of Nine is the top and means that it is times times as referred to in the Bible, or a thing reproducting itself by being multiplied by itself. Nine times nine equals 81 and six times 81 equals 486. We can also use 9 times 81, which would equal 729.

The number 5 is the most important number of the digits because it is the balance or main center. There are four numbers on each side of it. Note how it is shown as the balancing or center number in the Square of Nine.

We square the Circle by beginning at 1 in the center and going around until we reach 360. Note that the Square of Nine comes out at 361. The reason for this is it is 19 times, and the 1 to begin with and one over 360 represent the beginning and ending points. 361 is a transition point and begins at the next circle. Should we leave the first space blank or make it "0", then we would come out at 360. Everything in mathematics must prove. You can begin at the center and work out, or begin at the outer rim and work in to the center. Begin at the left and work right to the center or to the outer rim or square.

Note the Square of Nine or the Square of the Circle where we begin with 1 and run up the side of the column to 19, then continue to go across until we have made 19 columns, again the square of 19 by 19. Note how this proves up the circle. One-half of the circle is 180°. Note that in the grand-center, where all angles from the four corners and from the East, West, North and South reach gravity center, number 191 appears, showing that this point we are crossing the Equator or Gravity center and are starting on the other half of the circle.

We have astronomical and astrological proof of the whys and wherefores and the cause of the workings of geometrical angles When you have made progress, proved yourself worthy, I will give you the Master Number and also the Master Work.

Study the human body in every way and you will find that it is the work of a Master Mind, and when once you know yourself and know your body, you will know the Law and will understand all there is to know. Remember there is a source of all supply, and that you have within you the power to know all there is to know, but you must work hard, seek and you shall find.

CHAPTER 8

HOW TO FORECAST

HOW TO FORECAST

By studying the Tables and records given of past cycles and the time from tops to bottoms and from main bottom to main bottom and the time from main top to main top, you will be able to make up a forecast one year or more in advance. Then, by watching your weekly high and low chart and applying all of the other rules, you can tell when the main trend is changing.

After a bottom or top is made or at the beginning of any calendar year, you should go back over 3, 5, 7, and 10-year periods to see if the market is repeating and which one of these periods it is running closest to.

12, 20, AND 30 INDUSTRIAL AVERAGES

FROM MAIN TOPS TO MAIN TOPS OF BULL CAMPAIGNS

Year		Low	Time		From
1892	Mch. 4 and				
	Apr. 18	94½			
1895	Sep. 4	84½	42 months		Mch. 4, 1892
1899	Apr. 25	77.28	43 "	21 days	Sep. 4, 1895
	Sep. 5	77.61	48 "		Sep. 4, 1895
1901	Jun. 17	78.26	21 "	12 "	Sep. 5, 1899
1906	Jan. 19	103.	53 "		Jun. 17, 1901
1907	Jan. 7	96.37	11 "	19 "	Jan. 19, 1906
1909	Oct. 2	100.50			
	Nov. 19	100.53	46 "		Jan. 19, 1906
1912	Sep. 30	94.15	36 "		Oct. 2, 1909
1916	Nov. 21	110.15	49 "	22 "	Sep. 30, 1912
1919	Nov. 3	119.62	35 "	14 "	Nov. 21, 1916
1923	Mch. 20	105.38	40 "	17 "	Nov. 3, 1919
1929	Sep. 3	386.10	77 "	14 "	Mch. 20, 1923
1933	Jul. 17	110.50	46 "	14 "	Sep. 3, 1929
1934	Feb. 5	111.50	53 "	2 "	Sep. 3, 1929
1937	Mch. 8	195.50	37 "	3 "	Feb. 5, 1934
			43 "	19 "	Jul. 17, 1933
1938	Nov. 10	158.75	20 "	2 "	

It is important to study the TIME PERIOD between each important top and the next top.

During the period from 1892 to 1898 the time periods between the tops were as follows: There were 2 at 53 months apart; 7 at 42 to 49 months apart; 4 at 35 to 40 months apart; 2 at 20 to 21 months apart; and 1 at 11 months, 19 days.

One of the greatest Bull Markets of all time ... March 20, 1923 to September 3, 1929 ... was 77 months. This was abnormal, unusual, and an extreme, but it is well to know this time period because you may need to use it in the future.

From the above, you can see that most campaigns make tops between 3 and 4 years or between 35 and 49 months, only 2 cases running an extreme of 53 months and 2 running out in 20 to 21 months and 1 in a little less than a year.

FROM MAIN BOTTOMS TO MAIN BOTTOMS OF BEAR CAMPAIGNS

Year		Low	Time	From
1893	Jul. 26	62½		
1896	Aug. 8	28½	34 months 13 days	Jul. 26, 1893
1900	Jun. 23	53	46 " 15 "	Aug. 8, 1896
	Sep. 23	53	49 " 15 "	Aug. 8, 1896
1903	Nov. 9	42-1/8	40 " 17 "	Jun. 23, 1900
			37 " 16 "	Sep. 23, 1900
1907	Nov. 15	53	48 " 6 "	Nov. 9, 1903
1910	Jul. 26	73-5/8	32 " 11 "	Nov. 15, 1907
1911	Sep. 25	73-5/8	46 " 10 "	Jul. 26, 1910
1914	Dec. 24	53-1/8	39 "	Jul. 26, 1910
			48 " 28 "	Sep. 25, 1911
1917	Dec. 19	66	36 "	Dec. 24, 1914
1921	Aug. 24	64	44 " 5 "	Dec. 19, 1917
1923	Oct. 27	85¾	26 " 2 "	Aug. 24, 1921
1924	May 20	88-3/8	33 "	Aug. 24, 1921
1932	Jul. 8	40½	104 " 11 "	Oct. 27, 1923
			97 " 18 "	May 20, 1924
1933	Oct. 21	82½	15 " 13 "	Jul. 8, 1932
1934	Jul. 26	85	24 " 18 "	Jul. 8, 1932
1938	Mch. 31	97½	44 " 5 "	Jul. 8, 1932

The market always moves down in a shorter period of time than it moves up. It is important to study the distance between main bottoms in order to tell when the next one should come out.

There was only one period 49 months, 15 days apart; 6 at 44 to 48 months apart; 1 at 40 months; 6 at 32 to 39 months; 1 at 26 months; 1 at 24 months; and 1 at 15 months. Thus, you will see that more bottoms came out 3 to 4 years apart than any other time period.

The greatest time period was from the bottom of October 27, 1923 to the bottom of July 8, 1932 ... 104 months, 11 days. The next period was from the last bottom, May 20, 1924, to July 8, 1932 ... 97 months, 18 days. These great extremes occur at very rare intervals, but unless you know the greatest as well as the least movement, you cannot do accurate forecasting.

DOW-JONES 20 RAILROAD AVERAGES

FROM MAIN BOTTOMS TO MAIN BOTTOMS OF BEAR CAMPAIGNS

Year		Low	Time		From
1890	Dec.	76¼			
1893	Jul. 26	62	34 months		Dec. 1890
1896	Aug. 8	42	35 "	18 days	Jul. 26, 1893
1900	Jun. 23	73	46 "	15 "	Aug. 8, 1896
1903	Oct. 27	89-3/8	40 "	4 "	Jun. 23, 1900
1907	Nov. 23	81-3/8	48 "	27 "	Oct. 27, 1903
1910	Jul. 26	105-5/8	32 "	3 "	Nov. 23, 1907
1911	Sep. 30	109-5/8	14 "	4 "	Jul. 26, 1910
1914	Dec. 24	87½	38 "	24 "	Sep. 30, 1911
1917	Dec. 19	70¾	36 "		Dec. 24, 1914

The greatest time period between main bottoms was 48 months, 27 days; next 46 months, 15 days; next 40 months, 4 days; next 38 months, 24 days. There were 4 at 32 to 36 months apart and one minor at 14 months apart. Again, you will see that these important bottoms came at the end of 3 and 4-year periods.

FROM MAIN TOPS TO MAIN TOPS OF BULL CAMPAIGNS

Year		Low	Time		From
1886	Dec.	94½			
1890	May	99	41 months		Dec. 1886
1891	Apr.	89	11 "		May 1890
1892	Mch.	94½	22 "		May 1890
1895	Sep. 4	92½	41 "		Mch. 1892
1899	Apr. 25	87	43 "	21 days	Sep. 4, 1895
1902	Sep. 9	129.36	40 "	15 "	Apr. 25, 1899
1906	Jan. 19	138.29	40 "	10 "	Sep. 9, 1902
1906	Sep. 17	137.84	9 "		Jan. 19, 1906
1906	Dec. 11	137.56	51		Sep. 9, 1902
1909	Aug. 14	134.46	42 "	26 "	Jan. 19, 1906
1912	Aug. 14	124.16	36 "		Aug. 14, 1909
1912	Oct. 5	124.35	37 "	21 "	Aug. 14, 1912
1916	Oct. 4	112.28	48 "		Oct. 5, 1912
1918	Nov. 9	92.91	25 "	5 "	Oct. 4, 1916
1919	May 26	91.13	31 "	2 "	Oct. 4, 1916

There was one period between tops 51 months; one at 48 months apart; 6 at 40 to 43 months apart; 2 at 36 to 37 months apart; 1 at 31 months apart; 2 at 22 to 25 months apart; 1 at 11 months and 1 at 9 months apart. This again proves that most of the tops came out around 3 to 3-1/2 years apart and in extremes around 4 years apart. A few of them came out around 2-year periods and only 2 at less than one year, again confirming the working out of the 10-year cycle.

DOW-JONES 30 INDUSTRIAL AVERAGES

TIME FROM MAJOR AND MINOR TOPS TO MAJOR AND MINOR TOPS

High			Time				From
1895	Sep. 4		40	months	17	days	Apr. 18, 1892
1896	Apr. 22		7	"	17	"	Sep. 4, 1895
1899	Sep. 5		40	"	14	"	Apr. 22, 1896
1901	Jun. 17		21	"	12	"	Sep. 5, 1899
1906	Jan. 19		55	"			Jun. 17, 1901
1907	Jan. 7	Minor top	11	"	19	"	Jan. 19, 1906
1909	Oct. 2		44	"	12	"	" " "
	Nov. 19		46	"			" " "
	Dec. 22		47	"	3	"	" " "
1912	Sep. 30		36	"			Oct. 2, 1909
1915	Dec. 27		38	"	27	"	Sep. 30, 1912
1916	Nov. 21		84	"	2	"	Nov. 19, 1909
1917	Jun. 9	Last high	6	"	15	"	Nov. 21, 1916
1919	Jul. 14	Minor top	25	"	5	"	Jun. 9, 1917
	Nov. 3		35	"	13	"	Nov. 21, 1916
1920	Apr. 8	Second top	5	"	5	"	" 3 1919
1922	Oct. 14	Minor top	35	"	11	"	" " "
1923	Mch. 20		40	"	17	"	" " "
	" "		5	"	6	"	Oct. 14, 1922
1924	Feb. 6	Minor top	10	"	17	"	Mch. 20, 1923
	" "		15	"	23	"	Oct. 14, 1922
1925	Nov. 6		21	"			Feb. 6, 1924
1926	Feb. 11						" 6, 1925
	" "		34	"	22	"	Mch. 20, 1923
	Aug. 14		40	"	24	"	" " "
	" "		81	"	11	"	Nov. 3, 1919
	" "		76	"	6	"	Apr. 8, 1920
1927	Oct. 3	Minor top	13	"	19	"	Aug. 14, 1926
	" "		22	"	27	"	Nov. 6, 1925
1928	May 14		62	"			Mch. 20, 1923
	" "		27	"	3	"	Feb. 11, 1926
	Nov. 28	Minor top	27	"	14	"	Aug. 14, 1926
1929	Feb. 5		29	"	22	"	" " "
	" "		36	"			Feb. 11, 1926
	May 4		12	"			May 14, 1928
	" "		39	"			Feb. 11, 1926
	Sep. 3	Final top	118	"			Nov. 3, 1919
	" "		82	"	20	"	Oct. 14, 1922
	" "		77	"	14	"	Mch. 20, 1923
	" "		36	"	24	"	Feb. 11, 1926
	" "		9	"	6	"	Nov. 28, 1928
	" "		6	"	29	"	Feb. 5, 1929
	" "		4	"			May 4, 1929
	" "		1	"			Aug. 3, 1929

TIME FROM MAJOR AND MINOR TOPS TO MAJOR AND MINOR TOPS

1930	Apr. 17	Secondary top	7	"	14	"	Sep. 3, 1929
	Sep. 10	Top of rally	4	"	24	"	Apr. 17, 1930
1931	Feb. 24		29	"	21	"	Sep. 3, 1929
	" "		10	"	7	"	Apr. 17, 1930
	" "		5	"	14	"	Sep. 10, 1930
1931	Jun. 27		21	months	24	days	Sep. 3, 1929
	" "		14	"	10	"	Apr. 17, 1930
	" "		4	"	3	"	Jul. 23, 1931
	Nov. 9	Minor top	26	"	6	"	Sep. 3, 1929
	" "		18	"	23	"	Apr. 17, 1930
	" "		8	"	16	"	Feb. 24, 1931
	" "		4	"	13	"	Jun. 27, 1931
1932	Mch. 8		30	"			Sep. 3, 1929
	" "		22	"	20	"	Apr. 17, 1930
	Feb. 19		24	"			Feb. 24, 1931
	Mch. 8		4	"			Nov. 9, 1931
	Sep. 8		36	"	5	"	Sep. 3, 1929
	" "		28	"	22	"	Apr. 17, 1930
	" "		24	"	2	"	Sep. 10, 1930
	" "		18	"	15	"	Feb. 24, 1931
	" "		14	"	12	"	Jun. 27, 1931
	" "		10	"	1	"	Nov. 9, 1931
	" "		6	"			Mch. 8, 1932
1933	Jul. 17		10	"	9	"	Sep. 8, 1932
	Sep. 18	Lower top	12	"	10	"	" " "
	" "		2	"			Jul. 17, 1933
1934	Feb. 5		17	"			Sep. 8, 1932
	" "		6	"	19	"	Jul. 17, 1933
	" 15		5	"			Sep. 18, 1933
1935	" 18		19	"	1	"	Jul. 17, 1933
	" "		12	"	1	"	Feb. 5, 1934
1936	Apr. 6	Minor top	13	"	19	"	Feb. 18, 1935
1937	Mch. 8		90	"	5	"	Sep. 3, 1929
	" "		82	"	19	"	Apr. 17, 1930
	" "		78	"			Sep. 10, 1930
	" "		72	"	12	"	Feb. 24, 1931
	" "		54	"			Sep. 8, 1932
	" "		43	"	19	"	Jul. 17, 1933
	" "		37	"	3	"	Feb. 5, 1934
	" "		11	"			Apr. 6, 1936
	Aug. 14	Secondary top	49	"			Jul. 17, 1933
	" "		42	"			Feb. 15, 1934
	Oct. 29		7	"	21	"	Mch. 8, 1937
	" "		2	"	15	"	Aug. 14, 1937
1938	Jan. 15	Minor top	10	"	7	"	Mch. 8, 1937
	" "		5	"	1	"	Aug. 14, 1937
	Jul. 25		16	"	17	"	Mch. 8, 1937
	" "		11	"	11	"	Aug. 14, 1937
	Nov. 10		20	"	2	"	Mch. 8, 1937
	" "		10	"	5	"	" " "

DOW-JONES 30 INDUSTRIAL AVERAGES

BULL CAMPAIGNS---MAIN BOTTOMS TO MAIN TOPS

BEAR CAMPAIGNS---MAIN TOPS TO MAIN BOTTOMS

											Time			
1893	Jul.	26	low	62½	to	1895	Sep.	4	high	82½	25	months	9	days
1895	Sep.	4	high	82½	"	1896	Aug.	8	low	28½	11	"	4	"
1896	Aug.	8	low	28½	"	1899	Apr.	25	high	77.28	32	"	17	"
1896	Aug.	8	low	28½	"	1899	Sep.	5	high	77.61	36	"	28	"
1899	Apr.	25	high	77.28	"	1900	Jun.	23	low	53.63	14	"		
1899	Sep.	5	high	77.61	"	1900	Sep.	24	low	52.96	12	"	19	"
1900	Jun.	23	low	53.63	"	1901	Jun.	17	high	78.26	12	"		
1900	Sep.	24	low	52.96	"	1901	Jun.	17	high	78.26	8	"	24	"
1901	Jun.	17	high	78.26	"	1903	Nov.	9	low	42.15	28	"	23	"
1903	Nov.	9	low	42.15	"	1906	Jan.	19	high	103	26	"	10	"
1906	Jan.	19	high	103	"	1907	Nov.	15	low	53	21	"	27	"
1907	Nov.	15	low	53	"	1909	Oct.	2	high	100.50	22	"	17	"
1907	Nov.	15	low	53	"	1909	Nov.	19	high	100.53	24	"	4	"
1909	Nov.	19	high	100.53	"	1910	Jul.	26	low	73-5/8	8	"	7	"
1909	Nov.	19	high	100.53	"	1911	Sep.	25	low	73	22	"	6	"
1909	Oct.	2	high	100.50	"	1911	Sep.	25	low	73	23	"	23	"
1910	Jul.	26	low	73-5/8	"	1912	Sep.	30	high	94-1/8	26	"	4	"
1912	Sep.	30	high	94-1/8	"	1914	Dec.	24	low	53-1/8	26	"	24	"
1914	Dec.	24	low	53-1/8	"	1916	Nov.	21	high	110-1/8	23	"		
1916	Nov.	21	high	110-1/8	"	1917	Dec.	19	low	66	13	"		
1917	Dec.	19	low	66	"	1919	Nov.	3	high	119-5/8	22	"	14	"
1919	Nov.	3	high	119-5/8	"	1921	Aug.	24	low	64	21	"	21	"
1921	Aug.	24	low	64	"	1923	Mch.	20	high	105-3/8	18	"	24	"
1923	Mch.	20	high	105-3/8	"	1923	Oct.	27	low	85¾	7	"	3	"
1923	Mch.	20	high	105-3/8	"	1924	May	20	low	88-3/8	14	"		
1923	Oct.	27	low	85¾	"	1929	Sep.	3	high	386.10	70	"	7	"
1924	May	20	low	88-3/8	"	1929	Sep.	3	high	386.10	63	"	14	"
1929	Sep.	3	high	386.10	"	1932	Jul.	8	low	40½	34	"	5	"
1932	Jul.	8	low	40½	"	1937	Mch.	8	high	195½	56	"		
1937	Mch.	7	high	195½	"	1938	Mch.	31	low	97½	12	"	23	"

BULL CAMPAIGNS FROM BOTTOMS TO TOPS 1892-1939

There was one campaign 56 months apart; one at 36 months apart; one at 32 months apart; 4 at 24 to 28 months apart; 3 at 21 to 23 months apart; 1 at 18 months apart, 2 at 8 to 12 months apart. The greatest campaign ran from October 27, 1923 to September 3, 1929 ... 70 months, 7 days. Next from the last bottom, May 20, 1924, to September 3, 1929 ... 63 months, 14 days.

From the above, you will see that, except for the extreme move up to 1929, there was only one other period that ran above 4 years. The greater number of periods lasted between 2 years and 2 years, 4 months, only two periods running out in less than one year and one running out in 1-1/2 years, again proving the working out of the 1, 2, 3, 4, and 5-year periods in the 10-year cycle.

BEAR CAMPAIGNS FROM TOPS TO BOTTOMS

A Bear Market always runs out the same number of points or more in a much shorter period of time than a Bull Market. Like everything else that is going down hill, gravity helps to pull it down faster and momentum is gained faster on the downside than on the upside.

The greatest Bear Market of all time lasted from September 3, 1929 to July 8, 1932 ... a period of 34 months, 5 days ... a decline of 345-1/2 points, the greatest in history. The next periods were 2 campaigns of 26 and 28 months; 4 at 21 to 23 months; 6 at 11 to 14 months; 3 at 7 to 8 months. Thus, you will see that the greatest Bear Campaign ran out in less than 3 years and only 2 ran a little over 2 years, and 4 ran slightly under 2 years and 6 ran 11 to 14 months, about one-year periods, and 3 minor ones at 7 to 8 months apart.

This will help you to figure, after a market starts down in a Bear Campaign, how long it should run and by using your other tops and bottoms and time periods, you can tell about when it should run out. Before deciding that a Bear Market has made a final bottom, apply all of the rules and wait for a definite change in trend to the upside before deciding that final bottom has been reached.

DOW-JONES 30 INDUSTRIAL AVERAGES

BULL AND BEAR CAMPAIGNS

FROM TOP TO BOTTOM AND BOTTOM TO TOP

Year		Low or High		Points Up or down	Period of Time
1892	Mch. 4 and Apr. 18	high	94½		
1893	Jul. 26	low	62½	32	16 months 22 days
1895	Sep. 4	high	82½	20	23 " 9 "
1896	Aug. 8	low	28½	54	11 " 4 "
1897	Sep. 10	high	55-7/8	27-3/8	13 " 2 "
1898	Mch. 23	low	42	17-7/8	6 " 15 "
1899	Sep. 5	high	77-5/8	35-7/8	17 " 11 "
1900	Sep. 24	low	53	24-5/8	12 " 19 "
1901	Jun. 17	high	78¼	25¼	8 " 24 "
1903	Nov. 9	low	42-1/8	36-1/8	28 " 23 "
1906	Jan. 19	high	103	61	26 " 10 "
1907	Nov. 15	low	53	50	21 " 27 "
1909	Nov. 19	high	100½	47½	24 " 4 "
1910	Jul. 26	low	73-5/8	26-7/8	8 " 7 "
1911	Jun. 19	high	87	13-3/8	10 " 24 "
	Sep. 25	low	73	14	3 " 6 "
1912	Sep. 30	high	94-1/8	21-1/8	12 " 5 "
1913	Jun. 11	low	72-1/8	22	8 " 12 "
1914	Mch. 30	high	83½	11-3/8	9 " 9 "
	Dec. 24	low	53-1/8	30-3/8	9 " 2 "
1912	Sep. 30 to	high	94-1/8		
1914	Dec. 24	low	53-1/8	41	26 " 25 "
1916	Nov. 21	high	110-1/8	67	23 "
1917	Dec. 19	low	66	44-1/8	12 " 28 "
1919	Nov. 3	high	119-5/8	53-5/8	22 " 14 "
1921	Aug. 24	low	64	55-5/8	21 " 21 "
1923	Mch. 20	high	105-3/8	41-3/8	30 " 24 "
	Oct. 27	low	85¾	19-5/8	7 " 3 "
1924	Feb. 6	high	101¼	15½	3 " 10 "
	May 20	low	88-3/8	12-7/8	3 " 14 "
1929	Feb. 5	high	322	233-5/8	56 " 15 "
	" 16	low	295-7/8	26-1/8	11 "
	Mch. 1	high	321-1/8	25¼	13 "
	" 26	low	296½	24-1/8	25 "
	May 4	high	327	30½	39 "
	" 27	low	290	37	23 "
	Sep. 3	high	386	96	69 "
	Oct. 29	low	230	156	56 "
	" 31	high	273½	43½	2 "
	Nov. 13	low	195-3/8	78-1/8	13 "

INDUSTRIAL AVERAGES - FROM TOP TO BOTTOM AND BOTTOM TO TOP (Continued)

Year		Low or High		Points up or down	Period of Time
1924	May 20 to	low	88-3/8		
1929	Sep. 3	high	386	297-5/8	63 months 13 days
1929	Sep. 3 to	high	386		
	Nov. 13	low	195-3/8	190-5/8	71 "
1930	Apr. 17	high	296½	101-3/8	5 months 4 "
	Dec. 29	low	158½	138	8 " 12 "
1931	Feb. 24	high	196¾	38¼	57 "
	Jun. 2	low	120	76¾	98 "
	" 27	high	157½	37½	25 "
	Oct. 5	low	85½	72	100 "
	Nov. 9	high	119½	34	35 "
1932	Jan. 5	low	70	49½	57 "
	Mch. 8	high	89½	19½	63 "
	Jul. 8	low	40½	49	122 "
1929	Sep. 3 to	high	386		
	Jul. 8	low	40½	345½	34 months 5 days
1932	Sep. 8	high	81½	41	62 "
1933	Feb. 27	low	49½	32	5 " 19 "
	Jul. 17	high	110½	61	4 " 20 "
	Oct. 21	low	82½	28	3 " 4 "
1934	Feb. 5	high	111½	29	3 " 15 "
	Jul. 26	low	85	20½	5 " 21 "
1936	Apr. 6	high	163	77	20 " 11 "
	" 30	low	141½	21½	24 "
1937	Mch. 8	high	195½	54	10 " 8 "
1932	Jul. 8 to	low	40½		
1937	Mch. 8	high	195½	155	56 "
1934	Jul. 26 to	low	85		
1937	Mch. 8	high	195½	110½	31 " 10 "
1937	Jun. 17	low	163	32½	71 "
	Aug. 14	high	190½	27½	58 "
1938	Mch. 31	low	97½	98	12 " 23 "
	Nov. 10	high	158¾	61¼	7 " 10 "
1939	Apr. 11	low	120.07	38-5/8	5 " 1 "
1937	Aug. 14	high	190½		
1938	May 27	low	106½	84	8 " 13 "
1937	Aug. 14	high	190½		
1939	Apr. 11	low	120.07	70-3/8	20 "

INDUSTRIAL AVERAGES - FROM TOP TO BOTTOM AND BOTTOM TO TOP (Continued)

Year			Low or High		Points up or down	Period of Time
1939	May	10	high	134.66	14.59	29 "
	"	17	low	128.35	6.31	7 "
	Jun.	9	high	140.75	12.40	23 "
	"	30	low	128.90	11.85	21 "

MINOR TIME PERIODS 1892-1939

The above Table gives the number of points up or down and the time periods for major moves and minor moves of less than a year. There were 7 minor moves covering 8 to 9 months; 6 moves of 4 to 6 months; 2 moves of 7 months; and 5 moves of 3 months. This will show that you can watch for changes in trend around 3 months and then again around 4 to 6 months; a few changes around the 7th month and a greater number around 8 to 9 months. Many fast Bull Markets and Bear Markets have run out in 8 to 9 months once they got away from the Breakaway Point.

MINOR MOVES OF 17 TO 36 DAYS

These periods are runs that last over 2 weeks and culminate at the end of about 5 weeks. From 1896 to 1939, or in a period of 42 years, 10 months, 24 days, there were 204 moves on the averages running from 18 to 36 days. These were moves either up or down. This would mean that on an average every 2-1/2 months there was a reaction or rally lasting 18 to 36 days. Therefore, based on the average, when a market has advanced 3 to 4 months, with only 10 to 15-day reactions, you could expect a reverse move that would run possibly 36 days or more.

For 1929, 1930, 1931 and 1939, when the market was very active, we have shown the minor moves of 7 days or more and the number of points advance or decline, to help you check how far an active market will move in these shorter time periods.

DOW-JONES 30 INDUSTRIAL AVERAGES

FROM MAJOR AND MINOR BOTTOMS TO MAJOR AND MINOR BOTTOMS

	Low		Time	From
1896	Aug. 8	low 28½		
1898	Mch. 25		19 months 17 days	Aug. 8, 1896
1899	Dec. 18		40 " 10 "	Aug. 8, 1896
	Dec. 18		20 " 23 "	Mch. 25, 1898
1900	Jun. 23		46 " 15 "	Aug. 8, 1896
	Sep. 24		49 " 16 "	Aug. 8, 1896
	Jun. 23		6 " 5 "	Dec. 18, 1899
1901	Dec. 12		24 "	Dec. 18, 1899
	" 12		64 " 4 "	Aug. 8, 1896
	" 12		44 " 17 "	Mch. 25, 1898
1902	Dec. 15		12 "	Dec. 12, 1901
1903	Nov. 9		87 " 1 "	Aug. 8, 1896
	" 9		67 " 14 "	Mch. 25, 1898
	" 9		37 " 16 "	Sep. 24, 1900
1904	Mch. 12		4 " 3 "	Nov. 9, 1903
	May 18		18 " 9 "	" 9, 1903
1905	May 22		12 " 4 "	May 18, 1904
	" 22		18 " 13 "	Nov. 9, 1903
1906	May 3		30 "	" 9, 1903
	Jul. 13		32 " 4 "	" 9, 1903
1907	Mch. 14	and 25	40 " 5 "	" 9, 1903
	" 14		34 "	May 18, 1904
	Nov. 15	final low	48 " 6 "	Nov. 9, 1903
	" 15		42 "	May 18, 1904
	" 15		135 " 7 "	Aug. 8, 1896
	" 15		115 " 21 "	Mch. 25, 1898
1908	Sep. 22	low of reaction	10 " 7 "	Nov. 15, 1907
1909	Feb. 23		15 " 8 "	" 15, 1907
	" 23		5 "	Sep. 22, 1908
1910	" 8		11 " 16 "	Feb. 23, 1909
	" 8		16 " 7 "	Sep. 22, 1908
	" 8		26 " 24 "	Nov. 15, 1907
	Jul. 26		5 " 18 "	Feb. 8, 1910
	" 26		32 " 11 "	Nov. 15, 1907
1911	Sep. 25		46 " 10 "	" 15, 1907
	" 25		36 " 3 "	Sep. 22, 1908
	" 25		14 "	Jul. 26, 1910
1913	Jun. 11		20 " 15 "	Sep. 25, 1911
	" 11		34 " 15 "	Jul. 26, 1910
1914	Dec. 24		85 " 9 "	Nov. 15, 1907
	" 24		53 "	Jul. 26, 1910
	" 24		18 " 13 "	Jun. 11, 1913
	" 24		133 " 15 "	Nov. 9, 1903
	" 24		127 " 6 "	May 18, 1904
1916	Apr. 22		16 "	Dec. 24, 1914
	Jul. 13		18 " 19 "	" 24, 1914

FROM MAJOR AND MINOR BOTTOMS TO MAJOR AND MINOR BOTTOMS - 2

	Low			Time				From
1917	Feb.	2		25	months	9	days	Dec. 24, 1914
	May	9		28	"	15	"	" 24, 1914
	Dec.	19	low of decline	20	"			Apr. 22, 1916
	"	19		36	"			Dec. 24, 1914
	"	19		121	"	4	"	Nov. 15, 1907
	"	19		168	"	10	"	Nov. 9, 1903
1918	Nov.	25		11	"	6	"	Dec. 19, 1917
	"	25		47	"			Dec. 24, 1914
	Dec.	8	same low as 11/25					
1919	Feb.	8		19	"	6	"	Jul. 2, 1917
	"	8		48	"			Feb. 24, 1915
	Aug.	20	Minor bottom	20	"	1	"	Dec. 19, 1917
	"	20		56	"			" 24, 1914
	"	20		59	"	10	"	Jul. 30, 1914
	Nov.	29	and Dec. 22	60	"			Dec. 24, 1914
	"	29		24	"	3	"	" 19, 1917
	"	29		12	"			Nov. 25, 1918
1920	Feb.	11	and 25	61	"	18	"	Dec. 24, 1914
	"	11		26	"			" 19, 1917
	Dec.	21	low of big decline	60	"			" 24, 1914
	"	21		36	"	2	"	" 19, 1917
	"	21		25	"			Nov. 25, 1918
1921	Aug.	24		80	"			Dec. 24, 1914
	"	24		44	"	5	"	" 19, 1917
	"	24		165	"	9	"	Nov. 15, 1907
	"	24		134	"	2	"	Jul. 26, 1910
	"	24		119	"	1	"	Sep. 25, 1911
1922	Nov.	27	Minor reaction	15	"	3	"	Aug. 24, 1921
1923	Oct.	27	Last low	26	"	3	"	" 24, 1921
	"	27		70	"	8	"	Dec. 19, 1917
	"	27		11	"			Nov. 27, 1922
1924	May	20		33	"			Aug. 24, 1921
	"	20		18	"			Nov. 27, 1922
	Oct.	14		25	"	18	"	Aug. 24, 1921
	"	14		11	"	17	"	Oct. 27, 1923
	"	14		118	"			Dec. 24, 1914
	"	14		81	"	20	"	" 19, 1917
1925	Mch.	30		43	"	6	"	Aug. 24, 1921
	"	30		17	"	3	"	Oct. 14, 1923
	"	30		10	"	10	"	May 20, 1924
	Nov.	24		51	"			Aug. 24, 1921
	"	24		25	"			Oct. 27, 1923
1926	Mch.	30		12	"			Mch. 30, 1925
	"	30		22	"	10	"	May 20, 1924
	"	30		29	"	3	"	Oct. 27, 1923
	May	19		24	"	1	"	May 20, 1924
	Oct.	19		36	"			Oct. 27, 1923
	"	19		62	"			Aug. 24, 1921
	"	19		126	"			Apr. 22, 1916

FROM MAJOR AND MINOR BOTTOMS TO MAJOR AND MINOR BOTTOMS - 3

	Low	Time		From
1927	Jan. 25	10 months		Mch. 30, 1926
	" 25	22 "		" 30, 1925
	" 25	39 "		Oct. 27, 1923
	" 25	27 "	11 days	" 14, 1924
	" 25	119 "	28 "	Feb. 2, 1917
	" 25	110 "	6 "	Dec. 19, 1917
	Oct. 22 and 29	12 "	8 "	Oct. 19, 1926
	" 22	44 "	15 "	" 14, 1924
	" 22	48 "		" 27, 1923
1928	Feb. 20	16 "		" 19, 1926
	" 20	51 "	24 "	" 27, 1923
	Jun. 18	55 "	22 "	" 27, 1923
	Dec. 8	61 "	11 "	" 27, 1923
	Feb. 20	78 "		Aug. 24, 1921
	Jun. 18	82 "		" 24, 1921
	Dec. 8	87 "		" 24, 1921
1929	Feb. 16	90 "		" 24, 1921
	Mch. 26	91 "		" 24, 1921
	May 27	93 "		" 24, 1921
	Jul. 29	95 "		" 24, 1921
	Aug. 9	95 "	16 "	" 24, 1921
	Oct. 29	98 "	5 "	" 24, 1921
	Nov. 13	98 "	20 "	" 24, 1921
	Dec. 20	99 "	26 "	" 24, 1921
	Oct. 29	72 "	2 "	Oct. 27, 1923
	Nov. 13	72 "	17 "	" " "
	Oct. 29	60 "	15 "	" 14, 1924
	Nov. 13	61		" ", "
	Oct. 29	36 "	10 "	" 19, 1926
1930	Jun. 24	8 "		" 29, 1929
	" "	7 "	11 "	Nov. 13, 1929
	Dec. 17	61 "	23 "	" 24, 1925
	" "	120 "		Dec. 21, 1920
	" "	132 "	3 "	" 22, 1919
	" "	156 "	2 "	" 19, 1917
	" "	192 "	7 "	" 24, 1914
	" "	13 "	4 "	Nov. 13, 1929
1931	Apr. 29	17 "	16 "	" " "
	Jun. 2	18 "	20 "	" " "
	Aug. 6 and 10	20 "	24 "	" " "
	Oct. 5	22 "	22 "	" " "
	Aug. 6	119 "	13 "	Aug. 24, 1921
1932	Jul. 8	130 "	14 "	" " "
	" "	174 "	19 "	Dec. 19, 1917
	" "	210 "	23 "	" 24, 1914
	" "	247 "	23 "	Nov. 15, 1907
	" "	344 "		" 9, 1903
	" "	422 "	19 "	Apr. 19, 1897
	" "	431 "		Aug. 8, 1896

FROM MAJOR AND MINOR BOTTOMS TO MAJOR AND MINOR BOTTOMS - 4

	Low	Time		From
1932	Dec. 23	24 months		Dec. 17, 1930
	" "	36 "		" 20, 1929
	" "	85 "		Nov. 24, 1925
	" "	120 "	20 days	" 27, 1922
1933	Feb. 27	7 "	19 "	Jul. 8, 1932
	" "	26 "	10 "	Dec. 17, 1930
	" "	39 "	14 "	Nov. 13, 1929
	" "	112 "		Oct. 27, 1923
	" "	137 "	3 "	Aug. 24, 1921
	Jul. 21	12 "	3 "	Jul. 8, 1932
	" "	43 "	24 "	Nov. 13, 1929
	" "	120 "		Jul. 31, 1923
	Oct. 21	15 "	13 "	" 8, 1932
	" "	34 "	4 "	Dec. 17, 1930
	" "	47 "	8 "	Nov. 13, 1929
	" "	120 "		Oct. 27, 1923
	Jul. 21	4 "	24 "	Feb. 27, 1933
	Oct. 21	7 "	24 "	" " "
	" "	3 "		Jul. 21, 1933
1934	Jul. 26	24 "	18 "	" 8, 1932
	Sep. 17	26 "	9 "	" " "
	Jul. 26	17 "		Feb. 27, 1933
	" "	12 "	5 "	Jul. 21, 1933
	" "	9 "	5 "	Oct. 21, 1933
1935	Mch. 18	12 "		Mch. 27, 1934
	" "	17 "		Oct. 21, 1933
	" "	24 "		Mch. 21, 1933
	" "	24 "	19 "	Feb. 27, 1933
	" "	32 "	10 "	Jul. 8, 1932
	" "	120 "		Mch. 30, 1925
1936	Apr. 30	13 "	12 "	" 18, 1935
	" "	25 "		" 27, 1934
	" "	37 "		" 21, 1933
	" "	38 "		Feb. 27, 1933
	Dec. 21	12 "		Dec. 19, 1935
	" "	24 "		" 19, 1934
	" "	36 "		" 19, 1933
1937	Jun. 17	51 "	21 "	Feb. 27, 1933
	" "	59 "	9 "	Jul. 8, 1932
	Oct. 19	48 "		Oct. 21, 1933
	Nov. 23	32 "	5 "	Mch. 18, 1935
	" "	39 "	28 "	Jul. 26, 1934
	" "	49 "		Oct. 21, 1933
	" "	56 "	27 "	Feb. 27, 1933
	" "	239 "	4 "	Dec. 19, 1917
1938	Mch. 31	4 "	8 "	Nov. 23, 1937
	" "	23 "		Apr. 30, 1936
	" "	36 "	13 "	Mch. 18, 1935
	" "	48 "	4 "	" 27, 1934

FROM MAJOR AND MINOR BOTTOMS TO MAJOR AND MINOR BOTTOMS - 5

	Low	Time	From
1938	Mch. 31	61 months 4 days	Feb. 27, 1933
	" "	68 " 23 "	Jul. 8, 1932
	" "	117 " 13 "	Jun. 18, 1928
	" "	121 " 11 "	Feb. 20, 1928
	" "	132 " 9 "	Mch. 22, 1927
	" "	199 " 7 "	Aug. 24, 1921
	" "	243 " 12 "	Dec. 19, 1917
1938	May 27	11 " 10 "	Jun. 17, 1937
	" "	24 " 27 "	Apr. 30, 1936
	" "	48 " 13 "	May 14, 1934
	" "	60 "	" 22, 1933
	" "	84 "	Jun. 2, 1931
	" "	108 "	May 27, 1929
	" "	119 " 9 "	Jun. 18, 1928
1938	Sep. 26	5 " 26 "	Mch. 31, 1938
	" "	24 "	Sep. 25, 1936
	" "	48 " 9 "	" 17, 1934
	" "	59 " 25 "	Oct. 21, 1933
	" "	84 "	" 5, 1931
	" "	108 "	Sep. 29, 1929
	" "	120 "	" 27, 1928
1938	Nov. 26	60 "	Sep. 26, 1938
	" "	6 "	May 27, 1938
1938	" "	7 " 26 "	Mch. 31, 1938
	" "	12 "	Nov. 23, 1937
	" "	108 " 18 "	" 13, 1929
1939	Apr. 11	12 " 11 "	Mch. 31, 1938
	" "	16 " 19 "	Nov. 23, 1937
	" "	35 " 12 "	Apr. 30, 1936
	" "	48 " 24 "	Mch. 18, 1935
	" "	56 " 16 "	Jul. 26, 1934
	" "	65 " 22 "	Oct. 21, 1933
	" "	73 " 15 "	Feb. 27, 1933
	" "	81 " 3 "	Jul. 8, 1932
	" "	120 " 16 "	Mch. 26, 1929

The table below gives the re-actions in a Bull Market and the declines in a Bear Market, or the moves that are opposite to the main trend. The number of moves in each campaign is given and the number of weeks of re-action or rally in opposition to the trend. By going over these tables you will find that only six times in over forty-two years did a move in opposition to a trend last as much as eleven to fourteen weeks. We see that the average moves lasted from two to five weeks and a few from six to eight weeks. This will be a guide for you in future campaigns and enable you to figure about how many weeks a move will run in opposition to the main trend before the market again resumes the main trend.

Year	Moves	Weeks
	1st Bull Market Low Aug. 8, 1896	
1896	1	2
	2	5
1897	3	13
	4	7
1898	5	11
	6	8
1899	7	1
	8	5
	End of 1st Bull Market	
	1st Bear Market:	
1900	1	1
	2	3
	3	4
	4	2
	End of 1st Bear Market	
	2nd Bull Market:	
1900	1	1
	2	6
	3	2
1901	4	3
	5	1
	End of 2nd Bull Market	
	2nd Bear Market:	
1901	1	1
	2	3
	3	1
	4	5
1902	5	8
	6	3
	7	2
	8	4
	9	4
	10	1
	11	1
1903	12	3
	13	4
	14	1
	15	1
	16	1
	Nov. 9, 1903 End of 2nd Bear Market	

Year	Moves	Weeks
	3rd Bull Market	
1904	1	1
	2	6
	3	6
	4	1
	5	1
1905	6	6
	End of 3rd Bull Market	
	3rd Bear Market:	
1907	1	2
	2	5
	3	9
	4	4
1907	5	2
	6	2
	7	2
	8	2
	9	2
	End of 3rd Bear Market	
	4th Bull Market:	
1907	1	2
1908	2	4
	3	2
	4	5
	5	6
	6	6
	7	2
1909	8	2
	9	3
	10	4
	11	3
	End of 4th Bull Market	
	4th Bear Market:	
1910	1	3
	2	3
	3	2
	4	2
	5	2
	July 26 End of 4th Bear Market	

DOW JONES 30 INDUSTRIAL AVERAGES

Year	Moves	Weeks
	5th Bull Market:	
1910	1	4
	2	7
	3	4
1911	4	3
	5	14
	6	2
	7	2
1912	8	2
	9	2
	10	2
	11	2
	12	2
	End of 5th Bull Market	
	5th Bear Market:	
1912	1	2
	2	3
	3	2
1913	4	1
	5	2
	6	13
1914	7	6
	8	2
	9	4
	10	2
	End of 5th Bear Market	
	6th Bull Market:	
1915	1	4
	2	2
	3	12
	4	1
	5	1
	6	3
1916	7	5
	8	3
	9	6
	10	4
	11	1
	End of 6th Bull Market	
	6th Bear Market:	
1916	1	2
1917	2	7
	3	4
	4	3
	5	2
	End of 6th Bear Market	
	7th Bull Market:	
1918	1	7
	2	2
	3	2
	4	2

Year	Moves	Weeks
	7th Bull Market, Cont'd.	
1918	6	2
	7	3
	8	2
1919	9	5
1919	10	2
	11	5
	12	1
	End of 7th Bull Market	
	7th Bear Market:	
1919	1	2
1920	2	6
	3	2
	4	2
	5	5
	6	3
	7	2
1921	8	4
	9	2
	10	2
	11	4
	12	6
	End of 7th Bear Market	
	8th Bull Market:	
1921	1	2
	2	2
1922	3	3
	4	2
	5	2
	6	2
	7	7
1923	8	2
	End of 8th Bull Market	
	8th Bear Market:	
1923	1	1
	2	2
	3	2
	4	5
	5	1
	End of 8th Bear Market	
	9th Bull Market	
1924	1	1
	2	2
	3	6
	4	2
	5	2
	6	3
	Oct. 18, 1924	
1925	7	4
	8	4

DOW JONES 30 INDUSTRIAL AVERAGES

9th Bull Market, Cont'd.

Year	Moves	Weeks
1925	9	1
	10	1
	11	2
	12	3
	13	2
	14	7
	15	3
	16	1
	17	6
	18	6
1927	19	1
	20	1
	21	4
	22	1
	23	3
	24	2
1928	25	4
	26	2
	27	3
	28	2
	29	2
	30	2
	31	1
1929	32	2
	33	4
	34	3
	35	2

End of 1929 Bull Market

9th Bear Market

Year	Moves	Weeks
1929	1	1
	2	2

End of 9th Bear Market

10th Minor Bull Market or Rally in Bear Market

Year	Moves	Weeks
1929	1	2
1930	2	2

End of Rally in Bear Market

10th Bear Market

Year	Moves	Weeks	
1930	1	2	rally
	2	3	
	3	4	rally & 11 weeks from low
	4	1	
	5	2	
	6	3	
1931	7	5	rally & 10 weeks from low
	8	1	
	9	1	
	10	3	
	11	1	

10th Bear Market, Cont'd.

Year	Moves	Weeks
1931	12	1
	13	5
	14	2
	15	1
	16	2
	17	1

End of Bear Market July 8, 1932

11th Bull Market July 8, 1932 to Sept. 1932.

1st Sharp advance lasted 9 weeks no reactions followed by 25 weeks decline which was a reaction in a bull market or accumulation on the side. The greatest rally lasted 6 weeks and the last decline 7 weeks making bottom Feb. 27, 1933.

Bull Market Resumed

1933	1 move	2 weeks
	2 moves	1 week
	3 moves	1 week

July 17th to 21st declined 26 points. Then followed a trading market or accumulation on the side lasting 91 weeks until March 30, 1935 during this time the averages did not advance 2 points above the high of July 17, 1933 nor decline more than 2 points under the low of July 21, 1933. Holding in a range of 27 points. This long period of time indicated that when the averages crossed 112 the old tops in March 1935 that they would go very much higher and final top was made March 10, 1937 with the averages at 195½.

DOW JONES 30 INDUSTRIAL AVERAGES

From July 21, 1933 to March 30, 1935 the moves were as follows:

1 weeks rally
1 weeks reaction
7 weeks advance to Sept. 1933 making a total of 9 weeks rally.
4 weeks decline to 82½, Oct. 21, 1933. This was the extreme low of the reaction and was 13 weeks from July 21, 1933. The next rally lasted 14 weeks to February 5, 1934, high 111½, then declined to July 26, 1934. The last low 84½ - 24 weeks from February 5, 1934. There was no rally lasting more than 4 weeks and from this low the Bull Market was resumed. February 5, 1934 to July 26, 1934, 11-A Minor Bear Market or reaction in a Bull Market.

Year	Moves	Weeks
	11th Bull Market, Con't.	
1934	1	4
	2	2
	3	2
1935	4	3
	5	4
	March 18, 1935 last low	
	6	1
	7	2
	8	2
	9	4
1936	10	1
	11	1
	12	1
	13	3
	14	1
	15	1
	16	2
	17	1
	18	1
	19	5
1937	20	1
	21	2
	End of 11th Bull Market March 10, 1937.	
	11th Bear Market	
1937	1	2
	2	1
	3	2
	4	8 rally to Aug. 14, 1937
	5	1
	6	2
1938	7	2
	8	2
March 31, 1938 End of 11th Bear Market		

Year	Moves	Weeks
	12th Bull Market	
1938	1	2
	2	2
	3	1 August reaction
	4	4 weeks reaction or 8 weeks from top
Nov. 10, 1938 End of 12th Bull Market		
	12th Minor Bear Market	
1938	1	4
	2	6

DOW JONES 30 RAILROAD AVERAGES

Year	Moves	Weeks
	Reactions in Bull Market	
1897	1	5
	2	8
1898	3	8
	5	6
	6	8
1899	7	8
	End of 1st Bull Market	
	Rallies in Bear Market	
1899	1	13
	2	4
1900	3	15
	End of 1st Bear Market	
	2nd Bull Market:	
1900	1	5
1901	2	1
1901	3	8
	4	2
	5	3
	6	2
	7	3
	End of 2nd Bull Market	
	2nd Bear Market:	
1902	1	4
	2	3
	3	2
	4	2
	End of 2nd Bear Market	
	3rd Bull Market:	
1903	1	2
1904	2	7
	3	5
	4	2
1905	5	6
	6	2
	7	3
	End of 3rd Bull Market	
	3rd Bear Market:	
1906	1	3
	2	6
	3	9
	5	1
	6	2
	7	5
	8	4
	End of 3rd Bear Market	

Year	Moves	Weeks
	4th Bull Market:	
1908	1	4
	2	5
	3	2
	4	8
1909	5	2
	End of 4th Bull Market	
	4th Bear Market:	
1909	1	2
	2	4
1910	3	4
	4	2
	5	2
	6	2
	7	1
	End of 4th Bear Market	
	5th Bull Market:	
1910	1	3
	2	7
1911	3	3
	4	3
	5	10
1912	6	10
	7	10
	End of 5th Bull Market	
	5th Bear Market:	
1912	1	4
	2	1
	3	3
1913	4	3
	5	2
	6	13
	7	6
	8	2
	9	4
	10	2

5th Bear Market ended Dec. 24, 1914

CHAPTER 9

THE BASIS OF MY FORECASTING METHOD

TRUTH OF THE STOCK TAPE
WALL STREET STOCK SELECTOR
NEW STOCK TREND DETECTOR
HOW TO MAKE PROFITS IN COMMODITIES

AMERICAN ECONOMIC ASS'N
ROYAL ECONOMIC SOCIETY

W. D. GANN
82 WALL STREET
NEW YORK 5, N. Y.

THE BASIS OF MY FORECASTING METHOD

Mathematics is the only exact science. All power under heaven and on earth is given unto the man who masters the simple science of mathematics. Emerson said: "God does indeed geometrize." Another wise man said: "There is nothing in the universe but mathematical points." Pythagoras, one of the greatest mathematicians that ever lived, after experimenting with numbers and finding the proofs of all natural laws, said: "Before God was numbers." He believed that the vibration of numbers created God and the Diety. It has been said, "Figures don't lie." Men have been convinced that numbers tell the truth and that all problems can be solved by them. The chemist, engineer, astronomer would be lost without the science of mathematics.

It is so simple and easy to solve problems and get correct answers and results with figures that it seems strange so few people rely on them to forecast the future of business, stocks and commodity markets. The basic principles are easy to learn and understand. No matter whether you use geometry, trigonometry, or calculus, you use the simple rules of arithmetic. You do only two things: You increase or decrease.

There are two kinds of numbers, odd and even. We add numbers together, which is increasing. We multiply, which is a shorter way to increase. We subtract, which decreases, and we divide, which also decreases. With the use of higher mathematics, we find a quicker and easier way to divide, subtract, add and multiply, yet very simple when you understand it.

Everything in nature is male and female, white and black, harmony or inharmony, right and left. The market moves only two ways, up and down. There are three dimensions which we know how to prove--width, length and height. We use three figures in geometry--the circle, the square, and the triangle. We get the square and triangle points of a circle to determine points of time, price and space resistance. We use the circle of 360 degrees to measure Time and Price.

There are three kinds of angles--the vertical, the horizontal, and the diagonal, which we use for measuring time and price movements. We use the square of odd and even numbers to get not only the proof of market movements, but the cause.

HOW TO MAKE CHARTS

Charts are records of past market movements. The future is but a repetition of the past. There is nothing new. As the Bible says--"The thing that hath been, it is that which shall be." History repeats and with charts and rules we determine when and how it is going to repeat. Therefore, the first and most important point to learn is how to make charts correctly because if you make an error in the chart, you will make an error in applying the rules to your trading.

YEARLY CHART: You should keep a yearly high and low chart, that is, recording the extreme low and the extreme high price made during the calendar year on one line. The spacing for the price can be used one point to each 1/8 inch or two points or more, according to the activity and range of the stock.

MONTHLY CHART: You must always keep up a monthly high and low chart, which is the most important chart of all in determining the main trend. This chart records the extreme high and extreme low price for the calendar month on one line, and each space or 1/8 inch on the cross-section chart paper should represent one point or $1 per share.

WEEKLY CHART: The next and one of the very important charts to keep is a weekly high and low chart. Where stocks are selling below 50, it usually pays to make this chart up using each 1/8 inch to represent one-half point, or two spaces to represent one full point, or four points for each one-inch space. When stocks become very active, especially when they are selling above $100 per share, then you can make up the weekly chart using each space or 1/8 inch on the chart paper to represent one point or $1 per share.

SEMI-WEEKLY OR 3-DAY CHART: The next chart of importance to the Weekly Chart is a 3-day chart, that is, taking the extreme high and extreme low price made from the opening of the market on Monday morning until the close on Wednesday night, closing the chart on Wednesday night- then from the opening on Thursday to the close on Saturday, taking the extreme high and low and closing the chart on Saturday. This gives you a time period showing one-half of the week. This chart is very important as will be explained later on in the instructions. The spacing for this chart can be the same as for the weekly high and low chart.

WEEKLY MOVING-AVERAGE OR MEAN POINT: To get a Weekly Moving-Average, we take the extreme low for the week and the extreme high for the week and divide by 2, getting the half-way or mean point for the week. This can be recorded on the weekly high and low chart or on a separate chart, recording the Weekly Moving-Average with a dot and using one line on the chart for each week. Importance of this Weekly Mean Point will be explained later.

DAILY CHART: When you are trading in a stock that is active, you should always keep up a daily high and low chart, but for study purposes it is enough to keep up the Weekly and Monthly Charts, which give you the main trend. The Daily Chart shows the minor trend and shows a change in trend much oftener than any of the other charts, but the indication does not last as long or run so far. This chart should be kept up the same as the others, except when stocks are selling below 50 or when they are in an inactive trading range- then the spacing should be 1/2-point to each 1/8-inch on the chart paper, allowing two spaces to represent one full point or $1 per share. When stocks are active and advancing very fast, making a wide range each day, then you can make the Daily Chart the same as the Weekly or Monthly, that is, using one point for each 1/8-inch on the chart paper. This spacing cuts the chart down and keeps it in a range where it is easy to see and read when fluctuations are wide.

No spaces are skipped on the Daily Chart for holidays or Sundays, therefore the time period is for actual market days and not calendar days. However, you should carry the calendar days along at least every two weeks, as later, under rules for Time Periods for change in trend, you will find that it is necessary to check up and know when the stock is 30, 60, 80, 120, 135, etc. days from a top or a bottom, which means calendar days, the exact measurement of Time for the daily chart. Often the Daily Chart on actual daily movements comes out on an exact mathematical angle of time measurement at the same time the calendar days come out on exact time measurement, making it a doubly important point for change in trend.

GEOMETRICAL ANGLES

:::::::::: ::::::

After long years of practical experience, I have discovered that Geometrical Angles measure accurately Space, Time, Volume and Price.

Mathematics is the only exact science, as I have said before. Every nation on the face of the earth agrees that 2 and 2 make 4, no matter what language it speaks. Yet all other sciences are not in accord as mathematical science. We find different men in different professions along scientific lines disagreeing on problems, but there can be no disagreement in mathematical calculation.

There are 360 degrees in a circle, no matter howlarge or how small the circle may be. Certain numbers of these degrees and angles are of vast importance and indicate when important tops and bottoms occur on stocks, as well as denote important Resistance Levels. When once you have thoroughly mastered the Geometrical Angles, you will be able to solve any problem and determine the trend of any stock.

After 35 years of research, tests and practical applications, I have perfected and proved the most important angles to be used in determining the trend of the stock market. Therefore, concentrate on these angles until you thoroughly understand them. Study and experiment with each rule I give you, and you will make a success.

We use geometrical angles to measure Space and Time periods because it is a shorter and quicker method than addition or multiplication, provided you follow the rules and draw the angles or lines accurately from tops and bottoms or extreme highs and lows. You may make a mistake in addition or multiplication, but the geometrical angles accurately drawn will correct this mistake. For example: If you should count across the bottom of your chart 120 spaces, which represents 120 days, weeks, or months, then you begin at "O" and number vertically on your chart up to 120- then from this top point at 120 draw a 45-degree angle moving down, this will come out at "O" on 120 points over from the beginning. If you have made a mistake in numbering, this will correct it.

Angles drawn on a chart always keep before you the position of the stock and its trend whereas if you had a resistance point on time written down, you might mislay it or forget it but these angles are always on the chart in front of you.

These angles or moving-average trend lines correctly drawn will keep you from making mistakes or misjudging the trend. If you wait and follow your rules, these angles will show you when the trend changes.

The <u>moving-average</u> as commonly used is obtained by taking the extreme low price and the extreme high price of the calendar day, week or month, and dividing it by two to get the mean or average price for the day, week or month, and continuing this at the end of each time period. This is an irregular movement in spaces or points per week because at one time it may move up 2 points per week and at another 5 points per week, while the time period is a regular unit. Therefore geometrical angles, which are really moving-averages, move up or down at an uniform rate from any bottom or top on a daily, weekly or monthly chart.

HOW TO DRAW GEOMETRICAL ANGLES

There are three important points that we can prove with mathematics or geometry: the Circle, the Square, and the Triangle. After I have made the Square I can draw a Circle in it using the same diameter, and thereby produce the Triangle, the Square and the Circle.

The Angles or moving-trend-line averages measure and divide Time and Price into proportionate parts. Refer to Form "1", where I have drawn the square of 28. You will note that this is 28 high and 28 wide- in other words, 28 up and 28 across. It is the same as a square room which has a bottom or floor, a top or ceiling, and side walls. Everything has width, length, and height.

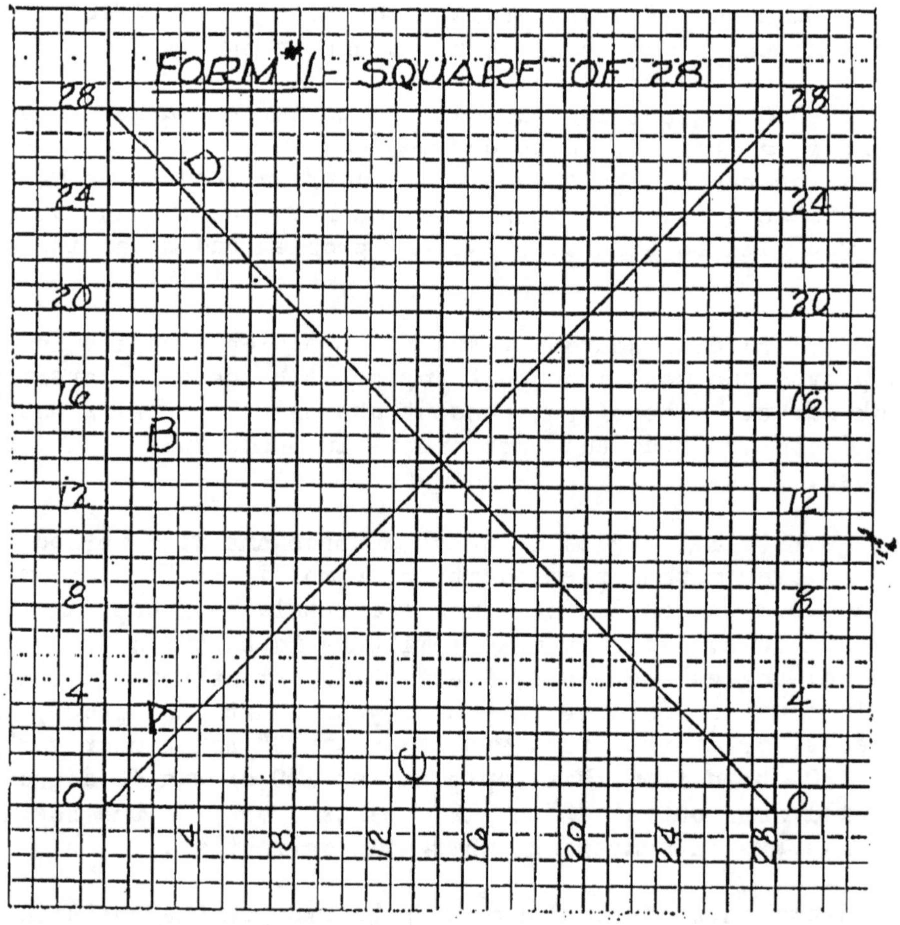

To get the strongest and most important points in this Square, I divide it into two equal parts by drawing a horizontal and a vertical line. Note angle marked "A", which divides each of the smaller squares into two equal parts and runs from "0" to "28" diagonally. This is a diagonal line moving on a 45° angle and divides the large Square into two equal parts. Then note angle "B" at "14" running horizontally across. This divides the Square into two equal parts. Note angle "C", which is a vertical line, running up from "14", which is one-half of "28". This crosses at the center or half-way point at 14, where the other angles cross, dividing the Square into two equal parts. Then note angle "D", which forms another 45° angle moving from the N. W. corner to the S. E. corner, crossing "14" at the exact half-way point. You see by this that if we draw the first line thru the center of the square, we divide it into two equal parts- then when we draw lines from the other directions, we divide it into four equal parts-then by drawing the two lines from each corner, we divide the square into 8 equal parts and produce 8 triangles.

As you look at this Square, it should be easy for you to tell with your eye where the strongest support point is or resistance point is It is at the center where all the angles cross. Four angles cross at this point, so naturally this would be a stronger support point than a place where only one angle crosses. I could divide each one of these smaller squares into four or eignt equal parts by drawing angles in the same way. Later, when I give you the rules and examples, I will explain how to square the Range of a stock, that is, the difference between the extreme low and the extreme high prices, or the difference between any low point and any high point, and also how to square the bottom price. For example: If the top of a stock is 28, this Square of 28 x 28 would represent squaring the Price by Time, because if we have 28 points up in Price, and we move over 28 spaces in Time, we square the Price with Time. Therefore, when the stock has moved over 28 days, 28 weeks, or 28 months, it will be squaring its price range of 28.

PATTERN CHART FOR GEOMETRICAL ANGLES

The Square of 90, or the Pattern Chart, shows all the measured angles that are important to use in determining the position of a stock. These angles are as follows: 3¾, 7½, 15, 18¾, 26¼, 30, 33¾, 37½, 45, 52½, 56¼, 60, 63¾, 71¼, 75, 82½, 86¼, and 90 degrees.

It is not necessary to measure these angles with a protractor. All you have to do to get the angles correct is to count the spaces on the chart paper, using 8 x 8 to the inch, and draw the lines or angles accordingly.

On the square of 90, which you will receive with these instructions, note how equal angles drawn from the top and from the bottom prove themselves by the point at which they cross. For example:

The angle of 8 x 1 drawn from "0" and the angle of 8 x 1 drawn from "90" down both cross at 45, 5-5/8 points over from "0" counting to the right. Then, the angle of 4 x 1 from "0" and the angle of 4 x 1 down from "90", you will notice, cross at 11¼ on 45, equidistant from the other angle and twice the measure. The reason why these angles prove this way is because the 45° angle or 45 points or degrees from "0" to 45 is one-half of 90. Therefore, parallel angles beginning at "0" going up and at 90 coming down, must cross on a 45° angle or at the gravity center.

HOW TO DRAW ANGLES FROM A LOW POINT RECORDED BY A STOCK

An example marked "Form 2" shows you the most important angles to use when a stock is working higher and advancing. (See page 6)

FIRST IMPORTANT GEOMETRICAL ANGLE: 45° or 1 x 1 The first and always most important angle to draw is a 45-degree angle or a moving-average that moves up one point per day, one point per week or one point per month. This is a 45° angle because it divides the Space and Time Periods into two equal parts As long as the market or a stock stays above the 45° angle, it is in a strong position and indicates higher prices. You can buy every time a stock rests on the 45° angle with a stop loss order one, two or three points under the 45° angle, but remember the rule— never use a stop loss order more than 3 points away. Unless stocks are near the low levels or just starting in a bull market or selling at very low prices, I always use a stop loss order one point under the 45° angle. If this angle is broken by one point, you will usually find that the trend has changed at least temporarily and the stock will go lower.

An easy way to calculate accurately how to put on this 45° angle is: For example: If the time is 28 days, 28 weeks, or 28 months from the point where the stock was bottom, then the angle of 45° must be 28 points up from the bottom and would cross at 28. This is one of the easiest angles to put on and one of the simplest to learn. You can beat the market by trading against the 45° angle alone if you stick to the rule—— wait to buy a stock on the 45° angle or wait to sell it against the 45° angle.

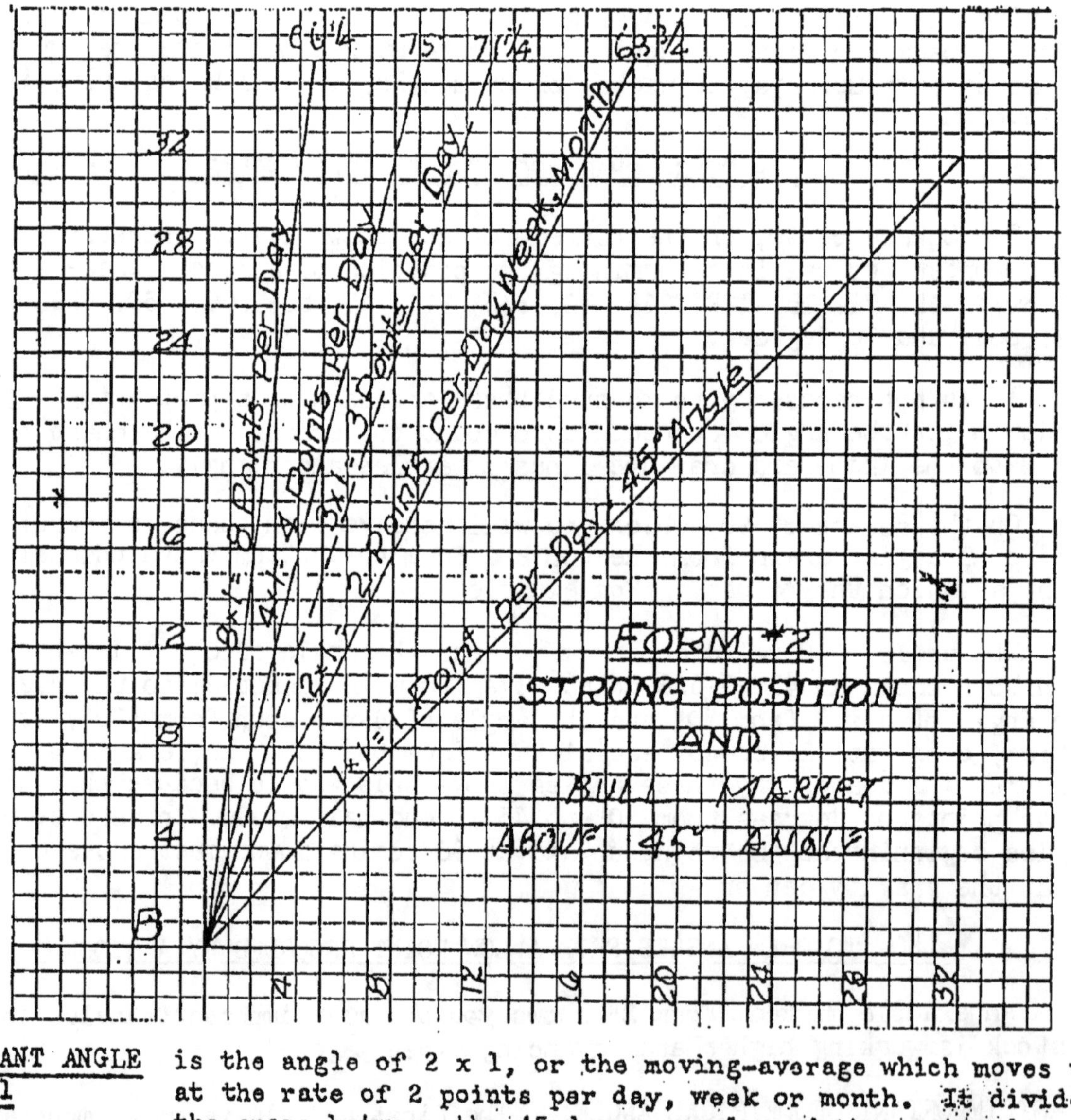

NEXT IMPORTANT ANGLE 2 x 1 is the angle of 2 x 1, or the moving-average which moves up at the rate of 2 points per day, week or month. It divides the space between the 45-degree angle and the vertical angle into two equal parts and measures 63¾°. That is why it is the next strongest and most important angle. As long as a stock holds above this angle, it is in a stronger position than when it is resting on a 45° angle because it is a more acute angle. When a stock breaks under this angle of 2 x 1, or two points for each time period, then it indicates that it will go lower and reach the 45° angle. Remember the rule of all angles: No matter what angle the stock breaks under, it indicates a decline to the next angle below it.

THIRD IMPORTANT ANGLE, 4×1 which is still stronger as long as a stock holds above it, is the angle which moves up 4 points per day, week, or month. This angle is 4 x 1, or 4 points of Space equal one period of Time. It measures 75° and divides the space between the angle of 2 x 1 and the 90° angle into two equal parts. Any stock that continues to advance 4 points per day, 4 points per week, or 4 points per month, and remains above this angle is in a very strong position as long as it stays above it, but when it breaks under, it indicates the next angle or next support point according to the position of the stock on Time.

FOURTH IMPORTANT ANGLE 8×1 is the angle of 8 x 1 or the one that moves up 8 points per day, week or month. This angle measures $82\frac{1}{2}^{\circ}$. As long as a stock can hold above this angle on daily, weekly or monthly chart, it is in the strongest possible position, but when it reverses trend and declines below this angle, then it indicates a decline to the next angle.

NEXT ANGLE: 16×1 It is possible to use an angle of 16 x 1, or 16 points of Price to one period of Time, which measures $86\frac{1}{4}^{\circ}$, but this angle is only used in fast, advancing markets, like 1929, when stocks are moving up or down 16 points or more per week or per month. There are very few stocks that will move up 16 points per day, week or month, and very seldom.

You will note that with these four important angles we show the strong or bullish side of the market. All the time by dividing the Space with angles we are getting the half-way point or the gravity center of Time and Price.

3 x 1 ANGLE: Note the angle drawn in Green, marked "3 x 1", which moves up at the rate of 3 points per day, week or month, measuring $71\frac{1}{4}^{\circ}$. This angle is important at times after markets have had a prolonged advance and are a long distance up from the bottom. It is an important angle to use on Monthly and Weekly charts.

These are all the angles you need as long as a stock continues to advance and work up and stays above the angle of 45° or the moving-average of one point per day, week or month.

While there are 360 degrees in a circle and angles can form at any of these degrees, all of the important angles form between "0" and "90" because 90 is straight up and down and the most acute angle on which a stock can rise. For example: The 45° angle divides the space from "0" to "90" in half. The angle of 135° is simply another angle of 45° because it is one-half of the next quadrant between 90 and 180. 225 and 315 in a circle are also 45° angles. Therefore all of the angles valuable in determining the trend of a stock are found between "0" and "90" degrees. When we divide 90° by 8 we get the most important angles to use– then divide it by 3 we get 30 and 60° angles, which are important to use for Time and Resistance Points.

WHAT KIND OF BOTTOMS TO DRAW ANGLES OR MOVING-AVERAGE LINES FROM

DAILY CHART: If a stock has been declining for some time– then starts to rally (by rallying from a bottom it must make higher bottoms every day and higher tops)– then after a 3-day rally on the daily high and low chart, you can put on the 45° angle and the angle of 2 x 1 from the bottom or low point. As a rule, it will only be necessary to put on these two angles at first. If this bottom holds and is not broken, then you can put on the other angles from the bottom.

WEEKLY CHART: If a stock is declining and reacts for more than one week and continues down, we will say, for three weeks or more, then starts to rally and advances two weeks or more, you would start to put the angles on from the low point of the decline, only using the angles above the 45° angle until the stock again breaks under the 45° angle- after that you would use the other angles on the lower or bearish side of the Square.

WHAT TO DO AFTER THE 45° ANGLE FROM BOTTOM IS BROKEN

After a stock makes top, either temporary or otherwise, and breaks under the 45° angle and starts moving down, then the first thing you do is to draw angles below the 45° angle, starting from the bottom or low point. Note example marked "Form #3":

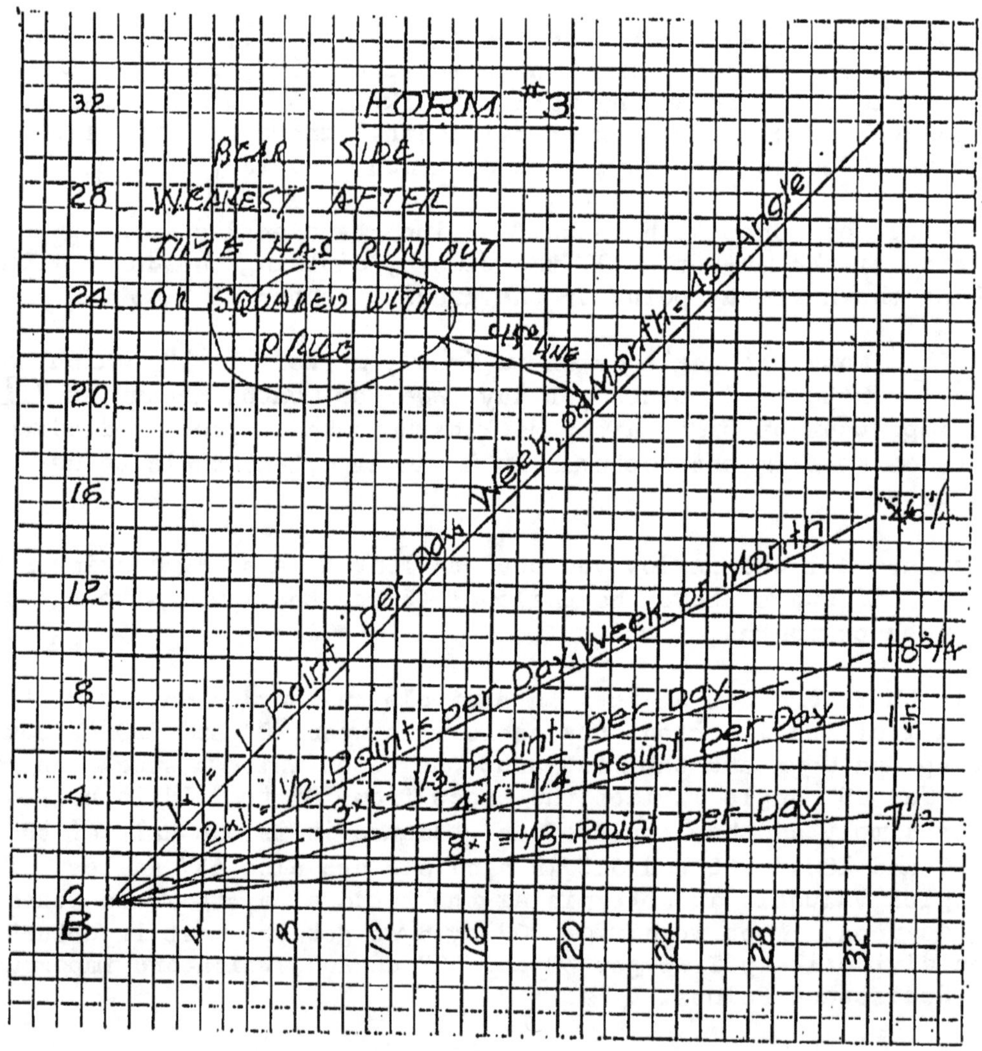

FIRST ANGLE ON BEAR SIDE OF THE SQUARE: 2 x 1

The first angle that you draw on the bear side of the Square is the angle of 2 x 1 or 2 points over and one point up, which moves at the rate of one-half point per day, week or month and measures $26\frac{1}{4}°$. This is the first support angle which the stock should reach after it breaks under the 45° angle. As a general rule, when the stock reaches this angle, it will receive support and rally. Sometimes it will rest on it for a long period of time, holding on this angle and making higher bottoms. But when this angle of 2 x 1, or moving-average of one-half point per day, week or month is broken, then you must draw the next angle of 4 x 1.

NEXT IMPORTANT ANGLE: 4 x 1 The next important angle on the bear side of the Square, which moves up at the rate of 1/4-point per day, is the angle of 4 x 1, measuring 15°. It will be the next strong support angle which the stock should get support on and rally from.

NEXT ANGLE 8 x 1: Then after the 4 x 1 angle is broken, the next important angle that you will put on your chart is the angle of 8 x 1, which moves at the rate of 1/8-point per day, week or month and measures $7\frac{1}{2}$°. This is often a very strong support angle. After a stock has had a big decline, it will often rest on this angle several times or may make final bottom and start up from this angle, crossing other angles and getting back into a strong position again. Therefore this angle is important to use on a monthly or weekly chart after a prolonged decline.

ANGLE 16 x 1: This angle can be used on a monthly chart after a long period of time has elapsed from an important bottom. It moves at the rate of 1/16 point per month and measures $3\frac{3}{4}$°.

ANGLE OF 3 x 1: This angle, drawn in rek ink, is a very important angle, measuring $18\frac{3}{4}$°. I strongly advise using it at all times and keeping it up on monthly charts from any important bottom. It can also be used to advantage at times on weekly charts, but is seldom of much value on a daily chart. It moves at the rate of one-third point per day, week, or month. By drawing this on the monthly chart for a long period of years, you will soon be convinced of its value and also by testing it on a weekly chart, will find it valuable.

This completes all of the angles that you will need to use from any bottom at any time.

HOW TO DRAW ANGLES FROM TOPS ON DAILY, WEEKLY OR MONTHLY CHARTS

POSITION UNDER 45° ANGLE DRAWN FROM TOP: After a stock has made top and declined for a reasonable length of time, say, three days, three weeks or three months, breaking previous bottoms, then you start to draw angles down from the top. Note example marked "Form #4", which is the pattern for drawing angles from the top under the 45° angle. (see page 10)

45° ANGLE FROM TOP: The first angle you draw is the angle of 45° or a moving-average which indicates a decline of one point per day, week or month. As long as the stock is below this angle, it is in the weakest position and in a bear market.

OTHER ANGLES: In many cases a stock will start declining an average of 8 points per day, week or month, or 4 points per day, week or month, or 2 points per day, week or month, therefore you should put on all of those angles from the top, which move down faster than the angle of 45°.

WEAKEST POSITION: The stock is in the weakest possible position when it declines and keeps under the angle of 8 x 1. It is in the next weakest position when it is dropping down at the rate of 4 points per day, week or month, or under the angle of 4 x 1. It is in its next weakest position when it is dropping down under the angle of 2 x 1.

STRONGEST POSITION: The stock is in a stronger position and indicates a better rally when it crosses the angle of 2 x 1, but this depends on how far it is down from the top and how far the angles are apart, as will be explained later under the rules.

CHANGING TREND: As long as a stock is declining one point per day, week or month, or falling below or under the 45° angle, it is still in a bear market and in a very weak position. When a stock rallies and crosses the angle of 45° after a prolonged decline, then you are ready to put on the angles on the other side of the 45° angle, which shows that the stock is in a stronger position in a bear market and may be getting ready to change into a bull market.

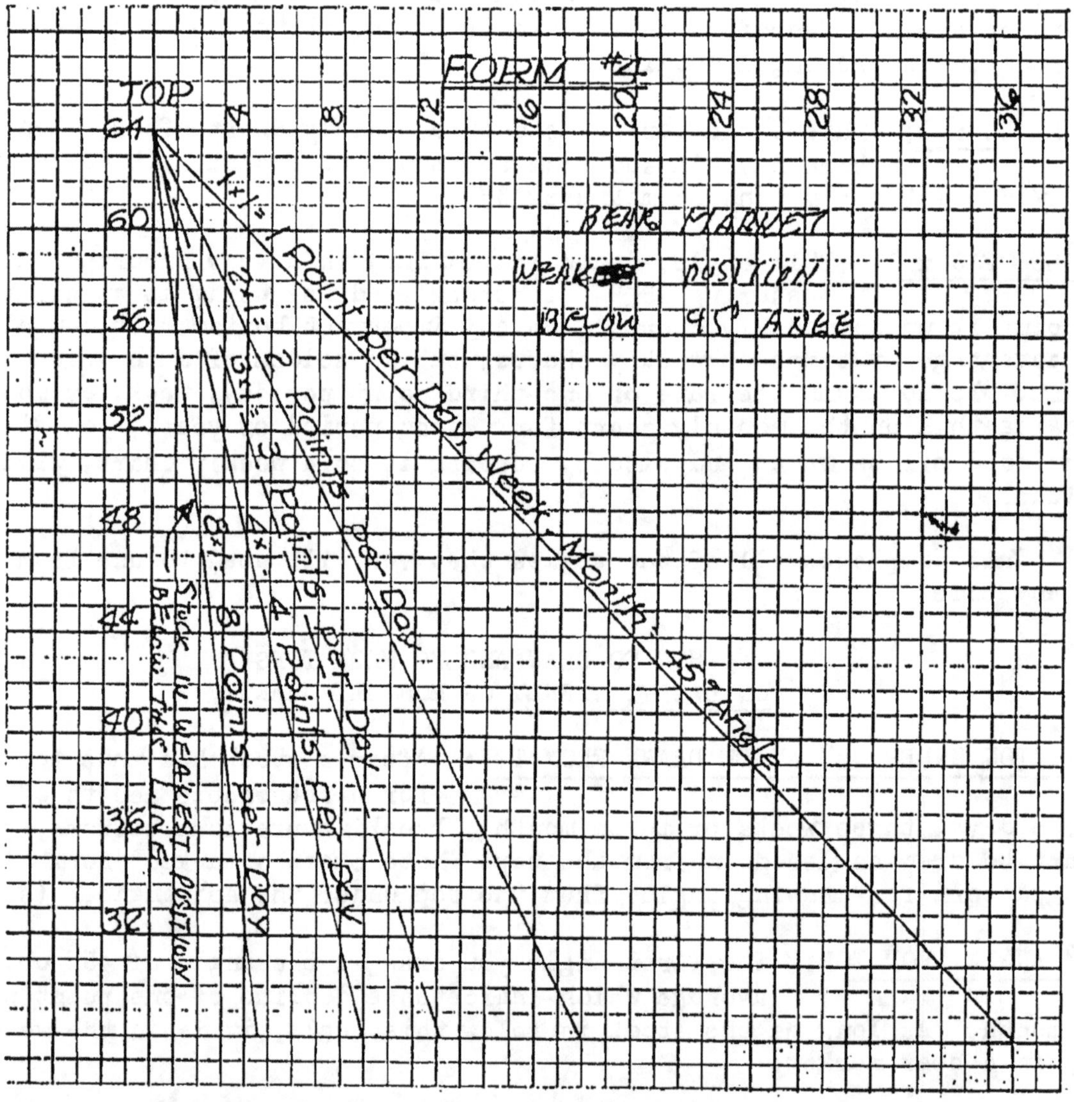

POSITION ABOVE 45° ANGLE DRAWN FROM TOP

Refer to Form #5, which is the pattern for drawing angles above the 45° angle from the top. (See page 11)

2 x 1 ANGLE FROM TOP: The first angle or moving-average you draw after the 45° angle from the top is crossed and after the stock indi-

cates that it has made a temporary bottom is the angle of 2 x 1, moving over 2 points and down one point, or 1/2-point per unit of Time. This is moving down at the rate of 1/2-point per month, week or day.

4 x 1 ANGLE: The next is the angle of 4 x 1 which moves down at the rate of 1/4-point per day, week or month.

8 x 1 ANGLE: The next angle is the angle of 8 x 1, which moves down at the rate of one point every 8 days, 8 weeks or 8 months, or 1/8-point per time period.

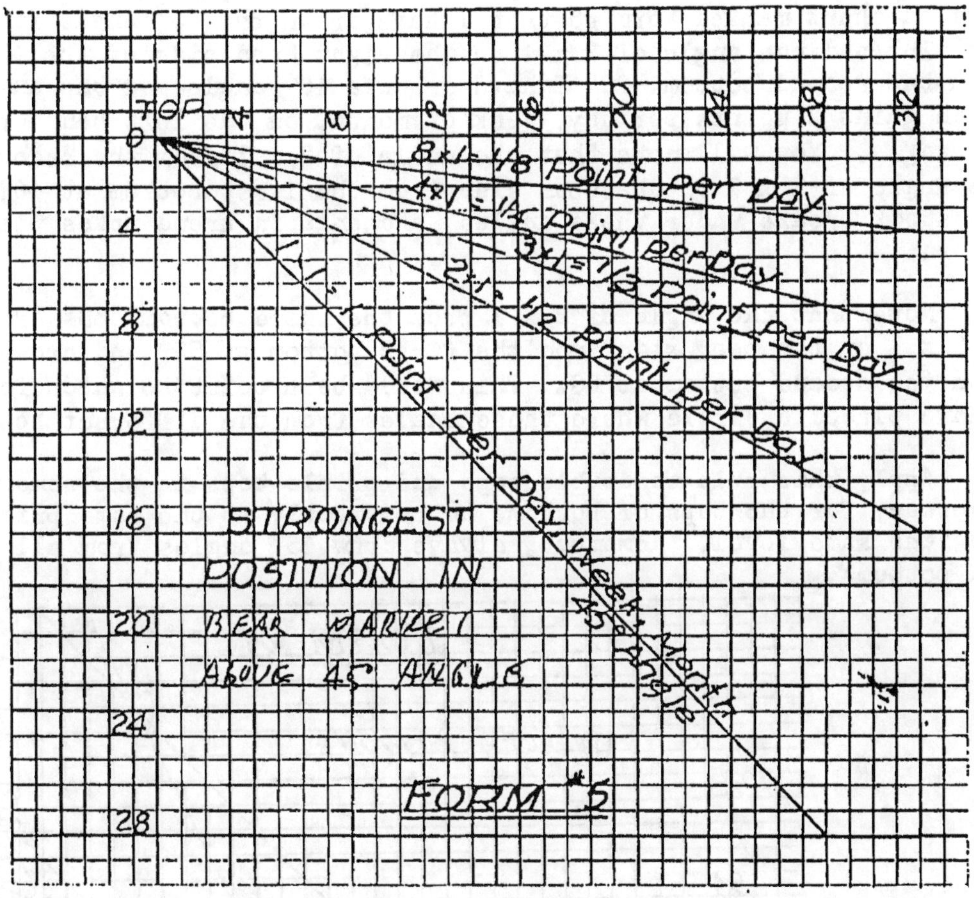

STRONG POSITION: After the stock has crossed the angle of 45° and rallied up to the angle of 2 x 1, it will meet selling and react to some angle coming up from the bottom of the last move, but it is in a stronger position when it holds above this angle of 2 x 1 and is in the next strongest position when it crosses the angle of 4 x 1. Crossing the angle of 8 x 1, which is of least importance, it indicates that it is in a very strong position again from the top. You must always consider a movement coming up from bottom and its position on angles from the bottom to determine its strength. It is important to consider the number of points it has moved up from the bottom and how many points it is down from the top.

3 x 1 ANGLE: The angle of 3 x 1 drawn in red on Form #5 moves down at the rate of one point every three days, three weeks or three months, or one-third point per day, week or month. This angle is important to use after prolonged declines.

This completes the forms of all the angles that you will need to use at any time from tops or bottoms. Practice putting these angles on tops and bottoms until you thoroughly understand how to do them and know that you are getting them absolutely accurate. Then you can begin to study the rules for determining the trend according to the position of the stock on angles.

DOUBLE AND TRIPLE TOPS OR BOTTOMS

ANGLES CROSSING EACH OTHER: When there is a double bottom several days, weeks or months apart, you draw angles from those bottoms, which are near the same price levels. For example: From the first bottom draw a 45° angle and from the second bottom draw an angle of 2 x 1- then when these angles cross each other, it will be an important point for a change in trend. Note on chart marked Form #6 that I have drawn the 45° angle from the first bottom "1B", and the angle of 2 x 1 on the right hand side of the 45° angle. Then, from the second bottom "2B" I have drawn a 45° angle and the angle of 2 x 1, which gains 2 points per day, week or month, on the left hand or bull side of the 45° angle. You will note that the angle of 2 x 1 from the second bottom crosses the angle of 2 x 1 on the bear side from the first bottom at 48, and that when the stock breaks under these angles, a change in trend takes place and it goes lower.

Note that the angle of 2 x 1 from the third bottom "3B" crosses the angle of 2 x 1 on the bear side from the first bottom at 53½ and crosses the 45° angle from the second bottom at 58. This would be a point to watch for change in trend. I have placed a circle where these angles from the different bottoms come together.

Apply this rule to double tops and triple tops in the same way. It is not necessary for the tops or bottoms to be exactly at the same price level, but near the same level. Remember, always draw 45° angles from all important tops and bottoms.

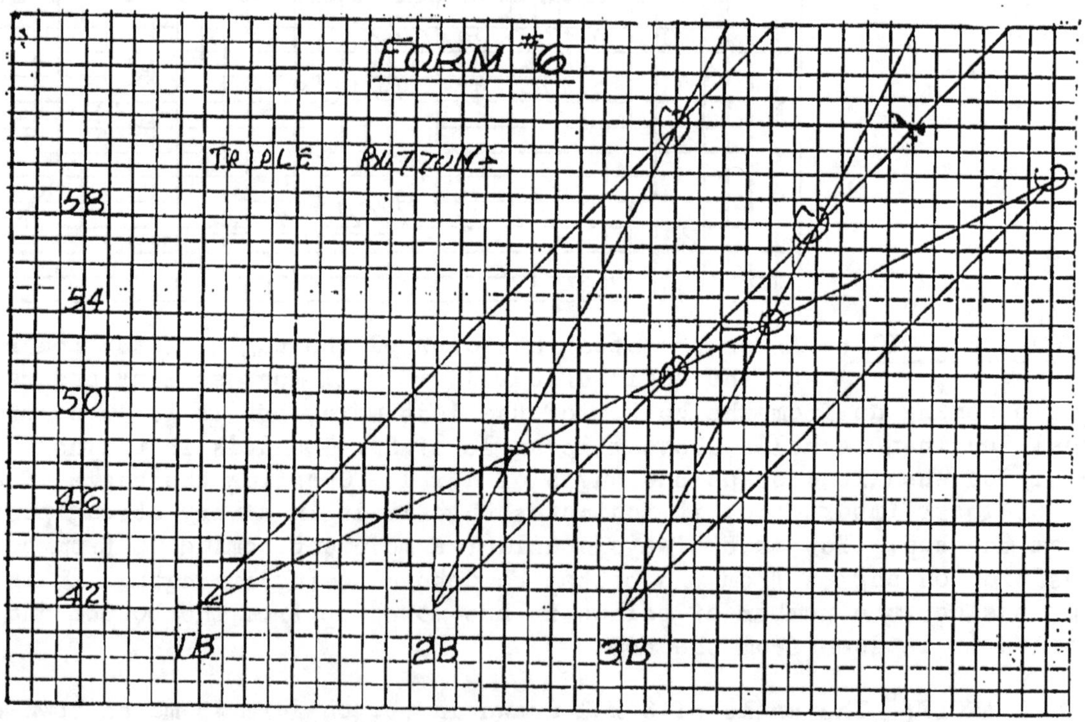

PARALLEL ANGLES

Parallel angles or lines run from important tops and bottoms. As previously explained, the 45° angle is the most important and should be drawn from all important tops and bottoms. If a stock starts advancing, we draw a 45° angle from the bottom- then if the stock makes top, declines and makes a higher bottom- then advances and makes a higher top, we draw a 45° angle from the first top, running the line up. This will give the oscillation or width of fluctuation in a parallel between the 45° angle from the bottom and the 45° angle running up from the top. Often a stock will advance to the 45° angle from the first top, fail to cross it, then decline and rest on the 45° angle from the first bottom- then advance again, working up for a prolonged bull campaign between these parallel angles.

When the angles are very far apart, you can draw another 45° angle equidistant between them, which is often a strong support angle from which a stock will rally, but when it breaks under, it declines to the bottom parallel.

Parallels can form between the angles of 2 x 1 or 4 x 1 just the same as between 45° angles, which often occurs in slow-moving stocks.

GEOMETRICAL ANGLES OR MOVING-AVERAGE LINES DRAWN FROM "O"

When a stock reaches bottom and starts up, you have been instructed to draw angles from this exact low point, which shows the support in time periods, but there are other angles that later on will be just as important and sometimes more important than the angles drawn from the bottom of a stock. These are the angles that begin at "O" or zero and move up at the same rate that they move up from the bottom. The starting point must be on the same line that the bottom is made on as the time period begins from this bottom, but the angles move up from "O". These angles should be started every time a stock makes a bottom, especially on weekly and monthly charts, and should also be carried up on important movements on the daily chart. Example: See chart marked Form #7 on page 14.

If a stock makes low at 20, as shown on the chart, starting the 45° angle from "O", when will this angle reach 20? Answer: It will reach 20 in 20 days, 20 weeks or 20 months from the bottom or its starting point. In other words, in 20 days, 20 weeks, or 20 months, it will be up 20 from "O" and at the price where the stock made bottom. Then the angle will continue on up at the same rate, and later, when the stock breaks under the 45° angle from the actual bottom made at 20 and breaks the other support angles drawn from the actual bottom at20, the next important point for support will be the angle of 45° moving up from "O". When this angle is broken, it is in the weakest possible position and indicates much lower prices, but this depends on how high the stock is selling and how much it has declined at the time it breaks the 45° angle from "O". These angles drawn from "O", especially the 45° angle, proves when Price and Time are balancing or when the stock is squaring out from its bottom.

"O" ANGLES STARTING AT THE TIME TOP IS MADE

When a stock reaches extreme top on a daily, weekly or monthly chart and the trend turns down, you should start an angle of 45° from "O" moving up from the exact space and date that the top is made. This will prove the square of the time period. It is very important when this angle is reached and indicates a change in trend. It is the last strong support and when broken, it will indicate much lower prices.

I have instructed you in each case to first draw the 45° angle from bottom, top and from "O" at bottom and top, but this does not mean that you must not use the other angles. All of the other angles can be used from "O", but the 45° angle is the first and most important. After this angle is broken, then you can use the other angles. It is not necessary to carry all of them along until you need them, but on the monthly chart, after a long series of years, those other angles should be carried along when the stock begins to approach the levels where they would be broken or where the stock would rest on them and receive support.

<u>45° ANGLE FROM "O" TO TOP AND BOTTOM:</u> When a 45° angle moving up from "O" reaches the line or price of the bottom, it is very important– then again when it reaches the point of the extreme high price, it is very important for a change in trend.

You should carry 45° angles and other angles up from "O" from all important first, second, and third higher bottoms, especially those where very much time has elapsed between these bottoms. You should also start the angle of 45° up from "O" from the first, second, and third lower tops, especially those which show much time period elapsed. These angles are the most important to be carried on the weekly and monthly charts.

Never overlook keeping up the angles from "O" because they will tell you when Time is squaring out with Price from tops and bottoms and will locate support angles or moving-average lines at a point on the bear side after the first 45° angle from a bottom is broken. You could not locate this support point in any other way except by the angles from "O".

You should go back over past records and bring up these angles and square out different tops and bottoms so that you can prove to yourself the great value of using these angles.

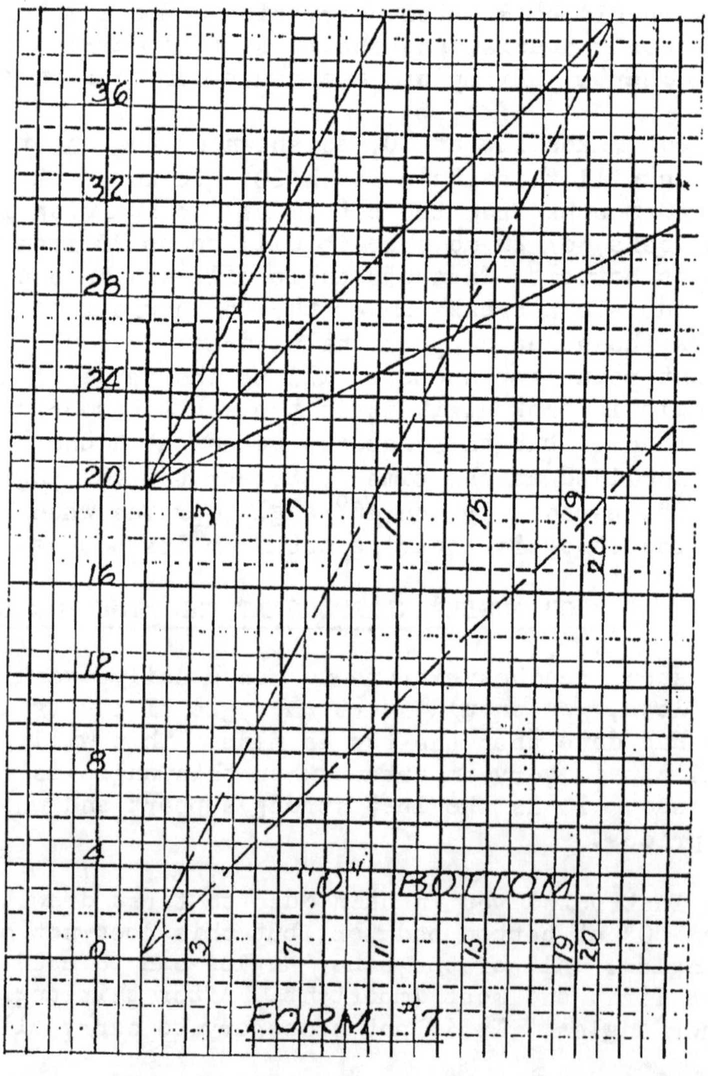

FORM #7

ANGLES FROM TOPS DOWN TO "O" AND UP AGAIN

A 45° angle starting down from any important top on a monthly or weekly chart should be continued down until it reaches "O" and then started up again at the same rate. After a long number of years between important tops and bottoms, this angle coming down and going up again is important. A 45° angle can also be continued down from any important bottom to "O" and then started up again. This will show the squaring of Price with Time from either top or bottom.

Angles can be started from "O" at the time any important time cycle runs out. For example: U. S. Steel made extreme low in 1904. May, 1924 would be the end of a 20-year cycle or 120 months. In May, 1924 Steel made top at 109 against a 45° angle beginning at "O" at the time bottom was made at 38 in February, 1915. On account of the importance of this top and a 20-year cycle running out here, we would start a 45° angle and other angles, if we need them, from "O" in May, 1924.

May, 1931 would end a 7-year cycle of 84 months from 1924. The 45° angle running up from "O" in May, 1924 crossed at 84 in May, 1931. Note that Steel made low at 83⅛ in June, 1931. In June, 1924 Steel made the last low at 94¼, showing the importance of the end of the 20-year cycle. The 45° angle moving up from "O" in June, 1924 crossed at 84 in June, 1931, and Steel declined and rested on this angle.

TWO 45° ANGLES FROM THE SAME BOTTOM

As we have previously explained, the 45° angle moves up at the rate of one point per month and moves down at the rate of one point per month.

Refer to example on Chart #8:

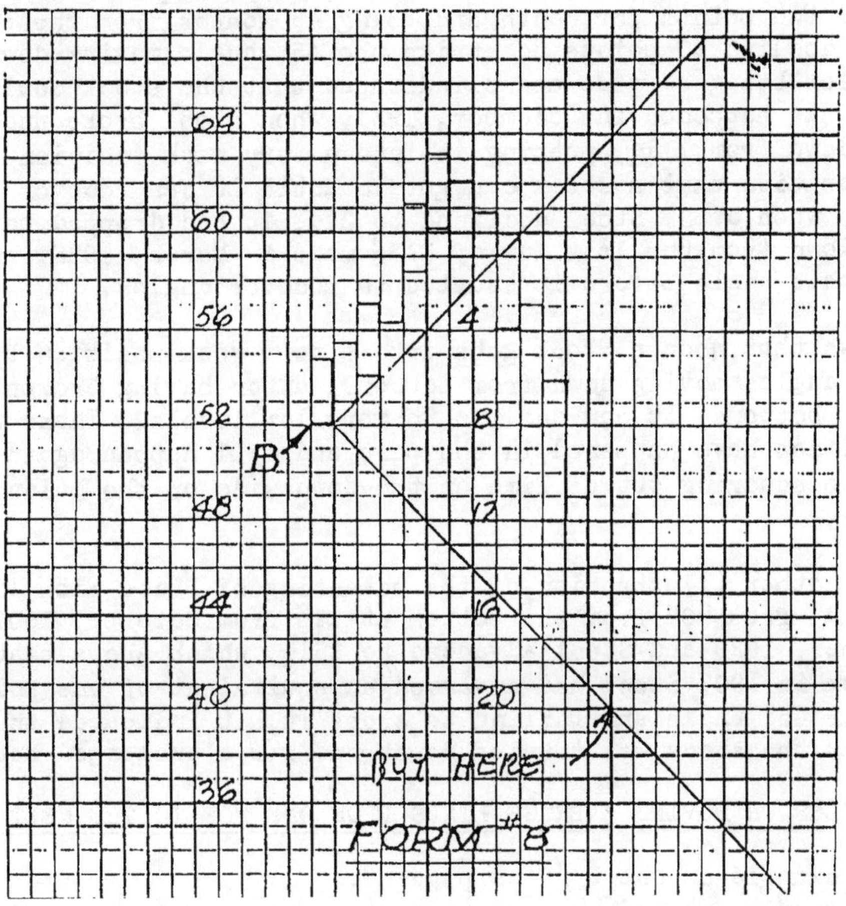

You will note that the low on this chart is shown as 52 and the stock moves up to a high of 63. A 45° angle is drawn up from the bottom, and after the stock reaches top and starts to work down, it breaks the 45° angle, getting under it at a price of 59. You will note that I have drawn another 45° angle down from the bottom at 52. At the point where the stock breaks under the 45° angle moving up from 52 to the 45° angle moving down from 52, the distance in points is 16, therefore the angles have widened until the stock could decline 16 points, if it went straight down, before it reached the 45° angle moving down from the bottom.

Note that I have shown on the chart that the stock continues down until it reaches 40, where it rests on the 45° angle from the bottom at 52. This would indicate the strongest support point and at least a temporary rally, especially as the stock is down 23 points from the top. Later you will find under "Resistance Levels" that $22\frac{1}{2}$ to 24 points is a strong support point.

<u>U. S. STEEL:</u> Take the extreme low point of U. S. Steel at $111\frac{1}{4}$ in January, 1927. Start a 45° angle on the monthly chart moving up at the rate of one point per month- then start a 45° angle moving down at the same rate. This shows the spreading of the angles and what can happen when Steel breaks under the 45° angle coming up from that bottom and the point where it can decline in extreme panicky markets, like 1931 and 1932.

The 45° angle coming up from the low of January, 1927 crossed at 156 in October, 1930. When U. S. Steel broke this angle it went right on down to $134\frac{3}{8}$ in December, 1930, where it rested on the angle of 2 x 1 from this bottom of January, 1927- then rallied to February, 1931, and at the time it broke under the angle of 45° from $111\frac{1}{4}$, it was on the 45th month, another indication of a sharp, severe decline. Here we look at the 45° angle moving down from $111\frac{1}{4}$ and find it is 90 points down from the 45° angle moving up from $111\frac{1}{4}$. These angles separate at the rate of two points per month and being 45 months from the bottom, the stock would have to decline 90 points to strike the 45° angle moving down from the bottom. The angles being so wide apart indicated that the stock could have a wide-open break. This happened in December, 1931, when Steel broke under the 45° angle moving down from $111\frac{1}{4}$, putting it into a very weak position- in fact, in the weakest position that a stock can get in until it can recover this angle. In June, 1932, when U. S. Steel declined to $21\frac{1}{4}$, it had dropped under the 45° angle moving down from the last low of $113\frac{3}{8}$ made in March, 1925, and closed two months below this angle before it started to recover angles.

This shows that when a stock gets into a very weak position by dropping under important angles moving down from bottoms, after having broken strong angles moving up from bottoms, it can decline to very low levels. These extreme fluctuations and declines have happened in the past and will happen again in the future. This proves the squaring out of Time on the down side or the balancing up of Price and Time.

Here is another illustration of the balancing of Price with Time: The angle of 45° moving up from "0" from the bottom at $21\frac{7}{8}$ from October, 1907 crossed at 262 in September, 1929 and Steel advanced to $261\frac{3}{4}$, which shows that in 262 months from the bottom in 1907 Steel had advanced an equivalent of one point per month. By striking the 45° angle and failing to cross it, it indicated that the Time was up and that the stock was turning downtrend for a prolonged bear market.

<u>ANGLES OR MOVING-AVERAGE LINES FROM ONE TOP TO THE NEXT TOP</u>

Refer to example on Chart #9 on page 17.

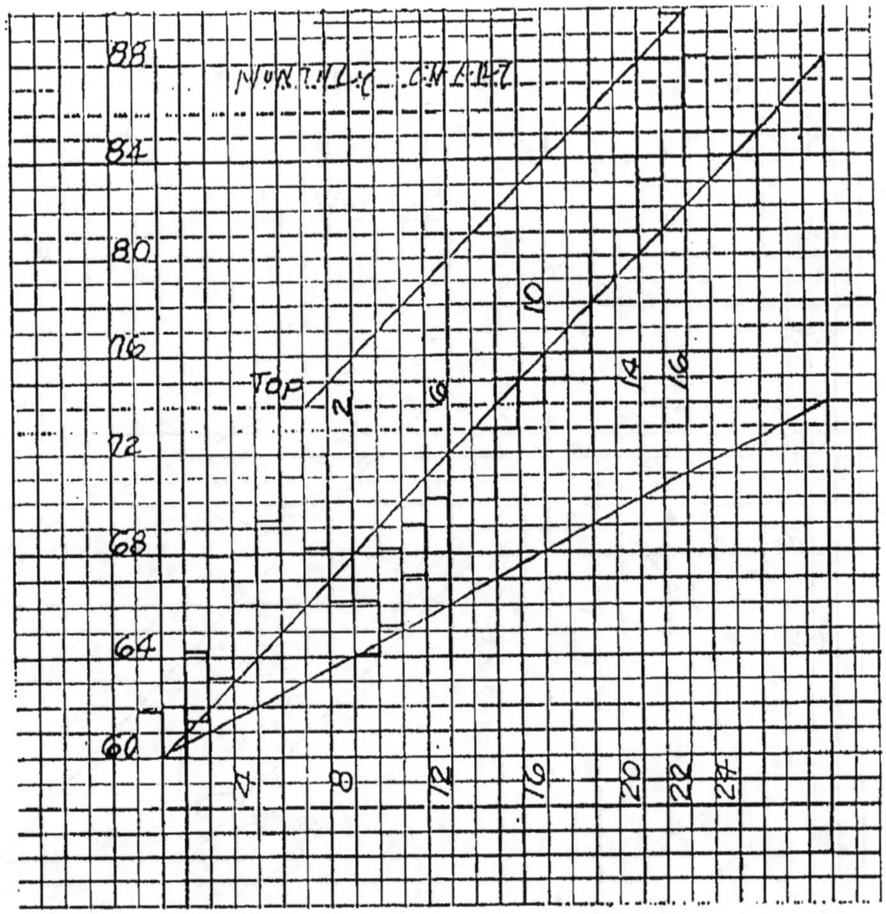

You will see that we have started the bottom at 60. The stock advances six months to 74, to a point marked "T" and makes top--reacts for three months to 64, breaking the 45° angle but resting on the angle of 2 x 1 from the bottom--then starts advancing and finally crosses again the 45° angle from 60, getting into a stronger position, having regained this angle. In order to determine where it might meet resistance, as it is in new high territory, we draw a 45° angle from the top at 74. The stock advances to 90 on the 22nd month from the bottom, striking the 45° angle from the first top at 74, on the 16th month from the first top. Being 16 points up above the first top, the Time equals the advance in the Price above the first top. The 45° angle shows that this is a strong Resistance point and a place to go short with stop one to three points above the 45° angle. A decline starts and in the third month the stock again breaks under the 45° angle from the bottom (at 60) at a very high level. In other words, it is 24 points up from the bottom and is now in a much weaker position, because it is so far from the base of support, and indicates a decline again to the angle of 2 x 1 (marked in green).

Don't overlook this rule: After a stock has advanced to a new high level, then declines to the old top at 74, this may be a support point unless it breaks 3 points under it. If it does and also breaks the angle of 2 x 1, it will be in a weaker position and the next point to watch for support and a rally would be the next bottom at 64.

ANGLES FROM BOTTOM OF FIRST SHARP DECLINE

When a stock that has been advancing for some time, makes top and holds for several days, several weeks or several months, then turns the trend down and has a sharp, severe decline, there is always a rally after this first decline. It usually makes a lower top on this secondary rally and then starts to work lower again. The bottom of the first decline is a very important point to draw angles from, especially the 45° angle moving down, as I have done on the chart marked Form #10.

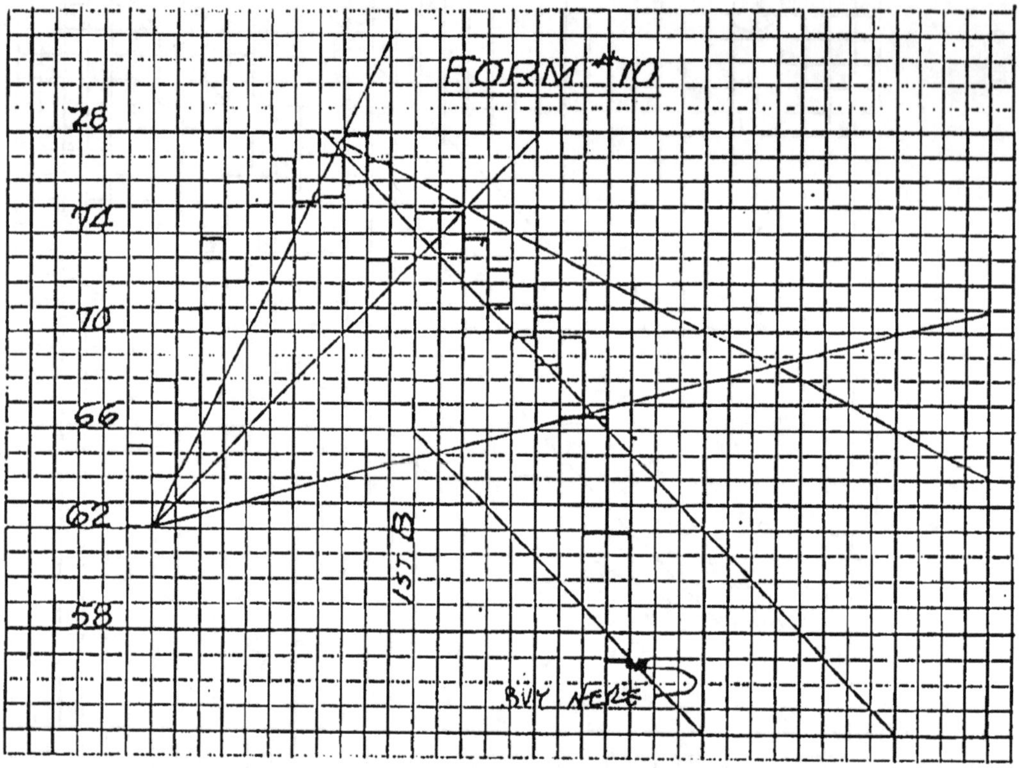

This chart shows the stock rallying up to around 75, where the 45° angle coming up from the last bottom crosses the angle of 2 x 1 coming down from the top. Then the decline started and at 66 the stock broke back under the angle of 45° from the top, which put it in a very weak position. It declined to the angle of 45° coming down from the bottom of the first sharp decline. This would be the squaring out of time from the bottom and would be a place to buy for a rally. A stock will often decline and drop a little below this angle from the bottom--then if it holds for several days or weeks under this angle or on it, it is a place to buy for a rally.

On a Monthly Chart always carry this angle down from the bottom of the first sharp decline, as it often becomes very important later on in a campaign.

After a stock has been advancing for some time and then has a sharp break lasting 2 to 3 days, 2 to 3 weeks, or 2 to 3 months--then rallies and afterward breaks under the lows of this first sharp break, it indicates that the main trend has turned down and that it is going lower.

Apply the same rule when a stock has been declining for a long time and then makes a sharp, quick recovery for 2 to 3 days, 2 to 3 weeks, or 2 to 3 months, then reacts and then crosses this first rally point that it made, an indication of higher prices.

LAST SWING IN A BULL OR BEAR MARKET

It is important to draw angles from the point where the market starts up and makes its last run in a bull market. Refer to Chart #11 on page 19.

In this example note point marked "last bottom". In the last stage of the bull market a fast advance follows to a price of 84. We have drawn the angle of 2 x 1 (a gain of 2 points per day, week or month) and the 45° angle from this bottom. When the angle of 2 x 1 was broken, it indicated that the trend had turned down. The stock declined and rested on the 45° angle--then rallied and made a second lower top-- then broke the 45° angle-- declined sharply and rested on the 45° angle drawn from the top at 84, which indicated that Time and Price had squared out or were equal. This would be a point to buy, with a stop loss order 2 to 3 points under this angle, for a rally back to the angle of 2 x 1 from the top, as shown on the chart.

In very active fast-moving markets a stock may stay above the angle of 4 x 1 or the angle of 8 x 1 from the "last bottom," but on the daily or weekly chart after this first acute angle is broken, it indicates that the trend has turned down.

Always remember that after a prolonged advance, when the main trend turns down, it is safer to wait for rallies and sell short than to buy against the trend.

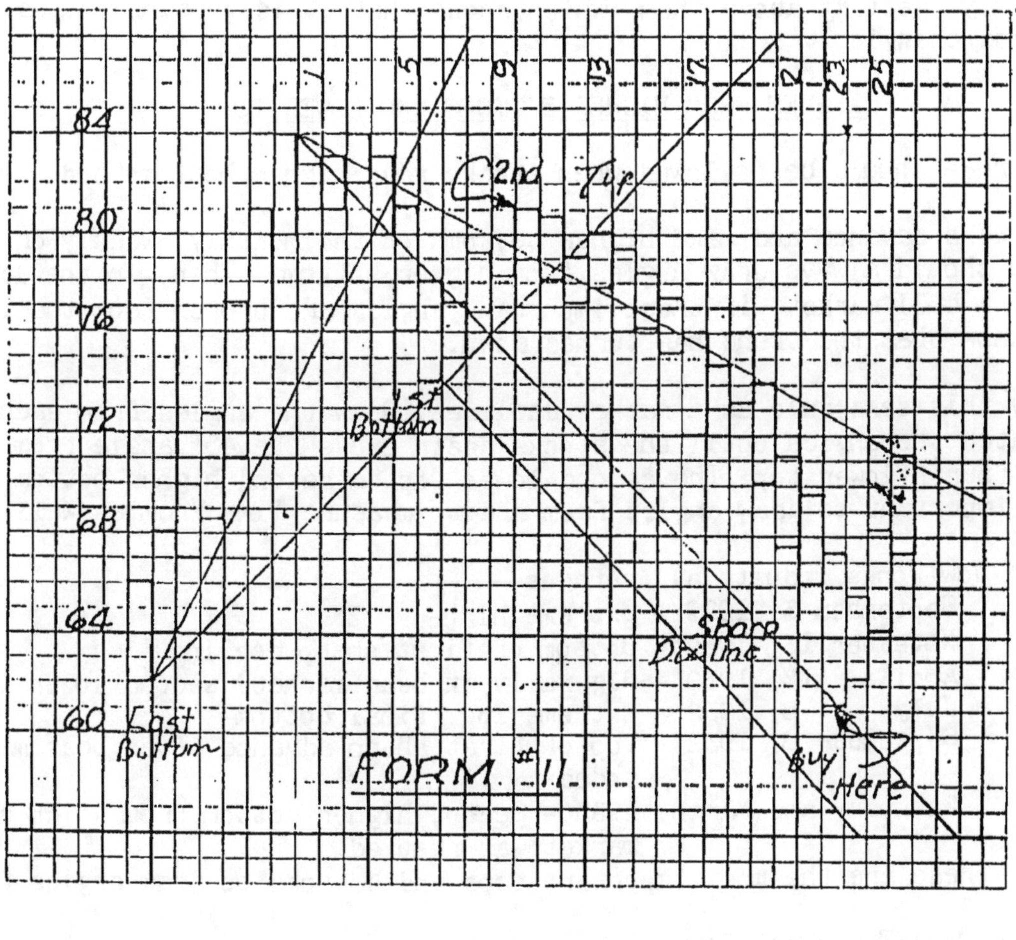

All of these rules are reversed at the end of a bear market or sharp decline. It is important to note when the market starts down from the last top or rally and makes its last run to bottom. Draw angles from this last top and watch when the market reaches these important angles and crosses them. For example:

On March 9, 1932 the Dow-Jones 30 Industrial Averages made last top at 90, from which a decline followed, with very small rallies, reaching bottom at 41 on July 8, 1932. Note on the weekly chart that the angle of 2 x 1 from the top at 90 crossed at 50 in the week ending July 30, 1932 and after they crossed this level they never declined to 50 again, and advanced to 81 in September, 1932. The crossing of this angle was the first definite indication that the main trend had turned up.

It is also important to review the major swing from November 9, 1931, when the Averages reached a high of 119½, to the low at 40½ in July, 1932. This was the last big swing of the bear market, a decline of 79 points. The half-way point of this was at 80. In September, 1932 the Averages rallied to 81-- then after they reacted to 50 and advanced, getting above the half-way point, and crossed 81, they indicated an advance to 119 anyway. After they crossed the half-way point the second time and advanced above 81, they never sold down to it again until they advanced to 149½ in November, 1935.

After a stock has been advancing for a long time, in the last run when there is a lot of momentum, it may cross angles from previous tops or bottoms, then fall back under them, which is an indication of weakness. When a stock has a sharp decline and is making bottom, it will drop under important angles and then recover quickly, getting above them, which shows that it is getting into a strong position and changing trend.

ANGLES FROM HIGHER BOTTOMS AND LOWER TOPS

What rule should be followed when stocks make higher bottoms and lower tops?

As stocks advance and make higher bottoms on the monthly, weekly or daily chart, you should always draw angles from higher bottoms. Then, in the last section of a bull market, if these important angles are broken from the last bottom, you know that the trend has turned down.

Apply this same rule as a market declines. Draw the angles from each lower top and watch the angles until the stocks again cross the 45° angle from a second, third, or fourth lower top. The second lower top or second higher bottom is always very important to draw angles from and to measure Time from as well.

Example: Dow-Jones Industrial Averages—

September 3, 1929 - Extreme high-
November 13, 1929 - Bottom of first sharp decline-
April 17, 1930 - Big rally in bear market, second lower top-
July 8, 1932 - Extreme low, final bottom-
September 8, 1932 - Top of first sharp advance after bear market ended-
February and March, 1933 - Second higher bottom from which bull market was resumed.

These are the most important tops and bottoms to draw angles from.

SECTIONS OF MARKET CAMPAIGNS:

All market campaigns, up or down, move in 3 to 4 sections. When an advance starts, the market runs for several weeks or several months and then halts for several weeks or months, moving up and down over a range of 5 to 20 points, according to the price of the stock--then the advance is resumed and the stock crosses the high level of the first section, moves higher, halts again, and reacts for a period of time-- then crosses the top of the second section and moves up again for another period of time and halts for the third time, which is a very important point to watch as markets often culminate at the end of the third section and a bigger decline follows,

Most markets run out in three important sections or campaigns. However, after resting and reacting, if a stock crosses the third top, it will then move up to the top of the fourth section. This fourth advance may be a shorter period of time than the previous sections, or in some cases may consume a greater period of time, especially if the stock is very active and high-priced. This fourth top is very important and generally marks a culmination and a reversal for a bigger decline.

For example: On March 12, 1935 CHRYSLER MOTORS declined and made low at 31--

FIRST SECTION of the advance carried the stock up to 49⅜ on May 16- then the stock declined to 41¼.

SECOND SECTION— On June 27 the advance started and the stock advanced to new high levels, reaching 62⅜ on August 10, which was top of the second section- then there was a reaction to 57½ and a resting period.

THIRD SECTION— Then there was another advance which started August 28. The stock crossed the top of the second section and reached high at 74 on September 11, top of the third section. Then followed a reaction to 68 on September 21.

FOURTH SECTION— In October the top of the third section was crossed and on November 18 Chrysler reached 90, top of the fourth section, where it held for 5 weeks in a 6-point range while distribution was taking place. This was a most important point to watch for a final top and a change in trend. Then the trend turned down.

Reverse this rule in a bear market. Watch the action of the market when it makes the third and fourth decline. But, remember, in a bear market when rallies come, they may make only one section or one move or in extreme cases only make the second section- then reverse and follow the main trend down.

You will find it very helpful to study and watch these various sections of a campaign and by applying the angles from tops and bottoms you can detect the first minor and major changes in trend.

STRENGTH OR WEAKNESS DENOTED BY POSITION ON ANGLES

The angles on the Monthly and Weekly Charts are of greater importance than those on the Daily Chart because the daily trend can change quite often, while only the major changes are shown according to the angles on the Monthly and Weekly Charts.

Always consider the distance a stock is from its beginning point when it breaks any important angle or crosses any important angle. The further away from the beginning point, the more important the change in trend, whether this is crossing an angle from the top or breaking under an angle from the bottom.

WHEN A STOCK IS IN THE WEAKEST POSITION:

A stock is in the weakest position when it has completed distribution and broken under a 45° angle from an important bottom on the weekly or monthly chart. It is also in the weakest position when it has broken under the half-way point between any important top or bottom. The longer the time period has run and the higher the price, the weaker the position. For example:

If a stock has advanced to 150 and has only moved down 25 points when the 45° angle from an extreme low on a weekly or a monthly chart is broken, then it is in a very weak position because it is so far above the half-way point on its price movement, already having squared out the time period with price.

Weakness in a stock develops when it breaks the 3/4-point, the 2/3-point, the 1/2-point, etc., but the position on the timing angles from the bottom tells you still more about the weak position. A stock shows its first weakness when it breaks the first important angle coming up from the last bottom in the final run in a bull market.

WHEN A STOCK IS IN THE STRONGEST POSITION:

A stock is always in the strongest position coming up from a bottom when it is holding above the very acute angles on the daily, weekly or monthly charts, especially on monthly and weekly charts.

As long as a stock holds above the angle of 2 x 1 (a gain of 2 points per day) on the daily chart, it is in a very strong position as far as the bottom is concerned. In fact, it is always in a strong position on the daily as long as it holds above the 45° angle. The same applies to weekly and monthly charts, which are the most important trend indicators.

I have found that the stocks which have the biggest advances are those that always hold above the angle of 2 x 1 on the monthly chart or gain 2 points per month for a long period of time. I have seen stocks rest 10 or 15 times on the angle of 2 x 1 and never break it until they have advanced 100 points or more. In this way a stock stays ahead of time and stays within the square of time by being far above the angle of 45°, and therefore is in a very strong position. But the time must come when the cycle has run out and the main trend begins to change from a bull market to a bear market--then the breaking of the angle from the last bottom shows a change in trend.

Another indication that a stock is in a strong position is when it advances and moves up above the half-way point of the previous price movement and then holds the half-way point, that is, advances above it and then reacts and fails to break under it. This is just the same as resting on a 45° angle and indicates a very strong position.

STRONGEST BUYING AND SELLING POINTS:

The cinch buying point is when a stock rests on a 45° angle, placing a stop loss order below it.

Another point to buy is on the half-way point of the price movement, placing a stop loss order under the half-way point.

When the main trend is up, it is also safe to buy when a stock reacts to the angle of 2 x 1 (a gain of 2 points per time period) on the weekly or monthly chart.

REGAINING ANGLES OR CROSSING LINES:

Remember, when any stock breaks under the 45° angle from the extreme low point of a move on the daily, weekly or monthly chart, it is then in a very weak position and indicates a decline to the next angle. However, when a stock can regain the 45° angle, it is in a stronger position.

The same rule applies to a 45° angle drawn up from any top. When a stock crosses the angle on the daily, weekly or monthly and stays above the 45° angle or any other angle to the left of the 45° angle, it is in a very strong position.

After a stock once drops below or gets above any important angle and then reverses its position by getting back above the angle or dropping back below it, it changes the trend again.

WHEN A STOCK IS IN STRONG POSITION FROM BOTTOM AND IN WEAK POSITION FROM TOP:

A stock is in a strong position from the bottom when it is keeping above the angle of 45° or the angle of 2 x 1, but at the same time it can be in a weak position when it rallies up and strikes against a 45° angle or the angle of 2 x 1 coming down from the top— then it is a short sale until it can cross these angles or cross previous tops. When it breaks the angles from the bottom, it is in a weak position and indicates lower.

A stock can be in a strong position from the top and in a weak position from the bottom, that is, it may cross some important angles from the top after a long period of time, but at the same time may break under the 2 x 1 angle or 45° angle from the bottom, which would indicate that it is in a weak position and getting ready to go lower.

WHEN ANGLES FROM EXTREME TOP ARE CROSSED:

The 45° angle drawn from the extreme high point of a stock is most important and when it is crossed, a major move may be expected. For example:

On the weekly chart of the Dow-Jones Industrial Averages, note the 45° angle moving down from 386, the high of September 3, 1929. January 12, 1935 was 279 weeks from the 1929 top. Taking 279 from 386, we get 107, the price at which the angle of 45° would cross. These Averages advanced to 106½ in the week ending January 12, 1935— then reacted to 100 in the week ending February 9. This was the first time that they had held within one-half point of this angle and the first time that they had ever reached it since the top was made. During the week ending February 16, 1935, the Averages crossed the 45° angle at 103 for the first time, and during the week ending February 23, 1935 advanced to 108, where they hit the angle of 45° moving up from the low of 85½ in September, 1934, and also hit the angle of 2 x 1 coming up from the low of July 8, 1932. This was a strong resistance point and the Averages reacted to 96 in the week ending March 18, 1935, where they rested on the 45° angle from the 1929 top and also where the 3 x 1 angle (a gain of 1/3 point per week) from September, 1929 coming up from "0" crossed the angle of 45° coming down from the 1929 top. This was a strong support point for a change in trend. The advance started and the Averages moved up to new high levels. This proves the importance of angles, especially the 45° angle drawn from any extreme top, and the point at which any other angle crosses the 45° angle.

Watch the 45° angle from 1929 top when it reaches "0" or when it is 386 weeks down from the top. This will be in the latter part of January, 1937. Note what happens at that time.

ANGLES FOR SEMI-WEEKLY CHART

The semi-weekly chart is a great help at the end of extreme advances or extremes declines. By applying all of the rules and using the geometrical angles from tops and bottoms on the semi-weekly chart, you will often get an indication of a change in trend two to three days before a change in trend is shown on the weekly chart.

A change in trend on the semi-weekly chart is of greater importance than a change in trend on the daily chart. It is much better to rely upon this chart than on the daily chart when markets are in a narrow trading range.

ANGLES FOR NEW LISTED STOCKS

Years of experience and research, which has cost me a large amount of money have enabled me to develop a method that will account for all market movements and give rules to determine the trend from any top or bottom.

It is important to know how to determine the trend when a stock is first listed on any exchange. When a stock has never fluctuated before, we have no top or bottom to draw angles from. Therefore, in order to determine the trend, we use the square of 90, which is 90 up and 90 across, and put all the natural angles on, like the Pattern Chart. As we have said before, the square of 90 is very important because it is one-quarter of a circle of 360°, and as 90° or the vertical angle is the greatest angle that can be used, all of the other angles are found between "0" and "90".

If a new stock opens at 18 or any point below 22½, then you could make out a square of 22½ to determine the position of the stock on angles. If the stock opened at 36 or any point between 22½ and 45, you could make up a square of 45. If it opened at 50 or between 45 and 67, you could make up a square of 67½. However, you could place any stock opening at any price below 90 in the square of 90 and get its proper position and strength or weakness on angles. If the stock opened at 100 or above 90 and under 135, you could make up a square of 135, or could make another square of 90 numbering from 90 to 180.

You could start a monthly chart on a square of 90 at the price where the stock opens or trading begins, as shown on U. S. Steel. (Refer to Special Analysis of U. S. Steel.) After the stock breaks any of these natural angles drawn from "0", it is just the same as breaking under an angle drawn from a bottom. When it crosses any of the angles drawn down from "90", it is just the same as crossing an angle from a top, as you can see by experimenting with U. S. Steel or any other stock, but always consider price resistance levels and how much the stock is up or down from the bottom or top. You can determine the first change in trend by the 3-day or semi-weekly Chart, daily chart, and weekly chart by bringing up the important Geometrical Angles from any higher or lower bottom as the market movements develop.

QUICK CALCULATION OF ANGLES

It is not necessary to draw these angles from a point a long way back. You can make the calculation and determine where they cross. For example: Suppose in 1900, in the month of January, a stock made bottom at 15, and we wish to calculate where the 45° angle will cross 10 years later in January, 1910. The 45° angle rises at the rate of one point per month-- then 10 years would be 120 points or months-- add this to 15 at the bottom-- then the 45° angle would cross at 135 in January, 1910. All of the other angles may be calculated a long period back in the same way.

ANGLES SELDOM USED

3 x 2 ANGLE: This angle of 3 x 2 on the left side of the 45° angle rises at the rate of 8 points in 12 months. A stock must show a gain of 3/4-point per month in order to keep above this angle. This angle can be used when other important angles from the bottom have spread far apart, as it will show the position and resistance or support point between the other angles.

LATITUDE AND LONGITUDE

On all charts--daily, weekly or monthly--the price must move up or down on the vertical angles. Therefore, the price movement is the same as latitude. You should begin with zero or "0" on any chart--daily, weekly or monthly--and draw the important angles and resistance levels across, which measure latitude.

Next, number the time points in days, weeks or months across, and draw the horizontal angle at each important natural angle, such as, 11¼, 22½, 33¾, 45, 56¼, 67½, 78¾, 90, 101¼, 112½, 120, etc. Then you will know when price reaches these important angles and meets resistance.

Longitude measures the time running across the chart, as it moves over each day, week or month. Therefore, you must keep your chart numbered from each important top and bottom in order to get the time measurements according to angles. These important angles, such as, 11¼, 22½, 33¾, 45, 56¼, 60, 67½, 78¾, 90, etc. from each bottom and top will show you where the strongest resistance in price and time takes place. These angles prove the parallel or crossing point. Study past records and see what has happened when prices on monthly charts reached these important angles or time periods.

For example: 90 points up in price from "0" we draw an angle horizonally across the chart. Then 90 days, weeks or months, going to the right across the chart, we draw a vertical angle up, which will cross the horizontal angle at 90 and prove the square. By keeping all these angles up and understanding them on your charts, you will know when important time cycles are running out.

If the price of a stock at 60 comes out on the 60th day, week or month, it will meet strong resistance because it has reached the square of price with Time. It is at the same latitude or price and the same longitude or time period. You can always put the square of 90 on a chart--either daily, weekly or monthly--and use the natural angles, but I advise only using this on the weekly and monthly. You can begin this square of 90 from any bottom or top, that is, going up 90 points, or from the natural points, which are 90, 135, 180, but you must not fail to square the extreme low and high price as well as the second and third lower tops and higher bottoms with Time.

RULE FOR KEEPING TIME PERIODS ON CHARTS

It is very important that you keep the time periods on all of your charts, carrying them across from the bottom and top of each important move in order to check up and know that you have your angles or moving-averages at the correct point and to see where major and minor cycles indicate changes in trend.

TIME PERIODS FROM BOTTOMS: When a stock makes bottom one month and then the following month makes a higher bottom and a higher top, or anyway, after it makes a higher bottom and rallies for one month or more, you can start numbering from that bottom. The month that it makes the low belongs to the old or downward movement and is the last move down. You count the first month up as one and then number across on the 1/2-inch squares, running them across, adding four each time.

For example: If a stock has made bottom and advanced 50 points, you look down at the bottom of the chart and find that you are on the 25th month- then the angle of 2 x 1, moving up 2 points per month, would cross at 50, while the 45° angle, moving up one point per month, would be at 25, and if the stock broke back under 50 the following month, it would be falling under the angle of 2 x 1 and indicate a further decline. Now, if you had an error on the chart in the timing or numbering across from the bottom, then the moving-average line or angle would not come out correctly.

TIME PERIODS FROM TOPS:

After a stock has advanced and made an extreme high and reacted for a few days, a fewweeks, or a few months, and you start putting on the angles from the top down, you must then begin to number the time periods across from the top. Apply the same rule for the top: The month, week or day that a stock makes extreme high finishes the upward movement and is not to be counted. You can count the number of days, weeks or months moving across after that, allowing the top month to be "0", the next month, week or day over to be "1", adding 4 across on the squares to get the correct position. If this Time Period is carried across on all the charts correctly, then you can always check up and find out if you have made any mistake in bringing down the angles or moving-average lines.

For example: After a stock has declined 75 points, either on a weekly or monthly chart, the angles move down the same, except where the spacing is different. Assuming that the spacing is one point per one-eighth inch, after it has moved down 75 points and all the angles are drawn down from the top, there may be an error in the angle of 2 x 1 because your ruler may have slipped and you may not have placed it correctly after it is down a distance from the top. Now, in order to prove exactly where the angle of 2 x 1 comes out, you determine the number of time periods there are. If 40 days, weeks or months have been required to decline the 75 points, the angle of 2 x 1 moving down 2 points per unit of time, would be down 80 from the top. If you find that this angle does not cross at 80, then you know that you made an error and should correct it.

This is a simple way to always know when the angles or moving-lines are correct because you simply add the movement to the bottom and subtract it from the top. Suppose the price referred to above, when the stock has declined 75 points, was 150, then subtracting 80 from the top at 150, the angle would cross at 70, and the price of the stock down 75 points would be at 75, therefore it would be above the angle of 2 x 1 from the top and in position for a rally if the time cycle indicated it.

POINTS FROM WHICH TO NUMBER TIME PERIODS

The most important point on the monthly high and low chart to carry the time period from is from the extreme low of the life of a stock and also from the date of incorporation or from the date trading in the stock began on the New York Stock Exchange. From the extreme low point the time period should always be carried across on the chart just the same as the important angles should be continued right along for years.

The next important point to number from is a second or third higher bottom,

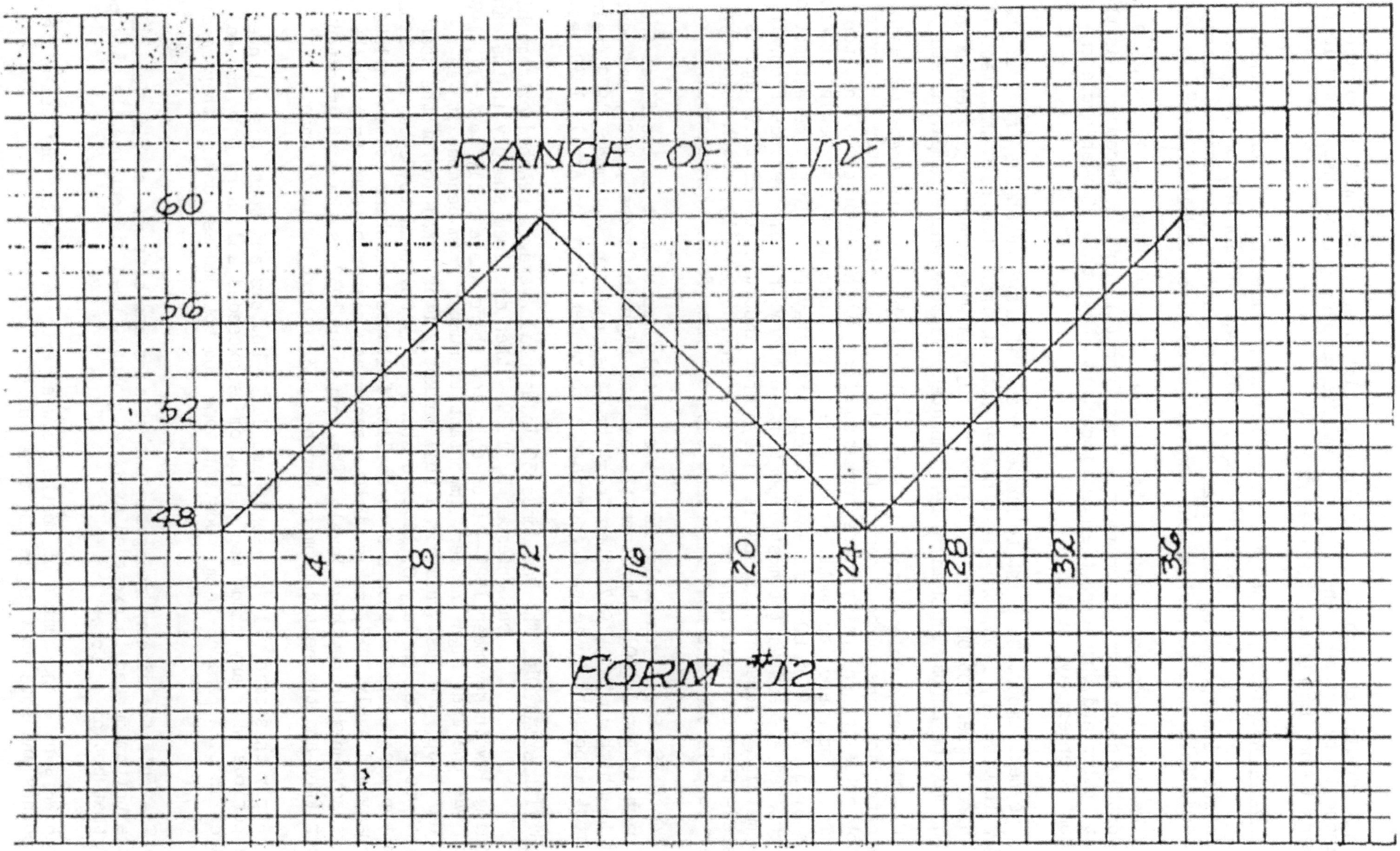
RANGE OF 12
60
56
52
48
4
8
12
16
20
24
28
32
36
FORM #12

but you should not consider a bottom established until the market has held up or advanced three to four months, then commence numbering from that bottom if it appears to be important. For example:

U. S. STEEL was incorporated February 25, 1901. Numbering the months across you will note that February, 1931, was 360 months, or 30 years, from the date of incorporation. Then start a new cycle and begin numbering across from "0". This will be working out the second cycle or circle of 360°.

The next important point is the extreme low of 8¾ made May 14, 1904. On the monthly chart carry the numbers across from this bottom, because it is the lowest bottom and therefore the most important. Note this 30-year cycle or 360 months ended May, 1934.

The next important point to number from and draw the angles from, is the low of 21⅞ in October, 1907, the first higher bottom. Then, the next important is the third higher bottom made in February, 1915. Always draw the angles and number the months across from any other important bottoms where campaigns start.

Use this same rule at tops. After top is reached and the trend turns down, then carry the time numbers across from the top, but after any top is crossed or bottom is broken that you are numbering from, then do not count that top or bottom of importance to number from; except to determine a time period on another cycle 3, 5, 7, 10 or 20 years ahead. Tops that stay for a long time without being crossed are always the most important to carry the Time Periods from. The extreme high reached by a stock is always most important until that high is crossed- then the next high point made on a secondary rally, which is always a lower top, is the next most important top to number from. For example:

On U. S. Steel you would carry the monthly measurement across first from the high in April 1901- then from the extreme high in October, 1909, and next from the high in May, 1917- then from the final high in September, 1929, being the most important to measure from, and also number from the April, 1930 top.

INDUSTRIAL AVERAGES: The Dow-Jones 30 Industrial Averages reached extreme high on September 3, 1929-- then declined sharply in the panic, reaching low in November 1929-- from this low there was a rally to April, 1930, which was the last high and very important to number from because it was a secondary top, the last rally in a bull market. After final low of the bear market was reached on July 8, 1932, a sharp rally followed to September, 1932, when top was reached-- then a slow decline followed, reaching bottom in late February and early 1933, making this a secondary higher bottom, from which stocks advanced to new high levels. The bottom in 1932 is the most important to number from and the next bottom of March, 1933 is next in importance.

Apply this same rule to weekly and daily bottoms and tops. Discontinue the time periods when any minor top or bottom is exceeded and carry only the main figures on time periods from important tops and bottoms as long as they remain unbroken.

The rule for discontinuing the use of tops and bottoms for Time Periods is: When a bottom or top is exceeded by three points, then discontinue the time period from that bottom or top.

Always note the number of months between extreme high and between extreme low points and note what angle the tops and bottoms come out on.

SQUARING THE PRICE RANGE WITH TIME

This is one of the most important and valuable discoveries that I have ever made, and if you stick strictly to the rule, and always watch a stock when Price is squared by Time, or when Time and Price come together, you will be able to forecast the important changes in trend with greater accuracy.

The squaring of Price with Time means as equal number of points up or down balancing an equal number of time periods--either days, weeks or months. For example: If a stock has advanced 24 points in 24 days, then moving the 45° angle or moving-average-line up at the rate of one point per day, the timing line or time period and the price of the stock are at the same level and the stock is resting on a 45° angle and you should watch for an important change in trend at this point. If a stock is to continue uptrend and remain in a strong position, it must continue to advance and keep above the angle of 45°. If it breaks back under this angle, then it is out of its square on the bear side of the 45° angle and in a weaker position. When you are squaring out Time on a daily chart, look at the weekly high and low chart and monthly high and low chart and see if the stock is in a strong position and has yet to run out the time periods, because on a daily chart it has to react and then recover a position, squaring its price many times, as long as the weekly and monthly point up. Market corrections or reactions are simply the squaring out of minor time periods and later the big declines or big advances are the squaring out of major time periods.

SQUARING THE RANGE: Refer to Form #12, where a range of 12 points is shown from 48 low to 60 high. Now, suppose a stock remains for several weeks or several months, moving up or down, in this range, never getting more than 12 points up from the bottom and not breaking the bottom: We start the 45° angle from the bottom of 48 and move it up to the top of the range to 60, then when we see the stock is holding this range and not going higher, we move the 45° angle back to the bottom; then back to the top of the range again, moving it up or down over this range until the stock breaks out into new low levels or new high levels. You will find that every time the 45° angle reaches the top of this range or the bottom of this range, there is some important change in trend of the stock.

You can also use the angles of 2 x 1 to the right of the 45° angle and the 2 x 1 to the left as they again divide the Time Period into two equal parts and are of some value.

If a stock finally moves out of this range on the up side, then the angles would begin at the new and higher bottom and move up, but from the point where the stock went into new high, or from any important bottom made while it was in the range, especially the last bottom that it made, which would be most important, you should then begin an angle at that bottom and continue on up again; watch when this angle is broken or when Time is squared out again with Price, which would be important for another change in trend, either major or minor.

THREE WAYS TO SQUARE TIME AND PRICE:

We can square the Range, that is, the number of points from extreme low to extreme high, with Time- then square the extreme low point with Time- and square the extreme high point with Time. When the market passes out of these squares and breaks important angles, the trend changes up or down.

1 - The range that a stock makes between extreme high and extreme low can be squared so long as it remains in the same price range. If the range is 25 points, it squares with 25 periods of Time-- days, weeks or months. Continue to use this time period as long as it stays in the same range.

2 - SQUARING TIME WITH BOTTOM OR EXTREME LOW PRICE:
The next important Price to square with Time is the lowest price or bottom of any important decline. For example: If the bottom of a stock is 25, then at the end of 25 days, 25 weeks or 25 months, Time and Price are equal. Then watch for a change in trend as based on its bottom or lowest selling price. As long as a stock continues to hold one bottom and advances, you can always use this time period running across and continuing the time period, noting every time it passes out of the squares. Watch especially when the stock reaches the third square, the fourth square, and again the seventh and ninth squares of its time period. These squares only occur frequently on the daily or weekly charts, as the monthly, in most cases, would move out of a range, up or down, before it squared a bottom as many as 7 or 9 times. However, this does sometimes happen when a stock is in a narrow range for many years.

3 - SQUARING TIME WITH TOP OR EXTREME HIGH PRICE:
The other important point to square Time with is the extreme high price of a stock. The Time period must be carried across from the high of the daily, weekly or monthly, and the square of the top price in Time must be noted and watched for a change in trend. If the top of a stock is 50, then when it has moved over 50 days, 50 weeks or 50 months, it has reached its square in Time and an important change is indicated. This can be determined by the position of the angles from top and bottom. For example:

Dow-Jones Industrial Averages-- The high of 386 on September 3, 1929 would require 386 calendar days to equal the Price in Time. This occurred on September 23, 1930. Look at the chart and note how the trend changed and turned down around that time. Then, on October 14, 1931, it run out this period again- and again November 4, 1932, November 25, 1933, December 16, 1934, and January 6, 1935. Look up those dates and you will see that important changes in trend occurred on the Daily Chart when this time period of 386 days balanced the price of 386.

Both major and minor tops and bottoms on all time periods must be watched as they square out right along. Most important of all is the extreme high point on the monthly high and low chart. This may be very high and work out a long time period before it squares the top, in which case you have to divide the price into 8 equal time periods and watch the most important points, like 1/4, 1/3, 1/2, 3/4, but most important of all is when Time equals Price.

When you are watching the position of a stock after it has squared out from a bottom or a top, always look up the time period and the angles from the opposite direction. If the market is nearing a low point, squaring out a top, see how its relation is to the bottom as it might be in the second or third square period from the bottom, which would be a double indication for a change in trend.

SQUARING WEEKLY TIME PERIODS:

The year contains 52 weeks and the square of this in Time and Price is 52 by 52. Therefore you can make up a square of 52 wide and 52 high; put on all of the angles from "0"; then chart the weekly high and low prices of any stock in this square. For example: If the low price of a stock is 50, then the top of this weekly square would be 52 added to 50, which makes 102 as top of the square. As long as the stock stays above 50 and moves up, it will be working in the weekly square of 52. On the other hand, if the stock makes top and works down, you would make up a weekly square 52 points down from the top and 52 over to get the time period.

You can take the past movement of any stock, put on a square of 52 by 52, and study the movement, noting 13 weeks or one-fourth, 26 weeks or one-half, and 39 weeks or three-fourths points on time, and the changes in trend which take place when the stock reaches these important Resistance Points in Time and Price. You would watch for a change in trend around these time periods.

SQUARING MONTHLY TIME PERIODS:

At the time a stock breaks a 45° angle, if it is selling at 135 on the 135th month, it is breaking a doubly strong Resistance Level-- a strong angle and a natural Resistance Level. This would be Time and Space balancing at Resistance Levels or geometrical angles and would indicate a big decline to follow. - Reverse this rule at the end of a bear campaign.

On a monthly chart twelve months completes a year, therefore the square of 12 is very important for working out time periods on the monthly chart. The square of 12 is 144 and important changes often occur on even 12 months' periods from a bottom or top of a stock. It will help you if you use the Resistance Levels on prices of the even 12's, noting 24, 36, 48, 60. 72, 84, 96, 108, etc. Watch how the stock acts on angles when it reaches these important Resistance points in Price.

PRICE AHEAD OF TIME

Why do stocks often cross the 45° angle on the daily, weekly or monthly chart, then have an advance for a short period of time, decline and rest on the same 45° angle? Because when the stock crosses the 45° angle the first time, it has not run out or overcome the square of Time with Price. Therefore, on the secondary reaction, when it rests on the 45° angle, it is at a time when the stock has reached the square of distance in Time. After that a greater advance follows.

Reverse this rule at the top of a bull market. When a stock breaks under the 45° angle a long distance from the base or bottom, it is most important. Many times a stock will rest on the 45° angle in the early stages of an advance, then later, on a reaction, rest on it again; then have a prolonged advance, react and rest on the 45° again, and then advance to a higher level; then break the 45° angle the next time, which places it in an extremely weak position because it is so far away from the base and so much time has elapsed since the stock made low. Don't forget--It is most important when angles are broken on the monthly and weekly charts.

This accounts for stocks that have a sharp, quick decline from the top and then advance and make a slightly higher top or a series of slightly lower tops, and work over until they overcome the square of the price range at a comparatively high level and break the 45° angle, then a fast decline follows.

STRONGEST ANGLES FOR MEASURING TIME AND PRICE

90° ANGLE: Why is the 90 degree angle the strongest angle of all? Because it is vertical or straight up and straight down.

180° ANGLE: What is the next strongest angle to the 90° angle? The 180° angle because it is square to the 90° angle, being 90° from the 90° angle.

270° ANGLE: What is the next strongest angle to the 180° angle? The 270° angle because it is in opposition to 90, or 180° from the 90° angle, which equals 1/2 of the circle, the strongest point. 270 months equals 22½ years, which is 1/2 of 45.

360° ANGLE: What is the next strongest angle after 270? It is 360°, because it ends the circle and gets back to the beginning point and is opposite 180° or the half-way point, or the angle which equals 1/2 of the circle.

120° AND 240° ANGLES What angles are next strongest to 90, 180, 270, and 360°? Answer: 120° and 240° angles, because they are 1/3 and 2/3 of the circle. 120° is 90 plus 30, which is 1/3 of 90. 240 is 180 plus 1/3 or 60, which makes these strong angles, especially strong for measurements of time.

45° - 135° - 225° - 315°: What angles are next in strength?
Answer: 45° angle, because it is 1/2 of 90,
135° angle, because it is 90 plus 45,
225° angle, because it is 45 plus 180, and
315° angle, because it is 45 from 270.
The angle of 225° is 180 from 45 and the angle of 315° is 180 from 135.

CARDINAL & FIXED CROSS: The angles of 90, 180, 270, and 360 form the first important cross, known as the Cardinal Cross. The angles of 45, 135, 225, and 315 for the next important cross, which is known as the Fixed Cross. These angles are very important for the measurements of time and space or price, and volume.

22½° - 67½° - 78¾°: Why is the angle of 22½° stronger than 11¼°? Because it is twice as much, being the same reason that a 45° angle is stronger than a 22½° angle. Again, the angle of 67½° is 1½ times 45, therefore quite strong when anything is moving up toward 90°. 78¾° is stronger than 67½°, because it is 7/8 of 90, and therefore one of the strongest points before 90 is reached--important to watch both on time, price, and volume. Many stocks have important moves and make tops or bottoms around the 78th to 80th day, week or month, but don't overlook 84 months or 7 years, a strong time cycle.

DIVISION OF $1: 1/8-POINTS Why are the angles of 1/8 of a circle most important for time and space measurement? Because we divide $1 into 1/2, 1/4, and

1/8 parts. We use 25 cents or one quarter, 50 cents or half dollar, and long years ago we had 12½ cent pieces. While the most important figures of our basis of money are the four quarters, we do use the 1/8 part or 12½ cents in all calculations. Stock fluctuations are based on 1/8, 1/4, 3/8, 1/2, 5/8, 3/4, 7/8 and the whole figure. Therefore, any price measurement as well as time will work out closer to these figures when changed into angles of time than 1/3 or 2/3 points for the simple reason that the fluctuations moving in 1/8 proportion must come out closer to these figures.

Figuring $100, or par, as a basis for stock prices and changing those prices to degrees, 12½ equals 45°, 25 equals 90°, 37½ equals 135°, 50 equals 180°, 62½ equals 225°, 75 equals 270°, 82½ equals 315°, and 100 equals 360°. For example:

When a stock sells at 50 on the 180th day, week or month, it is on the degree of its time angle.

On February 1, 1915, U. S. Steel made a low at 38, which is closest to a price of 37½, which is 3/8 of 100 and equals 135° angle. Steel was 14 years or 168 months old on February 25, 1915, and hit the angle of 135°, which showed that Steel was behind time, but that it was in a strong position, holding at 38 above the 135° angle or the price of 37½.

When Steel reached 200, it equalled 2 circles of 360°. When it advanced to 261¾, it was closest to 62½ in the third 100 or nearest the 225° angle or 5/8 point, which is the strongest angle after it crossed the half-way point at 250 or 180° angle.

W. D. Gann

November, 1935

CHAPTER 10

FORECASTING BY TIME CYCLES

FORECASTING BY TIME CYCLES

TIME is the most important factor in determining market movements and by studying the past records of the averages or individual stocks you will be able to prove for yourself that history does repeat and that by knowing the past you can tell the future.

The ancient hunters had a rule that when they were searching to locate an animal in his den, they always followed his tracks backwards, figuring that it was the shortest route to his lair. The quickest way for you to learn how to determine future market movements is to study the past

> "The thing that hath been, it is that which shall be; and that which is done is that which shall be done, and there is no new things under the sun." Eccl. 1: 9.

There is a definite relation between TIME and PRICE. In the previous lessons you have learned about FORMATIONS and RESISTANCE LEVELS around old tops and bottoms. Now, by a study of the TIME PERIODS and TIME CYCLES you will learn why tops and bottoms are formed at certain times and why Resistance Levels are so strong at certain times and bottoms and tops hold around them.

MAJOR TIME CYCLES

Everything moves in cycles as a result of the natural law of action and reaction. By a study of the past, I have discovered what cycles repeat in the future.

There must always be a major and a minor, a greater and a lesser, a positive and a negative. In order to be accurate in forecasting the future, you must know the major cycles. The most money is made when fast moves and extreme fluctuations occur at the end of major cycles.

I have experimented and compared past markets in order to locate the major and minor cycles and determine in what years the cycles repeat in the future. After years of research and practical tests, I have discovered that the following cycles are the most reliable to use:

10-YEAR CYCLES

The important cycle for forecasting is the cycle of around 10 years. Fluctuations of about the same nature occur which produce extreme high or low every 10 years. Stocks work out important tops and bottoms very close to the even 10 year cycle, although at times bottoms or tops come out around 10½ to 11 years in extreme markets.

The 10-year cycle equals 120 months. We divide this just the same as we divide the range between bottoms and tops to get Resistance Levels. One-half of the cycle would be 5 years or 60 months. One-fourth would be 2½ years or 30 months. One-eighth would be 15 months and one-sixteenth 7½ months. One-third would be 40 months and two-thirds of the cycle would be 80 months. All of these time periods are important to watch for changes in trend.

7-YEAR CYCLE

This cycle is 84 months. You should watch 7 years from any important top or bottom and 42 months or one-half of this cycle. You will find many culminations around the 42nd to 44th months. 21 months is one-fourth of 84 months, also important. You will find many bottoms and tops 21 to 23 months apart. At times prices make bottoms or tops 10 to 11 months from a previous top or bottom. This is due to the fact that this period is one-eighth of the 7-year cycle.

5-YEAR CYCLE

This cycle is very important because it is one-half of the 10-year cycle and the smallest complete cycle that the market works out.

MINOR CYCLES

The minor cycles are 3 years and 2 years. The smallest cycle is one year, which often shows a change in trend in the 10th or 11th month.

RULES FOR FUTURE CYCLES

Prices move in 10-year cycles, which are worked out in 5-year cycles---a 5-year cycle up and a 5-year cycle down. Begin with extreme tops and extreme bottoms to figure all cycles, either major or minor.

1 - A bull campaign generally runs 5 years -- 2 years up, 1 year down, and 2 years up, completing a 5-year cycle. The end of a 5-year campaign comes in the 59th or 60th month. Always watch for the change in the 59th month.

2 - A bear cycle often runs 5 years down -- the first move 2 years down, then 1 year up, and 2 years down, completing the 5-year downswing.

3 - Bull or bear campaigns seldom run more than 3 to 3½ years up or down without a move of 3 to 6 months or one year in the opposite direction, except at the end of Major Cycles, like 1869 and 1929. Many campaigns culminate in the 23rd month, not running out the full 2 years. Watch the weekly and monthly charts to determine whether the culmination will occur in the 23rd, 24th, 27th or 30th month of the move, or in extreme campaigns in the 34th to 35th or 41st to 42nd month.

4 - Adding 10 years to any top, it will give you top of the next 10 year cycle, repeating about the same average fluctuations.

5 - Adding 10 years to any bottom, it will give you the bottom of the next 10 year cycle, repeating the same kind of a year and about the same average fluctuations.

6 - Bear campaigns often run out in 7-year cycles, or 3 years and 4 years from any complete bottom. From any complete bottom of a cycle, first add 3 years to get the next bottom; then add 4 years to that bottom to get bottom of 7-year cycle. For example: 1914 bottom - add 3 years, gives 1917, low of panic; then add 4 years to 1917, gives 1921, low of another depression.

7 - To any final major or minor top, add 3 years to get the next top; then add 3 years to that top, which will give you the third top; add 4 years to the third top to get the final top of a 10-year cycle. Sometimes a change in trend from any top occurs before the end of the regular time period, therefore you should begin to watch the 27th, 34th, and 42nd months for a reversal.

8 - Adding 5 years to any top, it will give the next bottom of a 5-year cycle. In order to get top of the next 5-year cycle, add 5 years to any bottom. For example: 1917 was bottom of a big bear campaign; add 5 years give 1922, top of a minor bull campaign. Why do I say, "Top of a minor bull campaign?" Because the major bull campaign was due to end in 1929.

1919 was top; adding 5 years to 1919 gives 1924 as bottom of a 5-year bear cycle. Refer to Rules 1 and 2, which tell you that a bull or bear campaign seldom runs more than 2 to 3 years in the same direction. The bear campaign from 1919 was 2 years down — 1920 and 1921; therefore, we only expect one-year rally in 1922; then 2 years down — 1923 and 1924, which completes the 5-year bear cycle.

Looking back to 1913 and 1914, you will see that 1923 and 1924 must be bear years to complete the 10-year cycle from the bottoms of 1913-1914. Then, note 1917 bottom of a bear year; adding 7 years gives 1924 also as bottom of a bear cycle. Then, adding 5 years to 1924 gives 1929 top of a cycle.

FORECASTING MONTHLY MOVES

Monthly moves can be determined by the same rules as yearly:

Add 3 months to an important bottom, then add 4, making 7, to get minor bottoms and reaction points.

In big upswings a reaction will often not last over 2 months, the third month being up, the same rule as in yearly cycle — 2 down and the third up.

In extreme markets, a reaction sometimes only lasts 2 or 3 weeks; then the advance is resumed. In this way a market may continue up for 12 months without breaking a monthly bottom.

In a bull market the minor trend may reverse and run down 3 to 4 months; then turn up and follow the main trend again.

In a bear market, the minor trend may run up to 3 to 4 months, then reverse and follow the main trend, although, as a general rule, stocks never rally more than 2 months in a bear market; then start to break in the 3rd month and follow the main trend down.

NATURAL SEASONAL TIME CHANGES

While we do not use the calendar months for time periods, unless an extreme high or low should occur around January 2 or 3rd, we do use the Seasonal Time Periods which are more important and many of the important highs and lows have occurred around these Seasonal Time Periods. These periods are as follows:

December 21, any year
February 5
May 5
June 21
August 5
September 21
November 8

Then repeat, December 21, etc., for the 2nd and third years.

These Seasonal Time Periods divide the year into 8 equal parts of approximately 45 days each. You can divide these time periods into 2 equal parts which are approximately 22½ days. Example: December 21 to February 5 gives January 13 as the ½ period, and between June 21 to August 5 is July 14.

The variation from these Time Periods is usually 3 to 4 days before or after the actual dates. The most important changes in Grains occur during FEBRUARY, MAY, AUGUST and NOVEMBER, therefore; these dates and months are the most important to watch for major changes in trend, but always keep in mind the dates of the previous highs and lows of past years and watch for the change in trend around these dates.

CHAPTER 11

AUBURN MOTORS

W. D. GANN

91 WALL STREET
NEW YORK

SCIENTIFIC ADVICE
AND ANALYTICAL REPORTS
ON STOCKS AND COMMODITIES
AUTHOR OF "TRUTH OF THE STOCK TAPE"
"WALL STREET STOCK SELECTOR"
AND "THE TUNNEL THRU THE AIR"

MEMBER
AMERICAN ECONOMIC ASS'N
ROYAL ECONOMIC SOCIETY
CABLE ADDRESS
"GANWADE NEW YORK"

AUBURN MOTORS

The chart enclosed on Auburn Motors has all of the natural important angles placed on it which shows the natural resistance angles obtained by dividing up the circle of 360°. We have used only the 45° angles from tops and bottoms, the 90° angle and the horizontal angle, which is equal to an angle of 90°. Every stock squares itself according to price and time and when it breaks out of the square one way or the other continues to move in the same direction until it reaches another important 45° angle or resistance point according to the time or price. We use the angles of 11 1/4, 22 1/2, 33 3/4, 45, 56 1/4, 60, 67 1/2, 78 3/4, 90° and so forth. Then draw the 45° angle diagonally where the time crosses the 45° angle from either the important top or bottom.

The crossing of two right angles is very important for a change in trend as we will show on the example of Auburn Motors.

Auburn Motors made the extreme high on April 1, 1930, at 263 3/4; then made a second high on April 10th and a third final high on April 16, 1930, when the price reached 262 3/4. We draw the 45° angle from the top of April 1st and another 45° angle from the last top made on April 16th; then number the days across and draw the 45° angles bisecting the 45° angles from the top.

Example: April 15th the 45° angle from April 1st and the 45° angle from 11 1/4 days over crossed at the exact point where Auburn made the low price at this time. In other words, on April 15th Auburn made bottom on two 45° angles; then rallied to April 16th, broke the 45° angle and the trend turned down.

Note 23° or days over where we reach the angle of 22 1/2° and that Auburn made low on the 22nd day, rallied only one day, then broke the day angle or time angle of 33 3/4; next broke the more important 45° angle, showing that it was getting weaker all the time. It made bottom at 180 on the 27th day from the top. 180 is always an important resistance point because it is one-half of the circle of 360°. Auburn rallied to 201. The next important resistance level is 202 1/2, or 22 1/2° added to 180. Auburn at this top was just under the 45° angle. Next it broke the 45° angle from the day angle of 56 1/4.

May 20th, declined to 150, another important natural angle because it is 5/12 of the circle. This bottom was reached on the 40th market day. Auburn then rallied to 172 on the 45th market day, which is very important for a change in trend and top. Next it broke the 45° angle drawn from the bottom at 150; continued on down; broke the 45° time angle from 78 3/4, then broke the 45° angle from 90 timing angle. 90 is twice as strong as 45 and very important for a change in trend.

June 23rd, this is an important date for a seasonal change in trend. Auburn declined to 91, holding 1 point above the 90° price angle or resistance which is always important for tops or bottoms. It was on the 67th day and 67 1/2 is a strong angle.

July 17th, Auburn rallied to 141 on the 86th day and failed to reach the 45° angle from 101 1/4 days. Next it broke the 45° angle from 112 1/2 days; then broke the 45° angle drawn from the low of 91, which indicated that it was in a weak position and going lower. Note that 91 was the lowest parallel angle or lowest 45° angle from the 45° angles drawn from the tops of April 1st and April 16th. This parallel was 53 points wide from April 1st top and 59 wide from April 16th top. The bottom occurred on the 120th day time angle and 120 is important because it is 1/3 of a circle.

August 12th, Auburn declined to 102, which is just above the natural resistance angle of 101 1/4 and this bottom occurred on the 108th day and just above the 45° angle from the 135th day time angle.

September 8th, Auburn rallied to 135 and hit the 45° angle from April 1st top. It was on the 135° natural resistance angle, which is 3/8 of a circle and very strong. A stock is always a short sale the first time it rallies to the 45° angle from its top, protected with a stop-loss order 3 points above the angle, and at this point it was a safe short sale because the price was 135, which equals the crossing of two right angles. Auburn next broke under the 45° angle from the bottom at 102 and the 45° angle from the 135th day. It continued to break angles and to work into weaker squares until the final bottom was reached.

November 5, 1930, Auburn declined to 60 3/8. 60 is always important because it is 1/6 of a circle. It made this bottom on the 177th market day from April 1st top. Note on the 180th market day Auburn made a higher top and turned the trend up for the first time. The bottom was reached on the 190th day angle or on a 45° angle drawn diagonally from 190 days down from the top.

November 17th, for the first time since April 1930, Auburn crossed the 45° angle from the top of April 1st, when the price reached 77, where the trend turned up, and put Auburn in a very strong position because it crossed the 45° angle at such a low level.

Note the top of November 20th was made at 82 1/2, just under the 45° angle from the top of April 16th. Then a decline followed and bottom was reached at 72 1/2 on November 28, 1930.

November 29th, Auburn crossed the 45° angle from the April 16th top for the first time, indicating that it was in a stronger position and that the main trend had turned up because it had crossed the extreme outside parallel angle. This low was made around 78 3/4, the natural angle, and Auburn never sold lower after crossing this outside 45° angle until it advanced to 295 1/2 on April 14, 1931.

After Auburn regained or got above the 45° angle from the top of April 16, 1930, it started regaining 45° angles and making higher parallels to the left of the 45° angle from 60 3/8 just the reverse of its movement on the way down from 263 3/4 to 60 3/8.

December 18, 1930, Auburn advanced to 119 3/4. This was nearly twice the price of 60 3/8, and the natural angle, or 1/3 of a circle, is at 120. This top occurred on the 36th market day.

December 23rd, Auburn declined to 91 1/2 and made a second bottom at 92 on December 27th, holding above the 90° resistance point. Note that 90 was the half-way point from 60 3/8 to 119 3/4, which showed that Auburn was in a strong position. The last low of 92 was reached on the 43rd market day, and the price was above the 45° angle from 33 3/4 days.

1931, January 5th, Auburn rallied to 116 on the 225th market day from the top of April 1930. 225 is always strong because it is 5/8 of a circle. Auburn then declined and broke the 45° angle drawn from the bottom of 60 3/8.

January 14th and 17th, declined to 101 1/4, which is the natural resistance angle. Note the cross angle of 101 1/4 and that the price was bottom on the 60th market day, which your rule tells you is very important for a change in trend because it is 1/6 of a circle. The trend turned up and Auburn continued to get into a stronger position on angles.

January 22, 1931, Auburn crossed the 45° angle, marked in green, from the 60th market day and on January 26th crossed, or regained, the 45° angle drawn from the bottom at 60 3/8. The price was 128 on the 67 1/2 market day angle. When a stock regains the 45° angle from the bottom it is in a very strong position. Auburn never got back to the 45° angle from 60 3/8 until it made top on April 14, 1931, at 295 1/2. On the advance after crossing the 45° angle of 60 3/8, it continued to show strength because it worked into higher parallel angles to the left of the 45° angle from the bottom.

February 9, 1931, Auburn crossed the 45° angle drawn from the top at 119 3/4 made on December 18, 1930. This was another indication of a very strong position.

February 26th, Auburn made top at 217 on the 92nd market day from the bottom or just 2 days over the 90th day, which is always important for a change in trend. Note the natural resistance level at 213 3/4. Auburn then dropped back under this angle and broke back under the 120 day time angle marked in green, which put it into a weaker position and indicated a decline. You can see that Auburn on the way up worked to the 45th, 90th, and other important days on time just the same as it did on the way down.

March 7th, Auburn declined to 175, just 5 points under 180, which is half of the circle, and it reached the 45° angle which was 1/2 of the distance between the 45° angle drawn from the top of 119 3/4 and the 45° angle drawn from the first top made on November 20, 1930, at 82 1/2. Auburn made this top on the 100th market day and on the 101st day crossed the 120 green angle, which is the time angle. Then made two days tops on the 45° angle from 217 top. Then crossed the 45° angle from the top at 217 and never dropped back under it and continued to make higher parallels to the left of the 45° angle from 60 3/8.

April 14th, Auburn reached extreme high of 295 1/2. This was a date for a seasonal change because the last high occurred on April 16th, 1930, from which the big decline followed. Note that the same width of parallel from the lowest 45° angle drawn from 101 1/4 and 103 1/2 bottoms made January 14th and 19th, 1931, which was 59 wide. April 14th, the 180th day angle, crossed at 290. This was the crossing of 2 right angles—one the parallel angle of same width of the fluctuations from 263 3/4 to 91, and the other from the extreme of 101 1/4 to 295 1/2. The same day that Auburn advanced above the crossing of these parallel angles of 290 it declined and closed at 287, below these angles indicating a weak position. Auburn only closed 1 day above the width of the same parallel on which it declined. Then it started breaking parallel angles and getting into a weaker position right along.

It is important to note that 292 1/2 is an important resistance level because it is 270, which is 3/4 of a circle, plus 22 1/2, and Auburn failed to go over three points above this angle. Another thing to consider is that from 60 3/8 to

295 1/2 Auburn was up 235 1/8 points, which was nearly 2/3 of a circle and another reason for strong resistance. You should look up your resistance card and see the other important points around this level. For example, Auburn's extreme high was 514 and the low on the last move 60 3/8. This would make the half-way point 287 1/8. Auburn's extreme low of history was 31 3/4. This would make the half-way point 272 1/2. Then when Auburn broke back under the first half-way point of 287 1/8 it indicated weakness; next breaking the half-way point of the life fluctuation at 272 7/8, indicated greater weakness. The next important point was 257 or 1/2 of 514, the highest price at which Auburn ever sold. Therefore, when Auburn broke under 257 it was in a very weak position and indicated a further sharp decline.

April 20, Auburn declined to 180, getting support on the natural angle or 1/2 of the circle. This was on the 315th market day from April 1930, and on the 136th market day from the low of 60 3/8 and on the 166th calendar day. 165 is important because it is 1/2 between the angle of 150 and 180. Auburn made bottom on the 45th market day from the low of 101 1/4 made on January 14, 1931. It rested on the lowest parallel angle of 45°.

From 60 3/8 to 295 1/2 gives the half-way point at 177 3/4 and Auburn holding above this half-way point showed it was in a strong position and ready to rally. At that time 178 1/2 was on the 45° angle from 103 1/2, the low of January 19, 1931, and being the last and lowest 45° angle it was the strongest support point, from which a rally must take place and the stock was a purchase with stop 3 points under.

April 24th, Auburn rallied to 219 and hit the 45° angle from the bottom of 175 made on March 7th; then broke back under 213 3/4, the price angle, and broke 146 1/4 the day angle.

April 30, 1931, Auburn declined to 187, resting on the 45° angle from the low of 103 1/2. A sharp rally followed and on May 1st Auburn advanced to 227 1/2, just under the 45° green angle from 157 1/2 days. This was a cross-angle and also a 45° angle from the top of 119 3/4. The price of 225 was on a strong resistance, or 225°, which is 5/8 of a circle, and Auburn failed to go 3 points above it. A big break followed in the afternoon of the same day and Auburn declined to 184, which was 3 points under lowest 45° angle from 103 1/2, the bottom of January 19, 1931, and was just above the 45° green angle from the 135th market day and on the 146th market day from November 5, 1930, and on the 179th calendar day from the bottom, which was a strong indication for bottom or a change in trend. Auburn quickly regained the 45° angle from the lowest parallel; then crossed the 45° angle drawn from 60 3/8.

May 5th, Auburn advanced to 225 1/2, where it struck the same resistance of 225 on the natural resistance angles. It hit a 45° angle from the low point of 183 and the 45° angle from the top made on May 1st, and was just under the 45° angle from the 157 1/2 day, a strong resistance point.

May 6th, Auburn declined to 203 on the 45° green angle from the 146 1/4 day and being just above the natural resistance angle of 202 1/2, it received strong support, rallied and crossed the angle of 45° from 60 3/8 which put it again in a very strong position.

May 9, 1931, Auburn advanced to 252. This was just under the 45° angle from 219, the low of March 30th and on the 22nd day from the top of April 14, 1931.

You will note that 257 is 1/2 of the highest price at which Auburn ever sold—514. May 9th was 330 market days from April 1, 1930, which is important, and 103 market days from 60 3/8 and 185 Calendar days from 60 3/8. On May 9th Auburn dropped back under the 45° angle from the 168 3/4 day, declined to 237 where it rested on the angle of 45° from the top at 119 3/4 made January 18, 1931.

At this writing, May 9, 1931, Auburn is in a strong position on Angles, but is a short sale on rallies with a stop at 260, which is 3 points above the half-way point, or 1/2 of 514. The stock is in a strong position on angles and you have to watch the 45° angle from the top at 295 1/2 and the angle marked in green from 180. As long as Auburn can hold above the 45° angle from 60 3/8 it is still in a position to rally, but when it breaks the 45° angle from 60 3/8 and the lowest 45° angle from 101 1/4 and 101 1/2, the bottoms of January 14th and 19th, 1931, it will then indicate a big decline.

If Auburn can cross 260, the next resistance point will be around 273 and the next around 287 and should it get through the old top of 295 1/2 or cross 300, it will then indicate very much higher prices. You should always watch the 1/4 and 1/2 points from the last important bottom. In Auburn's present position, the point to watch would be between 180 and 252. Also 237 3/4 which is 1/2 from 295 1/2 to 180. Auburn closed just around this point on May 9th, which is near 240 and an important resistance level, which is 2/3 of the circle. Should Auburn break 234 now, or over 3 points under this half-way point it will indicate lower.

May 9, 1931.

CHAPTER 12

TIME AND PRICE RESISTANCE LEVELS

TIME AND PRICE RESISTANCE LEVELS
by
W.D. GANN

WEEKLY HIGH AND LOW CHART

The Weekly Chart is one of the most reliable trend indicators that we use. The Weekly Tables for Price and Time Resistance are very valuable and enable you to determine ahead of time the prices at which highs and lows will be made and the time or date when these extreme high or low prices will be reached.

These Weekly Tables cover periods of 7 days or 1 calendar week. Howeve you do not start to number time periods from January 1 or the 1st day of any month. You begin to count the time periods from the exact dates of any extreme high or low price. You also use the dates of the minor high and low prices both to begin to count time periods from and to get price resistance and determine a change in trend.

NATURAL SEASONAL TIME PERIODS

These periods do not start with the calendar year but start with the Spring Season March 20. The year is divided up into 8 equal parts and also divided into 1/3's which give two more time periods. These Time Periods are as follows:

Mar. 20 to May 5 is 1/8 of a year or 46 days
June 21 is 1/4 of a year or 91 days
July 23 is 1/3 of a year or 121 days
Aug. 5 is 3/8 of a year or 136 days
Sept 22 is 1/2 of a year or 182 days
Nov. 8 is 5/8 of a year or 227 days
Nov. 22 is 2/3 of a year or 242 days
Dec. 21 is 3/4 of a year or 273 days
Feb. 4 is 7/8 of a year or 319 days
Mar. 20 is 1 year or 365 calendar days

All of these periods are important to watch for changes in trend. The most important are 1/2 and the end of the season; next important 1/4 and 3/4, and 1/3 and 2/3.

MID-SEASON POINTS

These are May 5, August 5, November 8 and February 4. By checking over past records of prices, you will see how often highs and lows have occurred during these periods.

TABLES FOR TIME PERIODS AND PRICE RESISTANCE

The Tables for Time Periods and Price Resistance are made up to cover 40 years in the future. You can also use them for 40 years in the past

These Tables measure Price and Time Resistance from 6½ to 2080. Each period of one year or 52 weeks is shown at the bottom of the Table and the division of the yearly time periods are shown both for the Seasonal and Natural Time Periods and for the proportionate parts of a year starting from the date of any high or low price.

Below we give the Tables showing the Price and Time Periods.

1/8	of	year	46 days	6½	weeks	Price	6½
1/4	"	"	91 days	13	"	"	13
1/3	"	"	121 days	17	"	"	17
3/8	"	"	136 days	19½	"	"	19½
1/2	"	"	182 days	26	"	"	26
5/8	"	"	227 days	32½	"	"	32½
2/3	"	"	242 days	35	"	"	35
3/4	"	"	273 days	39	"	"	39
7/8	"	"	319 days	45½	"	"	45½
1		"	365 days	52	"	"	52

From the above you can see that the year is divided into 10 divisions of Time and starting with 6½ to 52, the price is also divided into 10 divisions. These Tables continue the same for 40 years or more, making equal divisions of Time and Price.

PRICE RESISTANCE

The Price Resistance is calculated in the same way at Time Periods from highs and lows. Always calculate how much the price is up from the low levels or how much it is down from high levels. In this way you are able to determine all of the important Price Resistance Levels. Example

Suppose the low price is 50 and the current price is 102. This is up 52 from the low and equals 52 weeks or 1 year in time, making this price important to watch for change in trend because it is a Time and Price Balance.

Suppose the high price has been 182 and at the time you look it up, the stock or grain is selling at 130. This is at 1/2 or 2½ years in time and the price is down 52 from the high which equals 1 year in time. This is also a Price and Time Balance and is important to watch for change in trend.

Suppose the price makes high or low on 1/4 and the next high or low is on 1/4 of 1/2. This would be important for change in trend.

From the low, suppose the time is on 1/4 and 3/4 and from the high the time is on 1/3 or 2/3, this is important for change in trend, especialy if the price is at 1/2 or 3/4 resistance. (for more proof see example of actual market moves in the past.)

INDICATIONS FOR CHANGE IN TREND

1. TIME AND PRICE BALANCE -- Suppose you wish to look up the time period for 5 years, you look at the bottom of column 5 where you find 260, which is 260 weeks. Suppose the price is at 260. This is a Time and Price Balance and is very important for a change in trend.
   Suppose at the end of 262 weeks the price is at 234, which is 1/2 and equals 4½ years in Time. This is next in importance for change in trend.

2. ANNIVERSARY DATES -- Always consider the anniversary date from extre highs and lows as important for a change in trend.

3. DIVISIONS OF TIME -- Next consider 1/4, 1/3, 1/2, 2/3, and 3/4 of th time periods important for a change in trend.

4. PRICE RESISTANCE LEVELS -- These same Resistance Levels in Price are also important to watch for change in trend, especially when the Time Period comes out at one of these important divisions of price.

5. WEEKLY BOTTOMS AND TOPS -- When you are studying the Weekly Chart, always look to see if a weekly bottom has been broken or a weekly high level has been crossed, which would be important for a change in trend. The greater the time period from any high or low level, the more important it is when prices cross these levels.

6. DOUBLE AND TRIPLE TOPS AND BOTTOMS -- When these occur on important Time Periods and at important Price Resistance Levels, they are very important to watch for change in trend and to expect a move to start that will last for a considerable length of time.

7. SWING BOTTOMS AND TOPS -- The breaking of a swing bottom or the crossing of a swing top is very important for a change in trend.

   SWING CHART -- You can make up a Swing Chart by moving the price up to the top of each week; then the first time the low of the previous week is broken, you move the swing line down to the low of that week When that week's bottom has been broken, continue to move the line down as long as the price makes lower tops and lower bottoms. The first week that the price makes a higher bottom and a higher top, you move the line on the Swing Chart up to the top of that week and continue to move it up each week until there is a reversal.

WHEN MOST IMPORTANT CHANGES IN TREND OCCUR

These are:

1. Anniversary dates of previous highs and lows
2. Next is 1/2 of each yearly period or 182 days from any high or low
3. Next in importance is 1/4 and 3/4 or 13 weeks and 39 weeks

4. Next is 1/3 and 2/3 or 17 weeks and 35 weeks.
5. Next is 3/8 and 7/8 of a year or 19½ and 35½ weeks.

You can prove to yourself how well these rules work by going back and checking the Time Periods from highs and lows for several years and checking the price at which the stock or commodity was selling and see how it compares on the Tables for Price and Time Resistance. This will give you the value of these Time Tables and Price Resistance Levels.

W.D. GANN

January 26, 1955

Chapter 13

How To Sell Puts And Calls

HOW TO SELL PUTS AND CALLS

Many people know how to buy Puts and Calls but very few know how to sell them or know that they can sell them and get the premium money for the option.

When you sell a Put or a Call on stocks, you are simply taking the opposite position to the one when you buy a Put or a Call, and there are more advantages on the selling side, especially at certain periods of the market.

Suppose you wish to buy U. S. Steel. Naturally, you want to get in the market and buy at the lowest level possible, but you cannot be sure of the exact bottom. For example: We will assume that U. S. Steel is selling at 66, and you feel that you would be willing to buy it if it declines to around 62. You have your account open with your broker and your money on deposit to cover the margin requirements to buy U. S. Steel. You give your broker an order to sell a Put on 100 U. S. Steel good 30 days -- which is always below the market, varying from 2 to 3 points to as much as 10 to 15 points. We will assume that the broker sells the Put on U. S. Steel at 62, good 30 days, and receives $112.50, which is credited to your account. This is the premium that you receive from the buyer. Then, we will assume that U. S. Steel does not decline to 62 before the 30-day Put expires. Therefore, you will have the $112.50 which you received for the Put.

Then, if you are still willing and want to buy U. S. Steel, you could sell another Put on 100 shares, good for 30 days, at whatever number of points below the market the broker could get it. In this case, we will assume that Steel is selling around 63 and the broker sells the Put for you at 59, again receiving $112.50 credited to your account. Then suppose U. S. Steel declines to 58 and closes at the end of 30 days at 58. The man who bought from you the Put on 100 U. S. Steel at 59 will put it to you or deliver it to your broker for 59 and you will have bought Steel at 59 and will have $250.00 to your credit, the money you received on the Puts sold.

Then, we will assume that you are willing to take 4 or 5 points' profit on U. S. Steel. You give your broker an order to sell a Call on U. S. Steel good 30 days. We will assume he sells it at 64 and again you receive $112.50 premium. If at the end of the 30 days U. S. Steel has not reached 64, you still have the stock and have $375.00 to your credit, which you have received for selling Puts and Calls.

We will assume that at the end of the 30 days U. S. Steel is selling at 63. You instruct your broker to sell a Call on U. S. Steel good 30 days, and he sells it at 67 and receives $112.50 for your account. At the end of the 30 days, or when the Call expires, U. S. Steel is selling at 69 and the man to whom you sold the Call demands delivery; then your broker delivers 100 U. S. Steel for 67. You have sold at 67 the Steel that you bought at 59 and have made 8 points' profit or $800.00, less commission and interest, and you have received $450.00 premium money for the Puts and Calls you sold, which is just that much extra profit because you did not take as much risk as you would if you had just bought U. S. Steel or sold it without selling the Puts or Calls.

SELLING CALLS TO GET SHORT OF THE MARKET

Suppose you think the market is about high enough to sell short but you are not sure just when and where the top will be reached. U. S. Steel is selling around 75 when you make up your mind to sell it short. Then you give your broker an order to sell a Call on 100 U. S. Steel good 30 days. He sells the Call at 80, which means that if U. S. Steel is selling above 80 at the end of 30 days, the man you sold the option to will call it or buy it from you at 80 and you will be short at 80 with a credit of $112.50 which you received for the Call.

You might be able to sell Calls twice, three times, five times or more and take in the premium money before the stock is called. Suppose, after you have been called for Steel at 80 — which puts you short at 80 — you decide to sell a Put. You get it at 75, which gives you 5 points' profit, and you again receive $112.50 for the Put good 30 days. We will assume that at the end of 30 days Steel is selling at 74 and the man you sold the Put to, delivers 100 shares of Steel to the broker for your account. This means that you have bought 100 shares at 75 and covered your short position, making a profit of 5 points or $500.00, less commission and taxes; and at the same time you have made $225.00 extra by selling the Puts and Calls and have taken no additional risk.

HOW TO PROTECT YOURSELF IN SELLING PUTS OR CALLS

Whether you want to enter the market or not, you can sell Puts or Calls and can protect yourself by buying or selling the stock before the Put or Call expires. *For example:*

Suppose you have sold a Call on U. S. Steel at 80 and you are not long or have not bought U. S. Steel. When it advances to 78 or 79 you decide that you do not want to sell it short as the market looks very strong. In order to protect yourself you buy 100 shares of U. S. Steel at 79. Then, we will assume that at the end of 30 days it closes at 87; the man you sold the Call to demands delivery of the stock and you deliver or sell it to him at 80. You have one point profit, because you bought it at 79, and you have $112.50 premium money that you received for the Call.

Suppose you sell a Put on U. S. Steel at 72, good 30 days. Then the market turns weak and is declining fast. When it reaches 74, you decide that it acts as if it is going very much lower, and in order to protect yourself you sell 100 shares of U. S. Steel short at 74. Then, we will assume that the stock declines and closes at 69, and the man you sold the Put to at 72, delivers you the stock at 72, which puts you out of the market and still gives you a profit of 2 points and the premium money of $112.50.

When you are long of the market or have stocks bought, it is nearly always to your advantage to sell Calls good 30 days until your stock is called, because if you are wrong and the market goes against you, you will be taking in the premium money you receive for the Calls, which will help to cover the loss on the stock.

When you are short of a stock, in most cases it will pay you to sell a Put good 30 days and take in the money, because if the market declines — as it often does — and fails to reach the Put price, you will still have the money you received for the Put and will still be short of the stock and can sell a Put for the next 30 days and take in another $112.50.

I know many traders, when they are long of the market or have stocks bought, who sell Calls every 30 days and sometimes carry the stock for six or twelve months before the man who buys the Calls has an opportunity to call the stock. During all that time they are making more than one point a month profit by selling a Call every 30 days.

BUYING A PUT AND SELLING A CALL AT THE SAME TIME

We will suppose that you buy U. S. Steel at 60 and want to be protected and limit your loss. Then you buy a Put, good 30 days, at 57, which is 3 points under your purchase price; and at the same time you sell at Call at 65. This leaves only a small expense or the difference between the price you pay for the Call and the price at which you buy the Put. Should the unexpected happen and some unfavorable news cause U. S. Steel to decline and close at 50 at the end of 30 days, you will be out at 57 because you can deliver on your Put at 57. This is what we call selling a Put or a Call on one side of the market to make the money to pay for protection on the other side.

ARRANGING TO SELL PUTS AND CALLS

You can arrange to sell Puts and Calls by getting in touch with your broker. Any brokerage firm that is a member of the New York Stock Exchange can endorse Puts and Calls. Many firms, however, do not handle this business, but your broker can recommend a firm that will be glad to endorse the Puts and Calls you wish to write. If your broker cannot help you out in this matter, you can get in touch with any member of the Put and Call Dealers Association.

In order to sell a Put or a Call, it is generally necessary that you deposit at least 30% of the value of the stock, or in case of a Call, you can deposit the stock itself, so that the broker will always be protected in case the stock is called for or is put to you.

Puts and Calls are sold not only for 30 days but also for 60 days, 90 days, and in some cases for longer periods of time, particularly in dull and inactive markets. Also, instead of selling at a regular rate, such as, $125.00 or $112.50, often they are sold for $250, $300, $400, or $500 AT THE MARKET; in other words, instead of getting points up or down, you receive an additional sum of cash which is equivalent to the points.

Your broker or a member of the Put and Call Dealers Association can furnish you with prices and quotations and the details for handling such transactions.

If you will read *"How to Make Profits Trading in Puts and Calls"* and supplement the information given, by the use of charts on a few active stocks, you should be able to protect yourself and also operate at a profit in both buying and selling Puts and Calls.

W. D. GANN

February 1941

Cosmological Economics

The Masters Of Technical Analysis Series

The Masters of Technical Analysis Series brings together a collection of the most important classical and modern works on technical analysis and financial market forecasting. These classic works from the Golden Age of Technical Analysis were carefully selected by the late Dr. Jerome Baumring of the Investment Centre Bookstore in the 1980's, as representing the most valuable and important works in technical analysis ever written. They were included as the foundational source texts for his program in advanced financial market analysis and forecasting, and serve as the ideal foundation for any analyst seeking a thorough education in market theory and technical trading.

The Golden Age of technical analysis was a period from the early 1900's through the 1960's where the foundational theories of modern financial analysis were initially developed. The ideas and technologies developed during this fruitful period have formed the basis for most modern technical market theory, which is considered to be mostly a repetition or reworking of these past ideas and techniques developed by the Old Masters of the Golden Age. In these historical works can be found the timeless trading wisdom which has laid the foundation for all modern investment theory and literature. These techniques are as useful in today's markets as they were in the past, providing rare and valuable insights, tools and strategies that give the modern trader an edge over traders and investors that are unaware of these time honored tools.

Each quality reprint of these classical texts has been reproduced as an exact facsimile of the original text, maintaining the original layout, typeset, charts, and style of the author and time period, helping to preserve and communicate a sense of the feeling of the original work that a reproduction in modern format does not capture. Many of these rare works and courses were originally printed in only very small private editions or as correspondence courses, so that the originals were easily lost or destroyed over time. Our reproductions of these important source works have been printed on acid free paper and bound in a quality hardcover format that will compliment any trading library and help to preserve this important resource for generations to come.

The series is also currently being digitized and archived for permanent digital preservation by the Institute of Cosmological Economics, creating a searchable reference library of market wisdom accessible globally and available in new digital formats to keep the knowledge fresh and accessible through new devices and technology as we advance further into the information revolution. To see our full catalog of hardcover reprints, new publications, and digital editions please visit our website at www.CosmoEconomics.com.

- **Samuel Benner, An Ohio Farmer** - Benner's Prophecies - *Of Future Ups and Downs in Prices* - (1879)
- **Geo. W. Cole, La Marquette** - Graphs & Their Application to Speculation - (1936)
- **Frank Tubbs** - Tubbs' Stock Market Correspondence Course - (1944)
- **R. N. Elliot** - Collected Works of R. N. Elliot - *The Wave Principle. Nature`s Law: The Secret of the Universe. "The Wave Principle": A Series of Articles Published in 1939.* - (1946)
- **Joseph A. Wyler** - Wyler Series on Stock Market Speculation - *Vol.1, The Application Of Scientific Principles To Stock Speculation. Vol.2, Trading And Trending* - (1960)
- **Edward Dewey** - How to Make a Cycles Analysis - *Correspondence Course in Advanced Cycle Analysis*- (1955)
- **Nikolai D. Kondratieff** - Long Waves In Economic Life - (1935)
- **Pickell & Daniel** - Pickell-Daniel Extension Course of Market Analysis - (1937)
- **Franklin Paul Jackson** - The I-S Method - *Individual Stock - Intermediate Swing* - (1972)
- **Richard Schabacker** - Technical Analysis & Stock Market Profits - (1930)
- **Richard Schabacker** - Stock Market Profits - (1934)
- **M. V. Woods** - Seven Studies In Stock Market Trading - (1943)
- **William Dunnigan** - Collected Works of William Dunnigan - *Gains in Grains. New Blueprints for Gains in Stocks & Grains; Barometers for Forecasting Stocks. One-Way Formula for Trading In Stocks & Commodities* - (1957)
- **Henry Ludwell Moore** - Collected Works of Henry Ludwell Moore - *Economic Cycles Their Law & Cause. Generating Economic Cycles. Forecasting The Yield of Cotton* - (1923)
- **Edwin S. Quinn** - Action - Reaction Signals - (1950)
- **Emil Schultheis** - Basic Trend Barometer - *A Long Term Stock Trend Study* - (1946)
- **Payson Todd** - The "Todd Theory" of Market Measurement & Price Projection - (1953)
- **Dr. Alexander Goulden** - Behind The Veil - (2010)
- **C. S. Johnson, C. P. A.** - A New Technique of Stock Market Forecasting - (1931)
- **William D. Gann** - The Collected Writings of W. D. Gann, Volume I - *Marketing Brochures, Interviews, Annual Forecasts & Trading Records* - (1909-1954)
- **William D. Gann** - The Collected Writings of W. D. Gann, Volume II - *The Master Time Factor: No. 3 Master Forecasting Method & Stock Market Forecasting Courses* - (1921-1954)
- **William D. Gann** - Collected Writings of W. D. Gann, Volume III - *Master Mathematical Formula & Calculators* - (1955)
- **William D. Gann** - Collected Writings of W. D. Gann, Volume IV - *The Complete Commodity Courses* - (1940)
- **William D. Gann** - Collected Writings of W. D. Gann, Volume V - *Introductory Stock Market Courses, Mechanical Methods, & Trend Indicators Courses* - (1935-1950)
- **William D. Gann** - Complete Collected Writings of W. D. Gann - In 6 Volumes - (1955)
- **Timothy Walker** - How To Trade Like W. D. Gann - *An Exploration of the Mechanical Trading Lesson on U. S. Steel* - (2014)
- **James P. Morton** - When to Sell to Assure Profits - (1926)
- **Daniele Prandelli** - The Polarity Factor System - *An Integrated Forecasting & Trading Strategy Inspired By W. D. Gann's Master Time Factor* - (2012)
- **Daniele Prandelli** - The Law Of Cause And Effect - *Creating A Planetary Price/Time Map Of Market Action Through Sympathetic Resonance* - (2010)
- **Perspectives, National Graphic Co.** - The Great Bull Market & Collapse - (1932)
- **Richard Martin** - An Introduction to Trend - Action - *A Scientific Method of Forecasting* - (1943)

- **George Bayer** - Money Investing In Stocks, Trading In Commodities, Or The Time Factors In The Stock Market - *The Art of Scientifically Detecting Direction & Distance of Swings* - (1937)
- **George Bayer** - The Egg of Columbus - (1942)
- **George Bayer** - Stock & Commodity Traders Hand-Book of Trend Determination - *Secrets of Forecasting Values, Especially Commodities, Including Stocks* - (1940)
- **George Bayer** - Gold Nuggets for Stock & Commodity Traders - (1941)
- **George Bayer** - Preview of Markets - *VOL. I, NOS. 1-10* - (1939)
- **George Bayer** - George Wollsten - Expert Stock & Grain Trader - (1946)
- **George Bayer** - The Collected Works of George Bayer - *9 Books In 2 Hardcover Volumes* - (1939)
- **Cliff Stewart** - Magic of Making Money in The Stock Market - (1951)
- **Dickson F. Watts** - Speculation as a Fine Art - *& Thoughts On Life* - (1865)
- **Henry Ansley** - I Like the Depression - (1932)
- **Henry Hall** - How Money is Made in Security Investment - *Or A Fortune At Fifty-Five* - (1908)
- **Dr. Jerome Baumring & Julius J. Nirenstein** - Gann Harmony: The Law of Vibration: The Complete Course Manuals & Lecture Notes - *The Complete Gann 1-9 Course Manuals. Compiled By Dr. Jerome Baumring With Notes On W. D. Gann's Hidden Material: The Complete Gann 1-9 Lecture Notes* - (1989)
- **Dr. Jerome Baumring** - Gann Harmony: The Law of Vibration. The Complete Course Manuals - *Course Manuals For Gann 1 Through Gann 9* - (1989)
- **Julius J. Nirenstein & Dr. Jerome Baumring** - Notes on W. D. Gann's Hidden Material: The Complete Lecture Notes - *Lecture Notes for Gann 1 through Gann 9* - (1989)
- **Alfred Friedman** - Lecture Notes from Baumring's Investment Centre Series - (1987)
- **B. Edlin** - Minor Swings of the Stock Market and their indications - (1924)
- **Henry Howard Harper** - The Psychology of Speculation - *The Human Element In Market Transactions* - (1926)
- **S. A. Nelson** - The ABC of Options & Arbitrage - (1904)
- **Daniel T. Ferrera** - The Gann Pyramid - *Square of Nine Essentials* - (2001)
- **Daniel T. Ferrera** - The Mysteries of Gann Analysis Unveiled! - *A Detailed Presentation of W. D. Gann's Technical Trading Principles* - (2001)
- **Daniel T. Ferrera** - Wheels Within Wheels – *The Art of Forecasting Financial Market Cycles* - (2002)
- **Daniel T. Ferrera** - W. D. Gann's Mass Pressure Forecasting Charts - (2004)
- **Daniel T. Ferrera** - The Keys to Successful Speculation - (2004)
- **Daniel T. Ferrera** - Spirals of Growth and Decay - *Exposing the Underlying Structure of Financial Markets* (2005)
- **Daniel T. Ferrera** – Gann for the Active Trader - *New Methods For Today's Markets* (2006)
- **Daniel T Ferrera** – Economic & Stock Market Forecasting – *W.D. Gann's Science of Cyclical Periodicity Sequencing* (2013)
- **Daniel T. Ferrera -** The Path of Least Resistance - *The Underlying Wisdom & Philosophy of W. D. Gann Elegantly Encoded in the Master Charts* - (2014)
- **Warren Hickernell** - What Makes Stock Market Prices - (1932)
- **William C. Moore (Market Expert)** - Wall Street - *Its Mysteries Revealed, Its Secrets Exposed.* - (1932)

www.ingramcontent.com/pod-product-compliance
Lightning Source LLC
LaVergne TN
LVHW081347011026
849161LV00013BB/3023